Literature in upheaval

R. Hinton Thomas
Keith Bullivant

Literature in upheaval

West German writers and the challenge of the 1960s

Manchester University Press
Barnes & Noble Books · New York

© 1974 R. Hinton Thomas and Keith Bullivant

Published by the University of Manchester
at the University Press
Oxford Road, Manchester M13 9PL

UK ISBN 0 7190 0576 0

USA

Harper & Row Publishers Inc
Barnes & Noble Import Division

US ISBN 0 6 496821 9

Printed in Great Britain by
Western Printing Services Ltd, Bristol

Contents

Preface

We wish to acknowledge our indebtedness to the papers and discussions in the graduate seminar in the Department of German Studies at Warwick University during the three years when it had as its theme what is now the subject of this book. Without the benefit of that experience we could hardly have written it. During the same period three German writers were at different times resident in the department, Wolf Wondratschek, Uwe Herms and Hermann Peter Piwitt. Their presence provided us with direct points of contact with the area of our inquiry, and our frequent discussions with them were of great value to us. We would likewise want to recall the help received from numerous other German friends, in particular Valy Schmidt-Heinicke and Ingo Weihe. Professor Roy Pascal most kindly read our typescript before its final revision and we have benefited in more ways than we can mention from the wisdom of his advice, so generously given. Whatever faults may remain are our responsibility. A word of thanks finally to Uta Goodfellow for her patience as our kind and tolerant typist.

As to who wrote what, the order of names on the title page indicates which of us was primarily responsible for Part I and which for Part II. Often, however, it would be hard to say where the contribution of one ends and the other begins. In conditions of such close collaboration the result can only properly be described as a joint enterprise throughout.

University of Warwick   R.H.T.
                                                                K.B.

Introduction

The political setting

The challenge of the sixties was varied and many-sided. There was, to begin with, the challenge of identity. Its impact was felt from the start of the decade and in particularly significant form. To a greater or lesser extent it was the theme of a group of novels that appeared around 1960, of Heinrich Böll's *Billard um halbzehn,* Günter Grass's *Die Blechtrommel,* Uwe Johnson's *Mutmassungen über Jakob* (and *Das dritte Buch über Achim*) and Martin Walser's *Halbzeit.* Identity is not the only theme of these novels, but it is central to them all, and these writers are among those who stand out by virtue of the quality of their literary achievement. There was the challenge, too, on the issue of the role and function of the writer, of the validity of fiction and narrative, of the authenticity of literature, of what is and what is not literature, of the range and character of the themes it should deal with, of the relation of literature and politics, of the possibilities of an 'alternative' culture. These issues overlap in various ways and none can be considered in isolation from the rest. The general setting of all of them, affecting them in different degrees, was the general political situation, and this we briefly sketch by way of introduction.

At the first federal elections in 1949 Adenauer's Christian Democratic Union (CDU) and Schumacher's Social Democratic Party (SPD) emerged as the two major parties, evenly balanced. The CDU increased its support in 1953, but without achieving an outright majority. The coalition that resulted included the Free Democrats (FDP), but not the SPD. Adenauer's prestige was growing, and the economic prosperity seemed to testify to the wisdom of his policies. Four years later the CDU did win an overall majority, but again there was a coalition, retaining the conservatively orientated Nationalist Party but excluding the SPD, the FDP having turned down the offer of continuing in the government. This was the high point of the fortunes of the CDU. Weakened at the 1961 elections, though still the dominant party, it ruled in coalition with the FDP (despite the latter's earlier decision not to collaborate again with Adenauer).

By now the period of political and economic stability which had characterised the fifties under the leadership of Adenauer and the CDU was drawing to its close, and strains and stresses were beginning to reveal themselves. 1962 was a year of crisis, largely as a result of the *Spiegel* affair. In that year *Der Spiegel*, a news magazine widely read and respected as a critical forum of opinion, published some facts and views affecting defence policy. This moved Franz Josef Strauss, leader of the Christian Social Union, the Bavarian partner of the CDU, as Minister of Defence, to have its offices raided and its editor arrested. His action was constitutionally improper and a storm of protest forced his resignation. The 1964 elections brought gains by both the CDU and the SPD, and led to another coalition (with the weakened FDP and without the SPD). There was by this time the embarrassment of the first prospects of inflation, trade union agitation for increased wages, the emergence of a new Nationalist Party (NPD), and the beginnings of the student protest movement. West German democracy was coming under pressure from right and left, and difficulties were apparent in the economic sphere. These were reflected in the decline of the hitherto favourable balance of trade, in the need for cuts in the budget, and in the problem of controlling the financial arrangements of the independent Länder. The FDP left the government and towards the end of 1966 Erhard, who had taken Adenauer's place as Chancellor, resigned and made way for Kiesinger.

This at last brought the SPD into the government in association with the CDU in what became known as the Grand Coalition. The opposition consisted virtually only of the FDP. With Willy Brandt now Minister of Foreign Affairs, the CDU had to make important policy concessions. Contrary to CDU principles hitherto, the government initiated discussions with the German Democratic Republic. Liberalising reforms of various kinds were made—changes in the Emergency Laws, for example—and long-term economic planning was provided for. The SPD, having been able to demonstrate that it was a responsible party, fit for government, reaped the benefit at the next elections. These took place in 1969, and the party gained only slightly fewer seats than the CDU. This put the CDU into opposition and made possible for the first time a coalition (with the FDP), headed by the SPD.

The CDU, which thus figures so prominently in the politics of West Germany throughout the fifties and during the sixties, was the successor of the older Catholic Centre Party. In the main its policies were conservative, though with liberal features. Its aim had been to free Germany from control by the Allies and, in the interests of security, to integrate it in the defence and economic system of Western Europe. At a time, however, when a younger generation was growing more radical in its demands, it lent itself to the suspicion of perpetuating reaction, if not, as some even went so far as to suppose, fascism—a view to which the *Spiegel* affair was interpreted as lending substance. When economic difficulties began to show themselves, its claim to respect as the guarantor of prosperity was weakened, and those set against capitalism were encouraged by the evidence that this looked less promising than it had a decade before.

Affluence prevailed all the same, but to a younger generation, armed with the theories of Marcuse, this appeared as a major obstacle to a wider appreciation of how wrong and unjust the workings of the existing society were. Parliamentary government, it was being said, masked the evils and delayed or even frustrated the means necessary to overcome them. Even the SPD did not necessarily command much respect among those convinced that only drastic methods were adequate. The latter tended to see it as controlled by men who came from an older socialism compromised by failure and defeat. The Grand Coalition seemed to them only to make matters worse, rendering effective opposition well nigh impossible and an energetic 'extra-parliamentary opposition' the more necessary. Accordingly in the phase of the Grand Coalition the radical movement, initiated and led by the students and the younger intellectuals, was at its most active and most aggressive. With the SPD victory in 1969 and Willy Brandt as Chancellor, the 'extra-parliamentary opposition' was wound up.

It is on these lines that, as far as political developments are concerned, the politicisation of the sixties as compared with the fifties and the quickening process of politicisation during the decade itself can be simply plotted. In addition there are social, as distinct from political, aspects to be considered, and we shall come to these in due course.

Part I

Chapter 1

Literature and identity

The question of identity has a long and important history in literature and thought. In Germany it has been particularly to the fore. Of all problems directly or indirectly occupying German writers from towards the end of the nineteenth century it is the most central and the most significant.

On the one hand there can be the sense that, deprived of the certainty of identity, man loses something precious and irreplaceable. Allusions to this have been common enough, and not only in Germany. 'Of all forms of impoverishment,' Charles Reich said in *The Greening of America*, the 'loss of self' is the 'most devastating', equivalent to 'death in life'. The opening, in the first instance about places rather than about individuals, of William Plomer's poem 'No identity' comments as follows:

> Against the name of the place we mean to move to
> The guidebook bleakly rules *No identity*:
> What Doctor Pevsner means is absence of ancient
> Or markworthy buildings.
>   What he implies
> Is a shallowly-rooted community, a huddlement
> Of not very settled commuters, interspersed with retired
> Couples, tending to dwindle to widows,
> Little communal sense or parish pride,
> And the usual private or commonplace fears
> Like that of being moved to some distant branch
> Of one's place of work, or of cold old age.

On the other hand, the weakening of personal identity may be felt as emancipation, liberation from the restrictions of confinement within a single self, so that Henri-Frédéric Amiel can say in his *Journal*, 'there are ten men in me, according to time, place, surroundings and occasion', 'I have lived a multitude of lives', 'I feel myself a kaleidoscope open to every kind of polarisation':

No identity can be a desirable thing:
To have a face with features noticed less
Than one's range of expression, so that photographed
It never looks twice the same, and people say
'But that's not you!'
  One would like to reply:
'No, that's not me, because I'm incapable
Of starting the very least personality cult.
I have freed myself at least from being me:
Don't think of me as chameleon or actor: if I take
Protective colouring, it is that I mean to be
A kind of medium, free to enjoy, well, *no identity*.'

Plomer's poem appeared in 1966. Just about this time a prominent German man of letters, Hans Werner Richter, convener of Gruppe 47, was reflecting on the same problem. Asked for his opinion as to whether it was any longer meaningful to keep a diary, he came to this conclusion: 'if I were now to sit down and start writing a diary, the doubts would begin. Is the person writing down his life—my ego —still identical with itself? It would be impossible to avoid the modern question of identity, and immediately everything would collapse.' For Richter, therefore, the diary had ceased to be a viable literary form. The forces of 'social changes and developments' were against it.[1]

The impact of the circumstances he was referring to had for some time been felt more powerfully in Germany than in England. It would hardly be an exaggeration to say that a good deal of modern German literature is about nothing less than a crisis of identity. So sensitive and in some respects so extreme a response calls for explanation.

Important above all in this connection is the part long played by the idealisation of the self, a characteristic of German culture from the second half of the eighteenth century. This was the critical phase of transition into the bourgeois era, establishing values long thereafter to the fore in the cultural tradition. Then, and in conjunction with a new insight into nature as more than a formal embellishment of existence, the area of subjective experience was discovered and validated, with a corresponding affirmation of the self. In the aesthetic theory of Goethe and Schiller, and in the concept of 'Bildung', the ego was idealised in the image of the organic personality, through which it was man's calling to fulfil himself. The terminology of 'Persönlichkeit' and 'Individuum', with overtones muted in the

English equivalents, came to acquire in the German vocabulary a quasi-metaphysical prestige, and it continued to enjoy this distinction long after changing circumstances began to undermine the basis which once had nourished it.

The question to be asked, therefore, is what kind of society it was that had made this concept of the individual possible in the first place. Whatever its limitations in scope and opportunity, it was a society undisturbed by industrialisation, and homogeneous enough for experience of it to be conceived—at least at the highest level of the artist—as totality, close enough to nature for organic unity to be able to present itself realistically as among the higher values, and slow-moving enough to make a sense of continuity more real than illusory. Continuity and identity support each other. The one by definition requires consistency, the latter the awareness of a past from which identity derives and a present that is more than a haphazard episode in time and circumstance.

This came to be most appreciated in the period in which identity ran into difficulties. It is illustrated by Friedrich Meinecke, writing in defence of historicism at a time when to a significant extent identity too was coming to be felt to be in obvious need of support. 'Beneficently guided both by the law of his own life and by the laws of life handed down from past ages,' he said, man 'recognises himself and his own nature in enlarged and intensified form'.[2] Similarly, quoting Max Scheler, E. R. Curtius linked 'preservation and tradition' with the 'complete development of the human personality'. He made the same point when discussing what seemed to him the unsatisfactory state of German literature around 1950: 'one of the reasons for this is certainly that writers evade the difficult problem of assimilating the great masters of the past and thus of enabling the precious individual self to absorb our intellectual heritage'.[3] At the opposite extreme, to a disorientated and fragmented ego like the narrative voice in Konrad Bayer's prose work *Der Kopf des Vitus Bering*, published (posthumously) in 1965, the past presents itself as fragmented and discontinuous.

Important therefore for their bearing on the 'social forces and developments' referred to by Hans Werner Richter are factors in the individual or in society damaging to memory. The situation in Germany towards the end of the nineteenth century is of significance in this connection. Belatedly but rapidly the country was making the transition to advanced industrialisation. Existence was coming rapidly to be conditioned by factors unfamiliar in the past of a society for so long only minimally affected by machine production, closer to nature, with a less hurried time scale, a more continuing awareness, less accustomed to frequent and rapid transformations, familiar with a view of history as something evolving gradually and organically. Ferdinand Tönnies, studying the consequences of the changes taking place around this time, and seeking to define the characteristics of the society being superseded and of the one replacing it, found a significant point of contrast in the matter of memory. Memory, he said, was most naturally at home under conditions of 'Gemeinschaft'. In those of 'Gesellschaft', represented by the new industrialised society, it was correspondingly precarious. Marcuse was later to go so far as to say that such a society, in its more fully developed form, has an interest in actually discouraging people from remembering too much, the 'progressing rationality' of advanced industrial production tending 'to liquidate, as an "irrational rest", the disturbing elements of Time and Memory'.[4] In modern industrial society, it might be said, time becomes a commodity. The less, then, does time other than the present and future matter. Materially unproductive, the past is 'useless'. There is a simple illustration of the idea in Max von der Grün's novel *Zwei Briefe an Pospischiel*: 'look, Pospischiel, you must realise that this plant was built in 1960. It's got no past . . . It was built for the future . . . What came before is of no interest.'

If, from the point of view of identity, continuity is important in man's relation to his past, it is equally so as regards his present. What struck many German writers in the situation created by advancing industrialisation was the variety, not to say incongruity, of the models and types of experience with which society faced the individual. One spokesman of the Expressionist generation spoke of the 'magic' of the new 'possibilities of mobility',[5] but adding, 'individual existence perished. . . . The isolated impression no longer meant anything. A myriad of thoughts and observations crowded in on the brain.'[6] Then a rather different style of life begins to be called for, whereby, simultaneously engaged in different fields, the individual has to develop a capacity to rearrange his self as circumstances require. Principles of wholeness and consistency are then an obstacle to adjustment to the heterogeneous demands and opportunities. The structure of language tends to fragment, as in the 'Sekundenstil' of the Naturalists, or later, for example, in a work like Jürgen Becker's

Felder (1964)—a pluralistic type of prose structure, one might say, without a firm centre, the response to the differentiated reality of a great city, where, in the image of the 'Radiokopf', consciousness is all the time tuning in to the multifarious messages of experience in the present and, through the effects of association, from the past. Identity then becomes a quality definable only in the plural: 'he is sucked up and swallowed, he multiplies himself in the figures which he finds before him . . . he hears all the voices which talk against each other in his heads. He sees in the plural, and in the plural hears and speaks.'

West German literature in the sixties offers many other notable examples of writers in whose work is reflected a response to experience as a pluralisation of awareness, and in which little if anything remains of identity as commonly understood, and their writings constitute some of the most characteristic literary productions of the decade. But what was it particularly about the sixties that led more forcefully than ever in this direction?

In the unreal situation in Germany in the period just after the war, with the economic processes suspended, problems of existence tended easily to appear as metaphysical ones. They could be of a directly religious kind, as in Elisabeth Langgässer's *Das unauslöschliche Siegel*, or of a more indeterminate sort, as with Hans Erich Nossack's *Interview mit dem Tode* or Hermann Kasack's *Die Stadt hinter dem Strom*. In these books, felt at the time and subsequently to be among the most representative, the theme of identity is present in one way or another. With Elisabeth Langgässer it is in terms of the recovery of the self through religion; in Nossack's book, of the crisis caused by the obliteration of his work—of his past, that is to say—in the bombing of Hamburg; in Kasack's of a state of limbo in a sort of shadow world. Nothing so concrete as the structure of the self in relation to the structure of society is under discussion. Identity was problematical because, in the aftermath of death and political disintegration, existence itself was problematical. When the currency reform came in 1948 no one could have foreseen in how short a time so apparently simple an economic readjustment could alter so much, and not only materially. At an earlier stage, in the Wilhelminian period, Germany's change from a situation of relative social and economic backwardness to advanced industrialisation had yielded important results as far as intellectual awareness was concerned. The transition from regression and stagnation after 1945 to the circumstances of the sixties was as decisive in a comparable way. The change can be dated fairly precisely. The critical point is 1957–58, when economic recovery was complete and prosperity firmly established. The basis was thus laid for affluence. From around 1960 it became a widely experienced fact of West German life, giving the decade a special character and significance by comparison with what had preceded it in the post-war phase. By the end of the nineteenth century there was advanced industrialisation in Germany, but without the country having become an advanced industrial society, meaning one which thoroughly transformed the wider aspects of life far beyond the world of industrial labour. Germany had become a sort of industrial feudal society, an authoritarian welfare state. In the Weimar Republic there still remained within the social structure features which complicate too facile generalisations about it as a free capitalist economy, and in any case it lasted effectively less than a decade. The situation taking shape in the fifties and reaching its climax during the sixties was different. In a fuller and freer sense the country acquired a capitalist economy through and through. Society became strikingly pluralistic as compared with anything previously known in West Germany. This means a society extensively characterised by the more or less free interplay of heterogeneous interests and values facilitated by the resources of affluence, with the emphasis on competition, conflict and diversity among coexisting groups and cliques, on the tolerance of inherently incongruous possibilities, without any one of these being allowed in principle effectively to monopolise authority and dictate the pattern. The result, a modern version of laissez-faire liberalism widely extended into the area of values and behaviour, is characterised by the pluralisation of values, of taste, of culture.

Identity, too, more freely than ever before, came to be seen as a matter of choice. In no book on West German literature of the fifties written at the end of the decade could the theme of identity have constituted a central feature. Only two writers really call for mention in this connection. One is Wolfgang Koeppen, whose novel *Das Treibhaus* appeared in 1953. Here a man, having lost faith in the values he publicly represents as politician, is moved to call into question the person he had originally taken himself to be. He is disorientated, but also induced to play with imaginary possibilities in the guise of experimental, sometimes incongruous roles. The other is Arno Schmidt whose *Aus dem Leben eines Fauns* (1953) includes the passage: 'my life?: is no continuum (not only broken up into black and white pieces by day and night). For even by day it is for me another person who goes for his train; sits in the office; flips through books; stalks through groves; copulates; chatters; writes; intellectual millipede; a fan falling open; who runs; smokes, pukes, listens to the radio—a tray of glittering snapshots.'

Koeppen's career as a novelist did not last into the sixties, but it was only then that his importance came to be properly recognised. Heissenbüttel paid this tribute to him: 'the most interesting of all aspects of recent German literature for me has been Koeppen's attempt to describe the self, as it experiences and contemplates the world, becoming increasingly, and ultimately totally, alienated from itself. Koeppen, moreover, attempts the impossible task of making the description of this alienated self a central theme of his work.' What follows in this concluding section of Heissenbüttel's essay[7] elaborates the problem of identity, focusing on a series of questions:

> Where does the self disappear to, when it has become totally alienated, so that it sees itself as terrifying, contemptible and disgusting? Where do the fragments of this self go, when it becomes objectified in the world of things, and what are the consequences of this for the real world in which we, though now without guidelines, must nevertheless exist? How is the world to be described in which I am no more than a partial self, and yet in part also the other, where, however, the other that confronts me already contains something of myself?

Heissenbüttel's *Textbuch 1* appeared in 1960. *Textbuch 6*, the last of the series, was published in 1967. It was dedicated to Koeppen, and the essay was written to explain why.

The problem presents itself less pessimistically in Arno Schmidt's *Kühe in Halbtrauer* (1964). The narrator 'as any totalised identity is all but abolished', existence 'seen as a series of discontinuities', and the self as what Schmidt calls the 'touching phantasy of a unitary, superior being created in God's image'. This is something other than 'Ich-Zerfall' as a negative concept. Schmidt's point is that 'experience needs to be looked at the other way round: the self, as it is represented by the narrator, is not in a state of disintegration; rather it is being constituted in a radically new way'.[8]

Such reconstitution of the self can be, and often is, a response to an incongruous variety of experience. Modern industrial society will frequently confront people with experience of this kind. It tends also to enforce a sharper division between on the one hand the sphere of imposed work, on the other of time over which the individual freely disposes, and so an area of existence in which life can be more emotionally expressive and the self given over to its own devices. This is the basis of Ruth Rehmann's novel *Illusionen*, which appeared in 1959.

It portrays a group of white-collar workers in a large industrial concern immured high up in a tall office block as in a realm apart, where human effort is directed to ends other than those which give sense and purpose to individual existence. Freedom comes at weekends, when the routine of the office is exchanged for various forms of escape, romantic and self-indulgent. There is the woman who finds compensation in memories of romantic passion on sunny beaches, only to come to realise that 'dreams have taken too much out of her', or the failed academic who, having had to sacrifice his scholarly ambitions for a translator's job with the firm, escapes to dream of 'a manly future' under the African sun. They illustrate the complementary relationship in this kind of society between 'the organisation of life rationally directed to material ends and based on the division of labour' and 'functionally impoverished private life': 'while most people are denied satisfactory expression as regards their personality, their innate possibilities and their feelings, they receive compensation for this—partly real, partly illusory—in a different sphere'. Daily the advertisements for consumer goods, and the like, 'all provide models as to how this could happen'.[9]

What the characters in *Illusionen*, imagining themselves in different situations and picturing themselves behaving accordingly, lack is the intellectual resources to do more than drift into daydreaming. In a sense this is a form of role-playing, but it affects only the leisure area of existence, and has no consequences as far as practical living is concerned. It is neither a way of organising their lives nor of improving their ability to turn social pressures to their advantage by self-adjustment and readjustment, as is illustrated in Heinrich Böll's *Billard um halbzehn* (1959).

In his earlier stories the figures were most characteristically the victims of circumstance, and the human appeal stemmed from the effects that Böll derived from this. If *Billard um halbzehn*[10] marks a new development in his work, it is partly in the resort to role-playing, which in this case functions as a defence against ideology from the Wilhelminian period into more recent times. Heinrich Fähmel is an expert in this field, and it is through the models he

finds in urban life that he becomes aware of what role-playing can
mean by comparison with the restrictions set to his personality in a
more narrowly based society. From the moment 'I entered the town
I had prescribed for myself all my actions, my movements, a precise
daily programme, I had sketched for myself a complicated dance
routine in which I was solo dancer and ballet-master in one; supporting actors and stage setting were at my disposal free of charge'. He
tries out a new way of life, stage-acting his personality, like the
waiters he observes in the café with such attentive and fascinated
interest: 'I liked that; I was pleasantly surprised; that was as things
were done in a town, I had never seen anything like this in any of the
out-of-the-way places where I had had to exist hitherto.' Human
existence comes to appear to him as a choice of roles; stage-acting
his life, in his inner monologue he is constantly talking in theatrical
terms.

It is rather similar in the case of Oskar Matzerath in Grass's *Die
Blechtrommel*, which appeared the same year as *Billard um halbzehn*. Culminating in the experience of city life, existence for him
too becomes an exercise in role possibilities. They offer him protec-
tion against pressures and also the freedom to make of himself what
at any particular time he wants to be. He manipulates circumstances
to this end, and his keen observation of detail, of what he sees
around him and of the way other people behave, helps to make him
the more successful in the roles which he is constantly assuming and
discarding. There would be a comparison with the central figure in
Max Frisch's *Mein Name sei Gantenbein*, published five years later,
except that Gantenbein's 'stories' are imaginary, only a potential
guide to behaviour. Oskar is a practitioner. Always elaborating the
range and diversity of role possibilities, towards the end of the novel
he is still pondering what else might offer itself when he resumes
life outside the mental home from which he writes the account of
his life thus far, having by this time reached the point when he is
led to wonder, in the light of an existence in so many guises, what
sort of a person he really is after all.

Previously, in 1957, the theme of identity had made its appearance in Martin Walser's first novel *Ehen in Philippsburg*, but incon-
spicuously. It is really only in the light of his later novels that we
recognise it as such. The action takes place mainly in the upper-
middle-class circles of a provincial town dominated by the new
prosperity. This is the world into which Hans Beumann, a student

from a working-class family, moves in search of a job. He has to make adjustments, and as a result his sense of identity is strained. What faces him, however, is little more than the choice of conforming to the demands of society or rejecting them. More a victim of circumstances than one able to turn them to advantage, except materially, he has not to any significant extent discovered the possibilities of role-playing, except in a crudely opportunistic sense, and he is left with a feeling of guilt, disorientation and resignation.

In *Halbzeit* (1960), however, with the scene transferred to a large-scale industrial centre and with its more complex and more differentiated picture of social life, the theme of identity is elaborated and diversified. A commercial traveller by profession, Anselm Kristlein is a 'comedian' in his way of life. Like Heinrich Fähmel and Oskar Matzerath, but more extensively, he draws on the language of stage and drama. He exemplifies, often down to the last detail of gesture and behaviour, the conduct of a man meeting the pressures of a pluralistic society by constantly adjusting and readjusting his self. Like Heinrich Fähmel he discovers the restrictions which role-playing can impose—once assumed, a role may not be so easy to drop—but it is the freedoms of such an existence that predominate, the possibilities that become available, with all the advantages of shifting and flexible identity. This is the case also with *Das Einhorn* (1966), which, with its more fully worked out picture of Germany's affluent society in conjunction with its varied cultural manifestations, and with the more complex psychology of its central figure, marks a further stage of development. With Kristlein now figuring as writer and intellectual, heavily in demand in the hectic cultural world of this society, identity is even more obviously in dissolution and more explicitly so. Kristlein has become the epitome of man as 'a pluralistic society Ltd', the 'collaboration of a million units'. 'Individuality' is rejected, 'dividuality' acclaimed: 'Vivat Dividuum. The thousandfold. And soon to be a hundred-thousandfold.'

The 'static ego', one might say, is portrayed as widely extendable into a set of possibilities—and this, incidentally, is exactly how Claus Bremer interprets one of the permutational 'texts' in his *Anlässe*, written between 1949 and 1969:

ich
ich e e
g ich e e
g ich ei e

g ichkei e
glichkei e
m glichkei e
m glichkei en
möglichkei en
möglichkeiten

As a picture of the pluralistic society *Das Einhorn* has its critical features—the commercialisation of culture, social and cultural snobbishness, the pressures to which in its own way it subjects the individual, and the strain put upon him by the adjustments and readjustments he is constantly called upon to make. Such a society may be destructive of the self in the sense of a unified and consistent ego, but, as in *Halbzeit*, ideas of selfhood are revised in the light of contemporary experience. Flexibility, adaptability, diversification are recognised as positive aspects which modern man in such a society is in position to turn to his advantage in a way denied to earlier generations. Incongruity in the pattern of behaviour is not viewed as a betrayal of man's essence. The validity of so metaphysical a concept is contested, and the principle of 'to thine own self be true' negated in favour of the other extreme of the pluralistic personality. In the interval between *Halbzeit* and *Das Einhorn* appeared Barbara König's novel *Die Personenperson* (1965), prefaced by a remark of Novalis: 'each one of us is a small society'. Its theme is the multiplicity of people in a single body, its principle that any 'ego-attempt' is tantamount to 'betrayal'.

The last of Walser's novels thus far, with *Fiction* and *Die Gallistl'sche Krankheit* a little way away, *Das Einhorn* appeared at a critical juncture, marking the point of full development of the pluralistic society in social and economic terms, and the point at which in literary and intellectual circles the initiative showed signs of passing to those whose ideology was incompatible with its principles and practices.

Das Einhorn was the last novel of the sixties which, taking the question of identity as its theme, orientated the decay of selfhood towards an image of the individual as productively pluralistic. The implications of such a view of man are to make the more traditional image of the individual, endowed with a firmer and more inherent structure, appear in terms of its limitations rather than its dignity. Up to about the mid-sixties it is the more positive aspects of the pluralistic personality that claim attention. Thereafter it begins to emerge in a more dubious light, suggestive of what might loosely be called schizophrenia, and of experience marked by a weakened hold on reality. In Rolf Roggenbuck's *Der Nämlichkeitsnachweis* (1967), the self is the 'many voices' constituting 'the loose arrangement', as in that novel Loeffler describes his consciousness. Such phraseology is close to Walser's in *Das Einhorn*, but now the implications seem at least problematical, epitomised in the remark about Europe requiring to be cured 'of its schizophrenia, its increasingly divided consciousness'. In Dieter Wellershoff's novel *Die Schattengrenze* (1969), a natural successor in this respect to his earlier *Ein schöner Tag* (1966), the theme relates to the 'shrinking' of a man who 'disintegrated in all directions', and in whose experience reality accordingly dwindles.

Das Einhorn, one of the most extreme portrayals in the sixties of the pluralisation of the self, is at the same time a book about the problematicalness of memory. Memory sets existence in perspective, and identity is firm and intact only with the self ordered in relation to what it has been and to what it might become, to a past carried into the present. Walser's interest in Proust is significant.[11] He earns Walser's praise for abolishing the 'distinction between what is important and what is not', for narrating 'in all their importance things that till then had not been noticed'. But this is not for Walser an affirmation of memory, rather a rejection of its claim to constitute a legitimate basis on which may be built the image of the self in terms of continuity and synthesis. So Proust is commended for 'not objectively narrating complete biographies'. The implications of Walser's essay can serve as a commentary on *Das Einhorn*, in which a pluralised image of the individual and a negative view of memory belong together: 'ENTSINNEN, ja. Von REMEMBERN keine Spur'. Memory preserves, so runs Walser's thesis in the novel as in the Proust essay, but only to destroy. Its method is a 'destructive method of preservation': 'instead of something only words remain'.

Memory, or liberation from memory, provides a motif in Zwerenz's *Casanova* (1968), a novel of picaresque-type adventure in the affluent society by one who well understands the opportunities for freedom of self-manoeuvre in modern urban society: 'a city like Cologne is a huge circus, you have the choice of appearing as ringmaster, spectator, clown, lion, aerial artist, or lion tamer. If you're agile enough, there's nothing to beat a city.' As to memory, 'one can't imagine how hard remembering is, even for people who have an adequately functioning memory. Man is so made that he leaves

his past behind him like a lot of old rags and walks away without
looking back.' Memory, negatively regarded, is thematic in Peter O.
Chotjewitz's novel *Die Insel* of the same year: 'did I travel to speed
up the collapse of the past? Was I a primitive, as far as the future
was concerned?'; 'I had nothing to hide from myself and, even if
there was something to hide, I could take the shock of forgetting
everything, and afford the luxury of wanting to forget everything, so
that ultimately I could virtually be devoid of personal history.'

A little while before, in Ror Wolf's *Fortsetzung des Berichts* (1964),
as in all his subsequent work, memory is an integral element, struc-
turally and thematically, and always problematical: 'This past time'
occurs in the first two lines, and 'I remember voices, words, in half-
full mouths, chewed up sentences...'. But the past gets mixed up
with the present, and memory sets other memory in movement ('this
image, and the sound linked with it, remind me of a similar image
from the past... We came...'). The relationship to the present is
no less problematical. This registers for the narrator only as fragmented, discontinuous and episodic, the details losing order, perspective and proportion. There is no linear continuity of narrative and,
as it turns out, one and the same person is at once on the way to the
meal and describing it. Since *Fortsetzung des Berichts* Wolf has
written no other large-scale work with an integrated structure, and
this is consistent with his remark: 'the book that interests me is one
that you can take off the shelf, open at random, begin to read at any
page, one that you can get into wherever you start, in which it is
therefore unimportant what happens before or afterwards... I tried
to do this in *Pilzer und Pelzer*.'[12] This book, published in 1967, and
consisting of forty short, numbered sections, presents reduced people
in a reduced milieu, in touch with the outside world only through a
shifting and tenuous kind of experience. This includes memory, but
it is never more than casual and haphazard: 'my memories, my
inability to remember', 'if only I could remember', 'once again the
ground has gone from under my feet'. Remembering yields only dis-
continuity. Fragments of episodes are recalled, then often quickly
abandoned. This is reflected in the structure of narrative: 'good, I
can start again from the beginning, back to where I broke off,
suddenly the widow, yes, back again to this meeting'.

The problematicalness of memory is a paramount motif of Wolf's
work. Another is the uncertainty of identity: 'was that really my
voice again?', or 'every time I looked in the mirror, I found that my

appearance had changed. I was shrivelled up or bloated, suddenly had a beard . . . or I found that I was puffing away at a pipe and wearing a hat with a very wide brim. I noticed that I suddenly took to wearing glasses, or I noticed nothing worth mentioning about myself. . . .' Fragmented in structure, *Pilzer und Pelzer* is still a single text. *Danke schön. Nichts zu danken* (1969) is a collection of separate pieces without semblance of coherence. In the opening story the narrator, characteristically uncertain about himself, discovers by chance what he might have been expected to know, namely that there is a pond by his house, but the memory of it has faded. It occurs to him casually that he has not seen his wife lately. In fact, he has killed her and buried her in the pond, noticing then that she has been missing for some time. Here, as in all Wolf's books up to this point, three things go together and condition each other—the self in disarray, reality fragmented, and memory at best confused and precarious.

By these standards, to affirm that the necessary condition of sound existence for the individual and society is awareness of historical continuity represents an essentially conservative position. This, to take one example, is illustrated in Hermann Lenz's *Spiegelhütte* (1962), a socio-critical picture of a State given over to the pursuit of pleasure and responsive to the attractions of freedom at the expense of obligation. In the story a 'governor' still rules, representing in an old-fashioned way, and with conviction, if not with confidence, 'peace, order and belief'. From him above all emanates the policy of 'restoring the magical connection with history', and he, incidentally, for his part has no doubts about his identity. It is hardly by chance that in the circumstances this work made little impact. Whatever its merits or demerits, such a book was bound to be a poor competitor in this earlier phase of the development of the novel in the sixties, with the prospects of the pluralistic society still apparently promising and the emphasis still positively on the pluralisation of the individual.

The decline of the novel with exploration of man's pluralistic possibilities as its central theme is reflected, as we shall see, in Walser's change of direction after *Das Einhorn*. In Grass's *Örtlich betäubt* (1969) belief in the values of the pluralistic society is associated with a middle-aged schoolmaster, who obviously has Grass's sympathy, whereas for the young he represents in the novel an old-fashioned liberalism. It is marked too by the close, with one or two exceptions,

of the sequence of neo-picaresque novels in the wake of *Die Blechtrommel*. Rudolf Krämer-Badoni's *In der grossen Drift* (1949),
born out of its time from this point of view, could not as yet inaugu-
rate a trend; the reprint in 1961 caught up with that initiated by
Grass's book. Now there was a certain shift of interest to stories with
other than large-scale urban settings. Curt Hohoff could comment in
1966 in *Der Spiegel* on the new attraction of stories with idyllic
characteristics and warm local colour: 'die hintergründige Idylle mit
Lokalgeruch ist jetzt im Kommen . . . Im Spiegel einer Kleinstadt
heisst jetzt die Parole.'

The previous year had seen the appearance of *Milch und Honig*
by Heinz Küpper, earlier himself the author of a neo-picaresque
novel. The story concerns a woman whose childhood had been spent
in rural East Prussia, now employed in the office of a West German
industrial concern. Her relationship to an executive of the firm is a
romantic love promising to free her from the mechanical existence
of an over-rationalised society and reunite her in spirit with the
values dear to her native landscape. She recalls the world of her
childhood, the basis of her true and natural self, a world with great
expanses of time at its disposal ('our countryside was still and vast.
It had time for lots and lots of snow'). In its own way it exemplifies
intact individuality: 'the towns and villages there retain their
appearance. Here people first cut up the face of towns and then
filled them up with cosmetics and tower blocks . . . they all look like
American film stars, all identical. . . .' Disorientated in industrialised
society, steadying her existence by reference to an earlier and simpler
life mediated by a remembered past, and in search of an identity of
her own now lost in urban existence, she yearns for a world socially
and geographically able to support her nostalgia with its own fixed
identity, in which continuity is assured and in memory secure. In
Hohoff's own *Die Märzhasen* (1966) the setting is a small town,
characterised by hearsay and gossip, whose 'history and prehistory
everyone knows'. Everyone knows about everyone else, and everyone remembers. The contrast is with Berlin: 'in a city like that people
just don't take any notice of each other'. Hohoff was a young man
when the events of the book took place in Nazi times, but the narrative perspective is that of a lad of ten, writing and recalling as a
grown man. His record does not claim to be accurate or objective:
'I combine report with hearsay. I imagine and invent. I get hold of
material and get to work on it.' 'I combine facts and invent links as

necessary. I connect ideas with feelings.' Memory may be tinged with irony, and the references to the little town are not necessarily idealising. Even so, it is portrayed as not without its attractions, a small, compact community in which memory is alive, may be in too trivial a way. Hence turns of phrase like, 'I write what I hear', 'the whole town knows', 'the whole town says ...'. Some reasons, amongst others, for the popularity of Siegfried Lenz's best-selling novel *Deutschstunde* (1968) may now suggest themselves. Describing a simple and compact society whose people know little of what goes on beyond its limits, it tells of a youth in penal detention near Hamburg, where he is given the task of writing an essay on 'The joys of duty'. He has so much in his mind that he cannot make a start, and is shut up in his cell until he can produce something. Working on his theme through an account of his father, a police official in a village in Schleswig-Holstein, the result turns out to be more than just an essay, and in fact substantial enough work to earn his release. Living with his memories and following his father's story further and further back in time, he recalls the past stage by stage, all the better able to do so since the events remembered are set in circumstances at a distance, in kind and geographically, from the fragmented and discontinuous world of urban civilisation.

But how reliable is memory, even in small and intact communities? Walser apart, this is a problem raised in the work of Peter Härtling, who in 1964 published his novel *Niembsch oder der Stillstand*, followed in 1966 by *Janek*. The former is to a great extent about identity, the latter the 'Portrait of a Memory'. The two aspects interplay, and *Das Familienfest* (1969) embraces both. The setting of the events in the past, with which this book is concerned, is the small town to which Georg Lauterbach, now a professor of history, returns in order, in the light of rumour and gossip, to test how memory works. Measuring the result against his own experience and knowledge, he concludes that what is remembered is a 'jumble of memories', and history is 'nothing more than the exposition of events that really cancel each other out'. If memory is one theme of Härtling's work, another is identity. In his first novel man is in the image of a person exploring the freedoms of role-playing, a 'comedian' viewing contemptuously 'an existence with roots and obligations'.

The two aspects can easily go together, the one encouraging the other—the self as an arrangement of possibilities freely and experimentally disposable, the past as weakened in significance and

authority. Too great a respect for the past, to paraphrase a passage in
Das Einhorn, fosters a false idealism: 'a giant, called the past, stands
with one foot on our chest, and when he changes legs we become
ecstatic. And we remember this far longer than is necessary. And
this excess, which makes us religious and ill, is called imagination,
soul, etc.'

The idealism thus rejected is defined in terms which had traditionally come to be commonly used to characterise creative personality.
With such a notion of the self coming to be felt as a restriction to be
got rid of, 'Kultur' was more and more being seen as representing
the authority of values incompatible with freedoms increasingly
insisted on in the name of democracy and emancipation. The need
is, we are told, in Chotjewitz's *Vom Leben und Lernen* (1969) to
clear 'Kultur' out of life; with the passing of 'bourgeois culture',
history 'becomes hazy and disappears'. In short: 'today, because the
fiction of the old culture is still strong, "Unkultur" still serves
authority. We defend "Unkultur", however, for the sake of the
future, and, with the fulfilment of its historical role, it too will disappear and with it everything that people see as historical.' Thus,
for example, the protagonists of sub-culture in Manfred Grunert's
Die verkommenen Engel (1970) are told, by a figure in the novel
attacking what he holds to be its illusions and its anti-authoritarian
obsessions: 'your ideology is the now'.

This may seem to bring us near the border dividing serious and
responsible discussion of the problem from its trivialisation. Profounder aspects come to light in figures, such as we encounter in the
work of the Austrian writer Thomas Bernhard—a major figure on the
West German literary scene—whose awareness of the limitation of
their situation is too deep-rooted to allow the illusion of short cuts to
easy solutions.

His first book, *Frost* (1963), is about a painter living in the seclusion of a little inn in a remote Austrian village, whose mental state
a medical student is commissioned to investigate. It is the case of a
man confined within a self so ill-adjusted to external experience as
to become a 'person living a precarious existence in the world of the
imagination' (*ein phantastischer Abgrunds-Mensch*). Lacking contact from early on with the outside world, he is in a state of complete
and unproductive detachment. 'Isolation' is his obsession. This, he
says, 'has concerned me as long as I can remember. Even the concept of isolation. Of total incapsulation within oneself.' It is as if

'nature had a right to push me further and further away, further in on myself and into myself'. He 'became completely involved . . . in his private world of ideas', but 'everything crumbled away', and all his thoughts grew 'false and valueless'. He is a person 'full of fractured harmonies'. Turned in upon itself too long, his individuality has decayed into eccentricity, into 'an addiction to the extraordinary and the bizarre', the 'unique and the unattainable'. 'Yes, I'm myself. You see, this is what I have been all my life'—'I'm always chasing after myself'—but 'I'm always bumping into the walls around me'.

Verstörung (1967), Bernhard's most famous work, is likewise set in a remote part of the Austrian countryside. A doctor going on his rounds with his son provides the perspective from which the other figures are viewed and presented. He feels no need 'for a non-scientific, poetical kind of literature', and he is indifferent to 'so-called belles lettres'. All this is a 'falsification of nature', since nature, if the truth be told, is beastly. The Jewish businessman Bloch is the only person 'with whom he could have a conversation that wasn't embarrassing'. This was due to his respect for him as a man able to face outwards on reality and to adjust it to his needs. He 'had the ability to control one's life, seeing life as a mechanism that was essentially easy to understand, and always resetting it according to his personal requirements'. The doctor's son, with his father's obvious approval, is studying in a town beyond the confinement of villages cut off from the outside world. A person open to the 'pleasures of life', he contrasts with Bernhard's more representative figures who are constantly 'irritated' by external stimuli intruding on the inwardness they cling to, but under which they suffer. This problematical inwardness is epitomised in those recurring 'closed spaces' which, it has been well said, signify both 'prison' and 'refuge'.[13] The doctor is, however, disturbed about his daughter. 'Irritated' by things around her, she lives an existence more and more 'cut off'. The 'victim of her terrible depression', she is 'completely at the mercy of her nervous system'. There is also the case of the industrialist, who, 'more or less mad', has withdrawn into solitude to concentrate on writing, but the seclusion makes his efforts all the more unproductive. He keeps on destroying what he has written, but is resolved not to leave his fastness till he has completed it. In touch with the outside world only by letters, he keeps it at a distance. He allows no book in the house 'in order to avoid being irritated': 'nothing irritates more than books if you . . . need to be alone with yourself'. Medically speaking, he may not be mad, but 'no one can exist in such isolation without suffering extensive damage, indeed the most extreme damage, to his mind and personality'. So he occupies himself 'entirely with objects of his imagination'.

Interest centres mainly on the Fürst, living apart in his castle, eccentric to the point of madness, and his monologue—which is what it amounts to—occupies the whole of the second half of the book. He embodies all the features which in these other figures make them desperately problematical creatures. Shut up amid nature, he is a man for whom 'isolation' is a 'pathological state'. Mad, with an 'unimaginable desolation' in his head, he delights in thoughts of decay and death. Mankind is just a 'community of the dying', life 'a school in which death is taught'. He is neurotically over-sensitive to whatever presses in upon him from the outer world, like all Bernhard's most typical figures, which is why they keep making superior comments about society. There are a number of such remarks in this novel, about this 'rotten state', and 'in this place this ridiculous state does not exist. . . . Here autonomous, natural laws are in force . . . not those of the Republic, of pseudo-democracy.' Such pronouncements are not to be taken as authorial opinions but as symptomatic of a fictional, and degenerate, character. Bernhard is not idealising existence so claustrophobic in terms of both place and self but exploring its problematical aspects. The deep melancholy running through all his work stems from his characters' sense of inwardness turned sour. Hence their preoccupation with death and decay. The motto quotation from Pascal thus gains its fuller significance ('the eternal silence of the infinite spaces makes me shudder'), as does the second part of the novel in which the Fürst, admirer of the 'art of the soliloquy', does nothing but talk. Nature, no longer guide, philosopher and friend, is now merely 'deception', 'comedy', and life no more than 'a constant learning to talk, walk and think, learning by heart, learning to deceive, learning to die'. The language of the theatre is invoked, but now to provide images of life in terms of helplessness and resignation. Existence is merely a 'rehearsal stage on which we rehearse non-stop', occupied by people who are 'nothing but actors who perform for us', 'people learning their parts', and 'each of us is continually learning one . . . or several or all imaginable roles possible without knowing why (or for whom) he is learning them. This rehearsal stage is a veritable torment.' Ultimately the 'object of our learning' is 'death'.

Already as a boy the central figure of Bernhard's latest and most explicit novel, *Das Kalkwerk* (1970), has been familiar with 'loneliness' and 'isolation', with a 'state of almost complete estrangement from his brothers and sisters, parents, relations, and finally from his fellow human beings'. Now he has withdrawn with his wife into the seclusion of the limeworks to devote himself to writing his 'study' (about hearing), but everything around him 'irritates' him—most of all his wife's illness—so in the end he kills her. Everything appears to him as 'one great conspiracy against oneself, namely against one's intellectual work': 'the world, and particularly the world about one, always and in every instance treats everything one does, as regards writing and research, as an abomination directed against it'. In the limeworks they had expected to be 'completely isolated and free of people', to have escaped the pressures of society (and now specifically the consumer society is mentioned). But still the couple found themselves 'irritated by people'. He is, as he knows, his own worst enemy, vulnerable because of a nature so 'awkward' and because of the 'powerlessness of his own being'. But, as he concedes, he cannot do anything about it. He must stick it out and live with it, and this demands 'the highest degree of uninterrupted intellectual and physical self-control'. The more he tries to be himself in this difficult and problematical sense, the more revolting, 'frightening' and 'ridiculous' the world around him appears: 'lies are all that matters in this country'. He cannot reconstitute his self to meet the problems that reality presents: 'one would simply have to change one's nature fundamentally', but no one can change his nature 'because nature cannot be changed'. Withdrawal to a setting calculated to bring his imaginative and intellectual activity to fruition defeats its purpose. He has good ideas, but they vanish as soon as he tries to set them down: 'words ruin everything that you think'. The ideal world would for him, he says, be a silent world without people. At the same time he recognises the futility of such a situation, even if it could be achieved: 'permanent lack of social contact is just as deadening as continuous social contact, and so on'. Marriage, friendship, companionship, however, ruin the intactness of the self, leaving him no choice but isolation. What does one then become? The answer is a 'highly intelligent mental case', like the Fürst in *Verstörung*. After taking refuge in the limeworks life became for him 'no human society at all', and 'that leads of necessity first to despair, then to intellectual and emotional desolation, then to disease and death'. His 'study', metaphor of a self incapsulated in its own self-sufficient world, in its own way refuses compromise with anything outside itself. Aspiring to totality, it cannot come to exist: 'every sort of alien image intrudes into my clear concept and destroys it for me, my study disintegrates beneath thousands upon thousands of alien images . . .'. Letters waiting to be answered make it impossible to get on with the 'study', and concentration on the 'study' disables him from meeting the extraneous demands. He neither answers the letters nor progresses with the 'study'.

Bernhard's work is about the psychological consequences of life in isolated places in Austria, but it is about much more than this, about existence gone rotten through being too long turned inwards upon itself, the victim of a self-sufficiency which can no more indefinitely be its own reward than 'the clear concept' can for ever dictate its too exclusive claims. The individual comes to live amid obsession with his own dissolution, and spirituality moves into the orbit of madness. Two observations among Walter's reflections in Bernhard's *Amras* clinch the problem. The one, 'life in its entirety: I don't want to be myself. *I* want to be, not be myself.' The other, 'the daily question: why am I made up of myself?'

At the other extreme the escape to the freedoms and possibilities of a more open type of existence, of which literature in the sixties offers manifold examples, can create problems of its own. They show themselves already in *Die Blechtrommel*. Living out his existence in many guises, Oskar learns to know not only the advantages of an alienated and alienating intellectuality. Becoming all the more conscious of the attractions of its negation, he conjures up in memory his early past—mother, childhood, Poland. His adventures finished, he enjoys being shut up in a mental home, with implications of the idea of return to the womb. But his adventuring, one may assume, is over only for the time being. He will surely be off again before too long. Ten years after *Die Blechtrommel* Manfred da Conta created in *Der Totmacher* (1969) a figure who likewise ends in a mental home. In his case it is not just another trick, a respite from the strains of what is after all a demanding kind of life. He has become genuinely deranged. For one so concerned to preserve his self intact, reality ('chaos in which he is drowning') makes more demands than he can cope with. With his 'perception' in danger of having 'too much demanded of it', his tactic is to seek a stance of superior detachment above 'the daily life around him': 'I won't join the crowd. I won't go into such darkness and confusion.' So he isolates himself 'further and further from social existence in order to be able to question everything that appears to him to stand in the way of the cognition of his supposed individuality'. This only drains the living substance of his being, the result of which, contrary to his intention, is 'the total loss of his individuality'. His problem, in short, is that experience is too complicated and demanding. In the sixties one way that suggested itself of simplifying things was political demonstration and public confrontation. The question now arising is whether the connection with problems of identity is not closer than at first sight might appear.

Confrontation can be a mode of behaviour through which the complexity of things may seem to be reduced to more manageable proportions and a person's relation to them simplified. It can be an easy antidote to alienation, a short cut to the sense of doing something and so of finding oneself closer to things than through intellect and ratiocination. It can be a great restorer of self.

The Vienna Group of writers and artists, which flourished in the fifties and broke up in the early sixties, was characterised on the one hand by an aggressive anarchism, reflected in interest in people in revolt against institutionalised authority, and on the other, as with Konrad Bayer, by an urge towards self-expansion. Of Oswald Wiener's *Die Verbesserung von Mitteleuropa* (1969), by a former member of the group, Jürgen Becker remarked that, if it has a unifying element, it is 'the continuous dissolution of an identity': 'one reads what sorts of voices a multiple ego releases and mixes'.[14] At the same time its intention is, as is stated at the end of the book, to awaken in the reader the feeling 'that he must direct all his energy against proof, against continuity and contingency, against formulation and against everything that is correct, unavoidable, natural and obvious, if he is to experience—however briefly—the full unfolding of his self'. In Helmut Salzinger's poem 'Das lange Gedicht', a text included in the symposium *Supergarde* (1969), one pole is represented by the necessity of revolt 'against everything that is / against reality and for possibility', the other by a view of revolution in the image of erection ('a revolutionary argument') and orgasm. Revolution 'goes on and on like orgasm / when you're turned on and feel eternal / a point stretching into infinity'. In Böll's *Gruppenbild mit Dame* (1971) interesting in this connection is the characterisation of Lev, one of a group which rejects social values

determined by competitiveness and efficiency. Towards the end of
the novel Böll makes use of a fictional report analysing his state of
mind. The author of the report refers to him as 'a person', but is
at this point 'inclined rather than disinclined, despite various misgivings, to talk of a personality', the problem being to take account
of Lev's concern to establish himself as an individual both to himself
and to others. The passage in question designates Lev as a 'person'
—or 'personality'—'whose highly developed sensibility and intelli-
gence left him no choice but to conform and thus to "betray" himself
and the fixed points by which he can identify his self, or else to
affirm himself and these fixed points by constant nonconformism',
and who was therefore 'in permanent conflict between the socially
attainable and his own talent'. Hence 'this person (personality?)
needed to resist in ever new, later artificial ways, in order to give
confirmation both to himself and his milieu'.

Discussion thus returns to the case of Walser, to his picture of the
weakened self in *Halbzeit* and *Das Einhorn*, and forward from there
to his concern, in the essay on Swift, with ways of recovering strength
and confidence. In Walser's analysis Swift,[15] having 'experienced no
stable environment in early childhood' and been 'put through pro-
grammings that were contradictory or at least got in the way of
each other', had 'later no positive view of the world in which he
lived'. He 'looks for contact. Would like to find refuge in this or
that opinion'. Echoing the tone of some remarks about Hans
Beumann in *Ehen in Philippsburg*, there is a comment on Swift's
'need to be accepted' and his efforts to 'make himself indispensable to
others'. Having never learnt 'to be confirmed as a stable individual
by continuing contact with a stable environment', the Englishman
chose to adopt the role of one who had a firm and definite position.
Only when he 'has an opponent' does 'he become aware of himself'.
To 'become more sure of himself' he 'had to attack'. Hans Magnus
Enzensberger argues on much the same lines in *Politik und Verbrechen* (1964) about the case of the American deserter Eddie Slovik.
He quotes Slovik's statement, 'and I'll run away again if they send
me to the front', with the comment: 'at that moment, for the first
time in his life, he knew what he was doing'. Previously he had 'his
whole life long, always done, said and thought what others said, did
and thought'. Lacking an identity of his own, he 'was at every
moment what "they" had demanded of him'. Now 'for the first
time . . . he defined himself by challenging "them", by confronting

"them"'. In doing so he affirmed himself: 'for the first and only time he said yes to himself, by saying no to "them"; a scarcely articulated, broken, endlessly painful yes, but a yes that couldn't be revoked'. In the moment 'when he said, I have done it and I'll do it again, Eddie Slovik discovered who he was'. Enzensberger associated himself with a very similar argument as signatory of an article in 1968 in which is described the action of a young man from Detroit who shot at the police from a rooftop as they approached him. Asked by a reporter what it felt like to do this, he is quoted as replying, 'It was incredible, baby, you can't imagine how beautiful it was.' The source of his exhilaration was that 'through his struggle he re-established a part of his ravaged identity . . . In that moment he became a human being.' Erich Fried might say that this supports his view that 'in late capitalist society man can only exist, if he does not wish to become totally alienated, by beginning to rebel continually against it'.

Similar in some ways, more complex in others, is the case of Peter Weiss. In *Fluchtpunkt* he described his early problem of a radical individualism plagued by 'anxiety about the loss of his ego', about the 'abandonment of an aura of privacy . . .'. Recognising as the 'sole truth' that 'I could only get involved in myself', Weiss had to pose the question as to who in any case he is, 'with this burden of filth and rubbish'. Already in *Fluchpunkt* there are indications of a guilty, confused and weak ego seeking strength by trying itself out against hostile experience. A crucial passage about memory, but with implications beyond it, articulates this very clearly: 'I conjure up objects and facts in order to sense my resistance, I confront myself with faces and words in order to accost myself and to get a statement out of myself that I can recognise.' Marxism and declaration of alignment with East Germany were then to provide him, *vis-à-vis* the given reality of the Federal Republic, with a form of confrontation, and this has to be seen in conjunction with the need for self-realisation in an identity crisis. Or one could say that, involving himself through Marxism in the great processes of history, Weiss finds a way of vicariously enjoying the sense of a strong and heroic self whose absence had been a burden on his conscience. In *Fluchtpunkt* he speaks of his feeling of guilt at having escaped the fate of murdered Jews: 'for a long time I bore the sense of guilt that I was one of those who had had that degrading number burned into their flesh, that I had escaped and been condemned to be an onlooker . . . I had fled and hidden myself away. I ought to have died, to have sacrificed myself, and since I had not been captured and murdered or shot on the field of battle I had at least to bear my guilt, that at any rate was demanded of me.' It is against this background that Weiss's idealisation of Che Guevara has to be seen—a man who realised himself in grandly heroic confrontation with a reality to be challenged and overcome in circumstances where, in contrast to modern industrial society, the individual is felt to count and is able to take upon himself the onus and honour of personal decision. Complementary to this is Weiss's idealisation of an opposite kind of society, and it is one that we can recognise as of the type least likely to make identity a problem. Features singled out for praise, for example, in *Notizen zum kulturellen Leben der Demokratischen Republik Viet Nam* (1968), and making their proper effect only in the original German, could be ingredients in any conservatively orientated definition of 'Gemeinschaft'—'Einheitlichkeit und Geschlossenheit', individual features 'gegenüber fremden Einflüssen und Überlagerungen', 'Geschichte mit ihren poetischen, ideellen Werten', 'poetische Kraft der Sprache', culture's 'tiefe Beziehung zur Poesie' as an 'Eigenschaft des Volkes'. 'Woe betide him who infringes the laws of the Gemeinschaft.'

These are qualities highly esteemed in the literature and theory of East Germany, whose social and political system Weiss came to affirm. 'Character' and 'personality' there stand in high regard. Typical themes of the novel include deviant behaviour stemming from inner weakness and uncertainty, and, as a corrective and a guide to those afflicted, the virtues of inner strength embodied most characteristically in Party representatives and those who learn from their example. The East German novel tends therefore to follow the pattern of an older type of 'Bildungsroman' and 'Erziehungsroman' familiar in Germany above all in the heyday of its bourgeois culture. Christa Wolf's *Nachdenken über Christa T.* (1968), about a figure craving to be fully and naturally herself, ran into official disapproval only because of the implication that this could not be achieved in the prevailing bureaucratised conditions. Her earlier *Der geteilte Himmel* (1963) had a different reception. Here the workers are part of a closely knit unity, with a very personal, not to say paternalistic, relationship to their brigade leader. They constitute a happy and harmonious group, operating in circumstances comparable less to the conditions of large-scale mass production than to those of an earlier stage of industrialisation.

Many East German novels prompt the question as to where in the

Federal Republic of the sixties, except among the most conservative and old-fashioned writers, a type of novel would still be possible patterned chapter by chapter on the succession of the seasons, the very structure idealising the notion of the organic continuity of experience and development. Where, except in the case of writers so regarded, would social change be viewed as the 'constant and unceasing process' of the 'unfolding' of 'continuity'? Who but those in West Germany would be able to speak so confidently of tradition? Or still find it possible to glorify the idea of the 'Volk', to affirm 'Heimat' and 'Heimatliebe' as 'wunderbar poetisch'?[16]

These questions serve to pull together a number of aspects bearing in their different ways on the problem of identity as we have come to know it in modern German literature. Two factors call for emphasis. First, in the case of East Germany, we have a society at the opposite extreme to the consumer society and to pluralism, one whose economy is tightly controlled and one that is governed by a unified ideology. In the second place, it is a society with a much more intact view of power and authority, implying, or seeking to imply, a greater coincidence of interest between those who are ruled and those who rule over them. An integrating ideology on such foundations calls for and encourages affirmation of the 'unified personality' ('die in sich geschlossene Persönlichkeit') which 'no longer succumbs to a divided awareness' ('die keinem gespaltenen Bewußtsein mehr unterliegt'),[17] as the official doctrine has it. It fosters idealisation of those features which draw society together and an image of the individual characterised by a synthesis equivalent to that which on this view should distinguish society itself. Reflecting the belief in socialism as the 'organic' goal of the 'process' of history and confirming the relation between the past, memory and identity, official approval is given to Becher's view that only through 'identification . . . with the great historical demands of our time' is 'deep and true personality' possible. It is in this sense, and with these implications, that literature in East Germany takes pride in being 'humanistic' and in linking up with the literature of the eighteenth century, with its high expectations of the individual, as such and as a social being. 'It is not a question of going back to Goethe, J. R. Becher said in his *Verteidigung der Poesie*, but 'of going forward to Goethe and forwards with him'. From no point of view is the contrast between the literature of East Germany and the Federal Republic more marked than from that of the model role of Goethe, including his idealisation of the obligations of selfhood ('so mußt du sein, dir kannst du nicht entfliehen') as an inherent and consistently developing pattern of organic form ('geprägte Form, die lebend sich entwickelt'). By and large, though not consistently, the writers of the Federal Republic in the sixties will have none of this, and its negation is exemplified in the work of Dieter Kühn, one who came on the scene at the very close of the decade.

Kühn's prose text entitled *N* (1970) takes the instance of a man, Napoleon, conventionally regarded as a great and powerful 'personality', and destroys the aura of this by fictionally diversifying it. Far from being destined to be what he became and none other, Napoleon is shown in other possible roles, among them priest, writer, mathematician, and so on. Only chance, it is implied, led him to what turned out to be his historical role, with a self to match, and even then, once in that role, his future was haphazardly determined. He could, for example, have been murdered on 17 Brumaire at the point of seizing power. This possibility, too, is fictionally explored, the last and grandly rhetorical section of the work listing the subsequent historical events that would then never have taken place. History is thus demythologised. No more than the individual self does it move to given ends as in the nature of things. Differently manipulated, it can, like the identity of the self, turn out quite unlike what on a more metaphysical view it could seem destined to become. Kühn's *Ausflüge im Fesselballon* (1971) is a variation on the same theme. Wolfgang Braemer had possibilities other than that of becoming a schoolmaster—German conversational assistant in the United States, public relations man, architect—and these are duly presented and demonstrated. He is a man characterised by a 'basic feeling of the provisional', reflected in the layout of his study ('a few slight pieces of furniture that were easily moved, and a small carpet that could be quickly rolled up'). Hence to some extent his fictional self (never realised in practice) as archivist: 'Braemer clearly tends towards improvisation, and this career offers him adequate possibilities for developing this.' If this is what he became, it was partly because of a tendency 'to a certain indolence and immobility', a desire for security, leading to the choice, among many other possibilities open to him, of 'one of the most secure professions'. He started life with many alternative possibilities, and the fact that only one materialised, and then by chance, is made to expose the illusion of 'a development characterised by its continuity'.

What applies to the individual applies no less to history. That is what we are to deduce from *N*. The relationship between the sense of the inherent continuity of history and the inherent continuity of the self, on which we reflected earlier in this chapter, is confirmed in its inversion. If the self is disposable, then so too is the course of history. If the identity of the self is not inherent, the pattern of history is not, either. If one can reconstruct and readjust the self according to desire and circumstance, then one can manipulate history. Heinrich Vormweg is quite right: behind Kühn's handling of the question of identity, corresponding to this view of the self and the course it follows or does not follow, is the idea 'that history is relative and can be changed'.[18] The political direction in this treatment of the identity question is obvious enough, and already at this stage—we shall return to the problem later—one is led to ask whether this had not been its hidden force all along. If so, the co-existence in West German literature of the sixties in so prominent a form of the problem of identity and, as we shall see in the next chapter, the demand that literature should be put in the service of social change—'politicised', that is to say—could have a deeper significance.

Notes

1 Uwe Schultz (ed.) *Das Tagebuch und der moderne Autor*, Munich, 1965, p. 109.
2 Quoted in W. Hofer, *Geschichtsschreibung und Weltanschauung. Betrachtungen zum Werk Friedrich Meineckes*, Munich, 1950, p. 537.
3 *Deutscher Geist in Gefahr*, Stuttgart and Berlin, 1933, p. 54, and *Französischer Geist im 20. Jahrhundert*, Berne, 1952, p. 526.
4 *One-dimensional Man. Studies in the Ideology of Advanced Industrial Society*, London, 1964, p. 99.
5 Cf. Paul Raabe (ed.), *Expressionismus. Der Kampf um eine literarische Bewegung*, Munich, 1965, p. 63.
6 Cf. Paul Pörtner (ed.), *Literatur und Revolution*, Neuwied, 1960, I, p. 138.
7 *Zur Tradition der Moderne. Aufsätze und Anmerkungen 1964–1971*, Neuwied, 1972, pp. 316 ff.
8 Tony Phelan, *Rationalist Narrative in some Works of Arno Schmidt*, University of Warwick Occasional Papers in German Studies, No. 2, 1972, pp. 25, 26, 27.
9 Dieter Wellershoff, *Literatur und Veränderung*, Cologne and Berlin, 1969, p. 40.
10 For a more detailed discussion of the relevant aspects of this novel, and of some others briefly mentioned in this chapter, cf. R. Hinton Thomas

and W. van der Will, *The German Novel and the Affluent Society*, Manchester, 1968.

11 Cf. *Erfahrungen und Leseerfahrungen*, Frankfurt a. M., 1965, pp. 124 ff.

12 Cf. Lothar Baier (ed.), *Über Ror Wolf*, Frankfurt a. M., 1972, pp. 154–5.

13 Cf. Anneliese Botond (ed.), *Über Thomas Bernard*, Frankfurt a. M., 1970, p. 68.

14 In his review in *Die Zeit*, 1 August 1969.

15 Introducing a volume of selected translations, *Jonathan Swift. Satiren*, Frankfurt a. M., 1965.

16 Cf. *Neue Deutsche Literatur*, 1, 1967, reporting the first annual conference of the (East German) Deutscher Schriftstellerverband, with an important editorial entitled 'Von der neuen deutschen Literatur'.

17 *Ibid.*, p. 71.

18 *Jahresring*, 1971–72, p. 288.

Chapter 2

Literature and politicisation

After 1945, with the war over and Germany defeated, literature was political only in the sense of being firmly anti-fascist. What it stood for in political terms is not easy to define. There was a general concern for democracy, a certain amount of optimism, and the sense of a fresh start with the advantage of experience. But this hardly amounted to a clear-cut set of attitudes and values. It would be fair to call literature in this phase politically committed in the main, but only in a rather general way. Broadly speaking, it was left-wing, but not in a very specific sense. In the fifties, with writers like Böll, Koeppen and Andersch, the emphasis shifted from anti-fascism to criticism of government and its policies. Characteristic themes included the misuse of authority, the failure of government to act wisely and humanely, the misguidedness of the Church. By the late fifties the Federal Republic had become a firmly established liberal democracy to the right of centre. There was no great internal dissension, and the situation offered little scope for radical opposition. The effect of government policy was more apolitical than otherwise, appealing to a general desire for security and prosperity and to a cautious attitude towards what could seem risky experimentation in the social and economic sphere—and, after the strains and hazards of the recent past, this, not unnaturally, was what many people wanted. Writers were often dissatisfied with the situation, but in the circumstances they could hardly have been expected to represent political extremes. Their socio-critical energy was alerted, though they found it difficult to associate their discontent with any particular cause which would solve the problems. This helped to give currency to talk about the 'unease' (*Unbehagen*) of the intellectuals as 'court jesters' of society. They enjoyed, it was said, the freedom to make fun of institutions and individuals without the obligations of responsible criticism, without positive solutions of their own, and without much influence on practical affairs. Martin Walser, in his 'Skizze zu einem Vorwurf' (1960),[1] was as cynical about the writer's situation in this respect as others sometimes were about the writer. Walser felt guiltily ineffective and spoke not only for himself. His use of the first person plural gave the piece implications beyond his individual case.

The inclination in the fifties towards the grotesque, especially in the shorter prose forms, reflected the situation of writers unable to identify concretely any overall source of discontent, still less to feel that there was much that they could do about it beyond giving it literary expression. A case in point is Reinhard Lettau's *Schwierig-keiten beim Häuserbauen* (1958). By comparison, his later stories (*Feinde*, 1968) have a sharper focus on a more specific theme, power, and with reference to a particular institution, the military. *Feinde* appeared after his return to Berlin from America in 1965. He had there been accumulating direct political experience, which he em-bodied in his explicitly political *Täglicher Faschismus* (1971). Impor-tant too in this connection was his exercise in direct and specific political analysis in several essays of 1966. With *Feinde* Lettau's grotesque stories 'have become political in that they are concerned less with general innovations in the sphere of cultural criticism and stem far more directly from immediate observation'.[2] The case of Lettau illustrates as concisely as could be the change in this regard from the one decade to the other.

The more in the sixties intellectual circles came to be politicised, the more common it became to stress the 'resignation' of the writers of the decade before, as in the case of Alfred Andersch. He had been actively engaged in left-wing politics, spent some time in a concen-tration camp, and in the 1939–45 war deserted on the Italian front. These experiences, portrayed in his autobiographical account *Die Kirschen der Freiheit* (1952), underlie his novel about the Nazi period, *Sansibar oder Der Letzte Grund* (1957). Here, as in his radio play *Fahrerflucht* (1958), is developed what had by this time crystallised as his characteristic theme, desertion and escape. Carried over into the circumstances of the new prosperity, it is the theme of *Die Rote* (1957) and it is still with him in *Efraim* (1967). A tone of resignation and contracting-out still colours Böll's *Billard um halb-zehn* and for that matter also *Ansichten eines Clowns*.

Enzensberger was attempting more particularly to come to grips with concrete social and political realities by detailed quasi-socio-logical analysis. He published some of the results in 1962 under the title *Einzelheiten*, a collection of essays written over the previous ten years. On general questions, he says, we are adequately informed. It is the particulars that call for attention. What 'can be localised' is too much neglected. To bother about it tends to be regarded as 'improper', but 'it alone allows the development of methods of observation that relate to the whole and can be applied to it'. Only through analysis of the whole by reference to what is specific within it can 'the whole be looked at critically'. Influenced by Adorno, but substituting 'consciousness industry' (*Bewusstseinsindustrie*) for Adorno's 'culture industry' (*Kulturindustrie*), with its less extensive implications, Enzensberger takes as of special importance the press and the mass media as the means whereby awareness is conditioned; 'only when basic industries have been built up, and the mass production of consumer goods has been assured, can the consciousness industry really develop'. We are still, however, some way from the radically revolutionary mood that within a very short time was to dominate the German intellectual scene, and with which by the close of the sixties Enzensberger, together with Walser and to some extent Böll, was to associate himself. Meanwhile, as regards the spirit in which his critical analysis was to be understood, he was at pains to point out that the purpose was 'revision, not revolution', without 'aggression' in mind; 'there is no wish to polish off or liquidate the objects of the criticism that is being attempted, rather to expose them to a second inspection'.

The phase in which for the most part these essays were written was one in which, after war and reconstruction, a new society was taking shape. Features of this society were emerging with sufficient clarity to command attention and offered material enough for analysis, but clearly it was too early for Enzensberger to advance towards revolutionary or overtly ideological generalisations. At this stage, anyhow, ideology was an ill-omened word, associated with National Socialism, Stalinism, and East Germany. True, in his study of *Der Spiegel* Enzensberger spoke disdainfully of a style of social criticism which starts with the assumption that it cannot fundamentally alter anything, and there are latent revolutionary implications in his analysis of the press and the media. It is inherent in his argument that, since the criticised features are an inevitable result of the position of the media in a particular kind of society, the one cannot be changed without the other. There are also aggressive implications elsewhere at the time in Enzensberger's work. The poem 'ins lesebuch für die oberstufe' (in *Landessprache*, 1960) concludes with the lines: 'wut und geduld sind nötig, / in die lungen der macht zu blasen / den feinen tödlichen staub, gemahlen / von denen, die viel gelernt haben / die genau sind, von dir', and 'schwierige arbeit' (in *Blindenschrift*, 1964), dedicated to Adorno, foresees the 'barricades of the future'. All the same, as the quotations show, the one is not quite a call to revolution, and the other retains the spirit of 'revision' by critical exposure in its reference to the need 'jeden gedanken wenden der seine rückseite verbirgt'. Moreover, in one of the essays referred to ('Poesie und Politik') Enzensberger defines the 'political task' of a poem as 'refusing any political task and to speak for all'.

By comparison with a good many writers of the fifties and into the early sixties *Einzelheiten* reveals a more self-confident and dynamic attitude to social and political change. If writers at that stage were not as forthcoming in this respect as came to be taken for granted in the sixties, one reason was the problem of discovering beneath a general mood of discontent exactly what was wrong. Another was that they lacked any significant degree of solidarity among themselves. Walser reflected this in his reference in the 'Skizze zu einem Vorwurf' to writers as a minority proud of 'our disinclination to organise ourselves'. Both aspects help to explain, as far as West German literature in its relation to politics is concerned, the significance of the *Spiegel* affair of 1962.

This served in the first place to unite a number of writers in a common and specific cause, on an issue where questions of power and authority did not present themselves in an abstract and elusive way. Also, it gave them the added confidence of feeling themselves allies under a common banner with powerful and organised opinion beyond their own ranks. On the day after the occupation by the police of the offices of *Der Spiegel* a number of them signed a telegram declaring solidarity with the paper, and later in the same year came the so-called 'Manifest der Gruppe 47', with a long list of signatories. Solidarity, publicly declared and in support of a victim of common concern, meant a step towards solidarity among writers thus aligned, and it aimed at a specific result, the resignation of a Minister wielding the power allegedly put to such misuse. The principle that it should be seen as a normal obligation to make military secrets public also had far-reaching and fundamental implications. For the writers involved the *Spiegel* affair was timely and advantageous. To become politically more effective they needed an issue to unite them, and, as an apparent threat to critical and dissident opinion, this was admirably calculated to rally diverse interests in literary and intellectual circles. It provided writers with the opportunity to improve upon their image as 'court jesters' of society, to demonstrate that their criticism of affairs was responsible and in the general interest, and to give courage to any who might have shared Walser's inclination to believe that, for all their talk, they were superfluous in a society able to manage just as well without them. In some quarters the *Spiegel* affair tended to harden opinion against intellectuals, but, with the affair ending ingloriously for the authorities, they were rewarded for their pains at least with the sense of having taken a lead in an issue seeming to prove that their intervention in a clear-cut political issue could bring a real measure of success.

The outcome, however, was not to transform those concerned into ideologists of revolution. Enzensberger, who was to come into this category in due course, did not do so for the moment. The 're-visionist'—in Enzensberger's sense—rather than revolutionary stance revealed in *Einzelheiten* still more or less represented his position in his debate with Weiss. The latter had not yet reached the point of declared political alignment with East Germany in the 'Zehn Arbeitspunkte eines Autors in der geteilten Welt',[3] but all the same was moved to attack Enzensberger, *à propos* of Vietnam, for his lack of political decision, for his 'double morality', 'doubts' and 'caution'. Enzensberger hit back hard with some contemptuous remarks about ideological extremism and revolutionary talk: 'you can keep your moral rearmament on the left. I'm no idealist. I prefer arguments to confessions, doubts to emotions. I hate revolutionary chatter, and I don't need ideologies free of contradictions. In cases of doubt reality is what decides.'[4] Walser's anti-ideological and anti-revolutionary position is still clear enough in some of his essays in the volume *Erfahrungen und Leseerfahrungen*, published in 1965 and written in the years immediately preceding. A pertinent essay in this connection is entitled 'Imitation oder Realismus', dating from 1964. The slightly involved argument turns on his use of the terms 'reality' and 'realistic', the meaning of which here is explained in the following comment: 'the tale that demonstrably draws on realistic observation cannot be hoodwinked by reality, but rather tells reality what reality is like. It plays with reality until this admits: that's me.' A 'realistic' work of literature—and this is what Walser is advocating—is on this view not one that offers ready-made solutions: 'the so-called positive does not appear in a realistic play . . . The play itself is the positive', and 'the dialogue should not be destroyed . . . by any exclusive attempt to explain things'.

Enzensberger's rejection of 'ideologies free of contradiction' and Walser's of any 'exclusive attempt to explain things' represent a position very close to that a few years later of the schoolmaster Starusch in Günter Grass's *Örtlich betäubt* (1969). At one stage of the novel, in a discussion with Veronika Lewand, he talks a language that she quickly and contemptuously rejects at once as that of the pluralistic society. Starusch retorts, 'and I hate confessions. I hate sacrifices. Hate dogmas and eternal verities. I hate the unambiguous.' By this time, with the growth of the New Left in Germany and the spread of its influence in literary and intellectual circles, Grass's novel, in which Starusch's position clearly corresponds fairly closely to his own, was regarded in more radical quarters as behind the times. Their ideology required that he should be discredited. As a writer of acknowledged distinction and committed to parliamentary democracy, he became an object of hostility. Criticism of him became frequent, brash and spiteful, and his position was caricatured to make him easier to hit at. He had reached a point, it was being said, at which he was prepared to accept things as they were rather than to take a stand on fundamental change. Already in certain poems ('Der Dampfkessel Effekt', 'In Ohnmacht gefallen', 'Irgendwas machen') in *Ausgefragt* (1967) Grass had very noticeably distanced himself from the more demagogic forms of protest, and this helped to divide him and the radical left. Events at the meeting of Gruppe 47 in the same year made matters worse. The students demonstrated outside the meeting, and Gruppe 47 passed an anti-Springer resolution. This being its first public political move since the *Spiegel* affair, the students were prompted to refer to Grass unflatteringly on one of their banners. When Lettau read the resolution to the students, Grass was so angered that he threatened to withdraw his signature, and this in turn led Erich Fried[5] to accuse him of 'an untroubled relationship to power and publicity' and to speak of him fighting as much against the students as against the right wing. Reviewing the performance of Grass's play *Davor*, thematically linked to *Örtlich betäubt*, in the same journal. Peter Hamm damned it as 'a work of integration by a completely integrated and corrupted author', the work of a 'whitewasher of the SPD, who now goes so far as to lump NPD and SPD together'.[6] The tension in the relationship between Grass and the radical left was matched by the now openly declared contempt in the same circles for Gruppe 47, as represented by an article in *konkret* in 1967 by one of its foremost commentators, Ulrike Marie Meinhoff. The fact, she said, that some of the decisive political developments—the entry of the Federal Republic into NATO, the communist ban, the issue of the Emergency Laws, the Vietnam war—'have left absolutely no trace on the character of the group and the style of its work', unmasks it as being 'in complicity with the ruling class'.[7]

It has to be appreciated in this connection that, roughly half-way between the appearance of Enzensberger's *Einzelheiten* and Grass's *Örtlich betäubt*, there had come vociferously into the foreground the demand that literature should be 'politicised'. This marked a decisive change of mood, with important consequences over the whole literary and intellectual situation. It represented the reaction above all of those who had come to regard awareness as now anaesthetised against any desire for radical change and who blamed particularly the mass media—a main concern of Enzensberger in *Einzelheiten*— for bringing this about. The Springer press was singled out for attack in this connection, and it was charged with 'fascist' treatment of minorities, as by Lettau in an article in *Kursbuch* in 1966 with reference, amongst other things, to its portrayal of beatniks. Opting out of the consumer world, they are bound, he said, to be felt as a disturbing factor in a society which, for all its declarations of liberal intent, can only regard them as irrational.[8] The point was to show that the freedoms and tolerance of the pluralistic society were illusory.

As to why in this regard the crucial point of change was around the mid-sixties, two factors above all have to be borne in mind. It could not have occurred before the new society was sufficiently advanced to manifest its characteristics in so developed a form as to reveal what were taken to be its hidden and fuller implications. Also, at this juncture a younger generation, born in the Nazi period, reached maturity, and a number of younger writers published their first work just about this time. Characteristic of this generation was the rejection of the idea, which they associated with bourgeois culture, of a spiritual dimension transcending the political. This made them more open to sociologically orientated attitudes and to the growing influence of Marcuse. The older intellectuals had seen the hopes they once cherished of a revolutionary transformation of society disappointed by the coming of National Socialism and then by prosperity and affluence. Marcuse was among the first to overcome this sense of frustration by a new relationship with Marxism through which socialism appeared less as a continuation than as a fresh beginning. Ironically, the new generation was exceptionally privileged, the beneficiaries of a society more generous in the freedoms it offered than any before in German history. The situation thus created would once have seemed like a dream come true, but its effect now was to awaken further and heightened expectations as practical possibilities realisable in the short-term future. With awareness now conditioned by a consumer society to regard every model— in the realm of style and values no less than in that of material production and the market—as inherently obsolescent, the imagination was alerted to factors hampering the exercise of the freedoms opened up, and willingness to tolerate them was correspondingly reduced. A generation now accustomed to the idea that, on the analogy of many an industrial product, there was nothing that could not in principle be quickly changed and improved, and whose intellectuals were far removed from the complications of political power and responsibility, was the less prepared to believe that social imperfections could not be quickly remedied. In short, the expectation of the increasing satisfaction of need and desire gave dynamic force and revolutionary energy to impatience with things as they are, materially, socially and politically.

If it is in the nature of advanced industrial society to offer greater variety, and a wider diffusion, of material resources, the freedom to take advantage of the choices offered can be affected by pressures influencing the exercise of it. In the consumer society both effects are maximised, and then most particularly one can speak of a dialectic of freedom and conformism, of what Chotjewitz in *Vom Leben und Lernen* (1969) calls the 'stages of increasing emancipation' and all the 'new fetishes' thrown up and commanding authority. There can even come a point when deviance needs the support of conformism, the extremes stimulating each other. Walter Höllerer, who in 1965 edited a novel by various hands entitled *Das Gästehaus*, commented on this in his postscript: 'its main theme— and it is hardly surprising in a contemporary existential novel—is the individual in the group, the extravagant and conventional behaviour of the individual in the larger unit of a society based on the division of labour'. In Gerhard Zwerenz's novel *Casanova* (1966) Casanova represents 'the type of totally unintegrated individual', but in the end 'the Casanovites did conform'. In Paul Schallück's *Don Quichotte in Köln* (1967) the hero, having explored to the full the liberties offered by the permissiveness of Carneval, adjusts himself to the *status quo*. Typical of mere entertainment literature of the more popular kind is that the adventuring is just self-indulgent escape, and the sole and simple norm is submission—as, for instance, in Willi Heinrich's *Schmetterlinge weinen nicht* (1969).

Conformism in the sixties becomes a major and characteristic theme as a corollary of the freedoms opened up. The greater the scope of licence, the more frustrating were such restraints as remained. In Peter Handke's play *Selbstbezichtigung* (1966) various voices are heard, leading from birth to growing awareness and then to guilty self-questioning, about their sins of omission in the matter of conforming. The list of things to be conformed to makes its effect by its range and diversity and by the mixing up, as if the voices cannot distinguish between them, of the important and the trivial— the 'laws of decency', the 'laws of love', the 'laws of cosmetics', the 'demands of piety'. The tone of the confessional heightens the solemnity of the obligations to conform, the smallest deviation being acknowledged as if amounting to mortal sin. In his play *Kaspar* (1968) the theme is provided by the biography of a well known foundling of the early nineteenth century. Wassermann once made this character the theme of a novel, but turned it to more idealistic purposes. In Handke's play reality, mediated by the various 'announcers', forces its claim on Kaspar through the process of his being taught the vocabulary needed to talk about the reality around him. The effect in the first place is to deprive him of the only sentence he naturally commands, and then to widen his range of speech by exercising him in what amounts to the clichés of conventional experience. His willing efforts to reproduce them, and his success in doing so, indicate the manipulation of his desire to accommodate himself. His reward is the sense of not being superfluous in society ('I'm useful') and the feeling that life makes sense ('I know where things belong'). 'Induced to speak', he has been 'ushered into reality'. Having thus become what society requires him to be, he is 'only coincidentally I', which is to say that as a self he is destroyed. It would, however, be quite wrong to leave the impression that for those whose gospel was the 'politicisation of literature' Handke was seen as belonging to their ranks. An extreme position of hostility is

exemplified in an article in *kürbiskern* in 1970, in which his 'neutral
linguistic structures' are condemned, as in *Kaspar*, for banishing the
'social context' and leaving intact the society from which they are
taken. This, as we shall see, is a type of criticism also directed sometimes against Heissenbüttel. On a related but different theme is
Renate Rasp's novel *Der Ungeratene Sohn* (1967), where for perversely idealistic reasons the parents have the idea of manipulating
their son into becoming a tree. Their success is due as much as anything to his lack of resistance, even to his collaboration. In Gisela
Elsner's *Der Nachwuchs* (1968) the son also shows himself keen to
conform to his parents' pressure, but in this case he makes it harder
for his manipulators.

Such concern about the individual as the victim of pressures to
adapt himself to other people's requirements does not go to prove
that society was, at least in any simple sense, repressive. It is fairer
to say of the circumstances in the sixties that the extent to which
society tolerated, and even encouraged, experiments in personal and
artistic freedom itself heightened sensitivity to residual restraint and
obligation. The process by which freedom of choice runs up against
factors restricting that choice becomes a characteristic theme of
literature in the sixties, and it lent itself to over-simplistic generalisations about these factors as merely the result of evil machinations
by people controlling the media. With expectations of freedom
pitched high, the checks and balances of a pluralistic society made
the latter appear less as a structure allowing people the chance to
follow their individual tastes than negatively as a system of calculated stability cunningly devised to protect itself from dissent and
change while allowing a harmless freedom of expression. Emphasis
then came to be placed more on aspects which led to the pluralistic
society being defined with the stress on stability and uniformity than
on freedom and opportunity, as 'uniform pluralism' (Oswald
Wiener), 'imposed democracy' (Heinrich Böll). Also, by contrast
with societies having a more clear-cut power structure of a simpler—
and less democratic—kind, a pluralistic society, with its diversity of
institutions and the complexity of their relationships, is made to
appear opaque, rendering it the more difficult to identify particular
points of authority. 'The system,' Walser said, 'admittedly creates
"ignorance" about itself' and 'produces in most people a feeling of
ignorance and incompetence, of insecurity and fear, because of the
multiplicity of conflicting opinions that exist within it. It is off this

that in turn other and privileged opinion-formers live, the so-called "experts".[9] Grass's *Örtlich betäubt* is partly about this. His dentist figure reveals his understanding of the mood of some of the younger generation in this respect when he says, 'I admit that this consumer society, because it gives the impression of being so compact, can appear uncanny to a seventeen-year-old, because it seems to him incomprehensible.'

Those set on quick and radical change were the more inclined to see such a society as governed by a complex and immutable rationality, and the authority of the whole as remote from, even immune to, individual initiative and intervention. The more in the consumer society the sense of choice is heightened and short-term desire fulfilled, the greater was the feeling of grievance against whatever did not lend itself to quick adjustment to the claims of individual satisfaction. What followed was the sense of a cold and mechanical 'system' with an inherent rationality protecting it from the forces of change generated within it. *Örtlich betäubt* catches this aspect too in the way it sets the development of more tolerant attitudes in relation to the experience, mediated in this case by the dentist and the technical sophistication of the treatment he provides, of science and technology. In these conditions alienation came into the foreground of discussion as a central topic of the sixties and in close conjunction with the 'politicisation of literature'. But those who spoke most about it were usually without experience of what it might mean in terms of industrial labour. What was objected to was ultimately the pressures of the technological age in connection with the experience, real or imagined, of political impotence in the presence of power structures which the individual might find it hard to grasp. To this extent the problem of identity is at work in the background here too, and there are also consequences affecting the attitude to the immediate political situation, the feeling namely that the parliamentary system no longer provides a satisfactory link between the individual and the process by which political decisions are made. Politics—at any rate, as understood in a liberal society—on this view tend to lose their relevance, governed, as they may then seem to be, by the hidden realities of a too complexly organised society.

A mood of protest was generated with few restraints in scope and expression, but with its own frustrations. At the time when Brecht's *Dreigroschenoper* was being most appreciated in the circles that it most criticised, Walter Benjamin had commented on the way the

culture of bourgeois society could absorb, even encourage, revolutionary material without endangering its own position. This notably
affected political cabaret. Already in Adenauer's time it had become
too respectable for the taste of those whose criterion was political
effectiveness and for whom the political cabaret as an institution
came to seem a contradiction in itself. Its role correspondingly
declined, and by the mid-sixties, for the time being at any rate, it was
more or less taken over by a type of 'song', designated 'politisch
engagiertes Lied', discussed later in this book. As if to prove Benjamin right, dissent was not only tolerated but subsidised in official
quarters. The city of Berlin helped to make it possible for Gruppe 47
to meet there, and while by this time it was viewed by some as so
respectable as to be part of the establishment, Berlin could even so
hardly expect a gathering of friends of the *status quo*. The short-lived
Frankfurt 'Forum für Literatur',[10] intended 'to open up a readily
available platform of discussion for the second post-war generation',
enjoyed official backing. While one of its declared aims was to take
advantage of what the cultural market offered in terms of the commercialisation of literature ('you have to be able to sell literature like
cheese'), the expectation could only be that it would be more socio-
critical than affirmative. Better examples might be Essen's financial
support of an underground festival (IEST) held some two years later,
in 1968, or the media support for the Waldeck festivals referred to in
a later chapter. There is a comment about this sort of situation in
Nossack's novel *Der Fall d'Arthez* ('you aren't even allowed to cry
out, because that doesn't disturb people any more, it is immediately
commercialised'), and to the same effect in Grass's *Örtlich betäubt*.
Trying to dissuade his pupil Scherbaum from burning a dog publicly
in Berlin as a protest against the use of napalm in Vietnam, Starusch
tells him, 'and a fortnight later no one will be talking about it,
because something else has turned up, maybe a cow with two heads'.
If, however, protest was being rendered ineffective enough to cause
resentment, all the blame could not be put on the 'system', if only
because the failure of people to be adequately shocked was partly
at least a result of the progressive erosion of taboos, and this was one
of the things the radical left wing in Germany, and a good deal of
its literature, had been working to achieve.

All these considerations help to explain the demand in the sixties
for the 'politicisation of literature'. This came in the first place from
outside literary circles. It owed almost everything to the movement

dominated by the students in close association with the New Left, hardly anything in the first place to writers, many of whom it was to influence so decisively. As to why things happened this way round, it is useful, in order to set the developments now to be described in perspective, to compare them with the situation in the fifties as far as the effect of certain main political issues was concerned, such as the remilitarisation of West Germany, the decision to enter NATO, and the proposal to equip the Bundeswehr with atomic weapons. These had all produced lively critical responses in literary intellectual circles, but the opposition had in the first place been more moral than political, trusting rather in the power of rational persuasion, and also the younger generation had not been publicly in the foreground. Of the issues mentioned, the most important from our present point of view is the last. Out of it came the journal *Das Argument*, started in 1958, and this was to play a particularly significant part, both in itself and in conjunction with the discussion groups of the Argument Club, in preparing the way for the 'movement' of the Berlin students.

By the time in 1964 they first took to the streets tension had been building up between radical students and the authorities within the universities, especially in Berlin. The sit-in there in 1966, resulting from the refusal of the authorities to allow a lecture in the university by a prominent left-wing journalist, helped to make the conflict more openly political, and it decisively advanced the self-awareness of the students as an oppositional body. So too did the protests, and the consequent police action, about the visit of Vice-President Humphrey and, a little later, of the Shah of Persia in June 1967, when a student, Benno Ohnesorg, was shot. This was the critical juncture at which the radical students first really became aware of themselves as a 'movement'. Beyond that, the impulse of the students' movement came to owe a lot to the debate about the Emergency Laws, which, providing for certain parts of the constitution to be suspended in the event of a threat to the security of the State, lent themselves to the interpretation of validating the arbitrary misuse of power. An important practical outcome was the creation of the organisation Notstand der Demokratie in 1966, which, supported by virtually all the 'extra-parliamentary opposition', became a focal point of real significance. In the same year it organised a congress, at which intellectuals (including Ernst Bloch and Enzensberger), trade unionists and students were represented. Then, on the grounds that opposition to the laws was not properly represented in parliament, the Grand Coalition—and the parliamentary system itself—came under attack as embodying a false consensus. Grass had already expressed anxiety on this score. If the coalition came about, he had warned Willy Brandt in an open letter,[11] the result would cause the younger generation to abandon moderation and turn away from the accepted form of government. As the struggle passed from the universities into the streets it drew strength from the study of American policy in Vietnam in the wider context of the social and political factors operating in the Third World, highlighted in the influential second number of *Kursbuch* in 1965. At home, it was being said, capitalism had succeeded in concealing the class struggle and dulling the awareness of large numbers of people, but they were now at last coming to realise how great was the contradiction between the slogans of liberal democracy at home and what was happening world-wide. The assassination attempt on Rudi Dutschke served further to widen the issues into general questions about the basis and values of German democracy. The role and character of the 'extra-parliamentary oposition' changed. A term used already in the fifties to describe the body of socio-critical writers, it assumed sharper political energy and operated with a better trained, more ideologically motivated and more sociological understanding. In this more militant phase, restyled by abbreviation APO, it now amounted to a vigorously combative opposition spearheaded by the radical students. The position was intensified by the recession of 1966–67, a relatively minor one in itself, but appearing significant as seeming for the first time to break the pattern of prosperity. Interpreted as proving illusory the hopes attached to the stability and growth of capitalism, it was an encouragement to those set on destroying the latter.

The climax of the students' protest movement in 1968 coincided with the escalation of the war in Vietnam. In the same year attention was directed to the Frankfurt Book Fair. The object of attack was the capitalist basis of book production, and the practice of some of the big houses, pre-eminently Suhrkamp and Rowohlt, of publishing books of contradictory political tendencies and making money out of it, though this could be seen as helping the radical cause as much as its enemies. Only in this way, too, could the conflicting sympathies within a liberal society be duly represented, but those whose ideological sympathies ran counter to moderation spoke of duplicity and dishonesty, and the publishing trade was accused of institutionalising in its own way the corruptions of capitalism. As the 'shop window' of the book trade, the Frankfurt Book Fair was in a particularly exposed position. The authorities controlling it came under violent criticism, supported by demonstrations. There were calls for the 'self-organisation of the anti-authoritarian camp', and the 'boycotting and breaking up of bourgeois businessmen making money out of the left-wing movement', and for an 'Anti-Book Fair'—as such, in fact, the Mini-Pressen Messe, set up in 1970, was conceived. To make matters worse, it was discovered that certain books published by Rowohlt had been bought in quantities by the Defence Ministry and dropped, in disguised form, over East Germany by way of propaganda. In the course of the disturbances the police were called in, proving to the protesters that the establishment was ready to use force to preserve the evil situation.

The increasingly militant belief in the 'politicisation of literature' was also reflected in events affecting the internal organisation of publishing houses and the management of certain types of publication. Lektors in the Suhrkamp Verlag began to demand more widely shared decision-making as to what books should be published. The outcome was agreement that a general meeting of Lektors should settle the programme, but the managing director was to have the final say. Other firms, too, adopted the principle of joint decision-making by the collective of Lektors. Then again there was the demand that profits should revert to those who made the goods, namely the writers. Both ideas, as regards decision-making and profits, came to affect the administration of the journal *Kursbuch*, which had been founded by Enzensberger and which, now occupying a representative position on the left, clearly felt the obligation to set an example. Transferred from Suhrkamp to Wagenbach—whose own organisation on a democratic and collective basis had meanwhile fallen victim to internal dissension—it adopted a constitution in which participatory principles were acknowledged, while recognising certain inescapable realities—the need for advertisements, for instance, and discount for booksellers. Care was to be taken 'that our organisation no longer succumbs to the logic of the utilisation of capital'. Capital was to be invested and the interest employed to pay contributions or to hold down the price. Decisions about content were to depend on 'permanent and informal' discussion, with readers and contributors taking part. Organisationally there was to be only a 'minimal administrative organisation'. The avoidance of a large bureaucratic structure, prone to establish and perpetuate its own authority, remote from democratic pressures from below, was clearly seen as an alternative to the managerial arrangements associated with capitalist enterprises. The outcome was to be to put a left-wing journal 'into the hands of the producers'. Similar considerations applied to the creation of the Verband Deutscher Autoren. Exploitation of writers by publishers, the press and the media was a central theme at the foundation meeting in 1969. The main speaker on that occasion was Böll, who called on writers to take power into their own hands 'over the things we produce'.

The events thus summarised, significant in their own right in the context of the 'politicisation of literature', serve to bring out two aspects essential in the meaning to be attached to the term. One is the notion of the function of literature as primarily, even exclusively, an instrument of social and political change, with the stress on direct and quick results. The other is the shift of emphasis to the economic basis of literature within a system of production.

The 'politicisation of literature', as we have seen, owed its energy in the first place and above all to impulse and example from outside the literary sphere. Thus from around 1966 a position was quickly created in which, as has been nicely said, writers suddenly found themselves 'overtaken on the left'.[12] Enzensberger was quick to catch up with the new state of affairs. The erstwhile 'revisionist' in 1968 denounced 'the sickly parliament' and 'the system' as at the 'end of its legitimacy', called for unity of action on the broadest possible front of writers, students and workers, and declared: 'the capitalist and party bosses who rule us will never listen to us. They'll pretend to be deaf and dumb ... until we go out on to the streets with the students and the workers, and express ourselves a bit more clearly. The lesson is obvious: misgivings aren't enough. Our aim must be: let us create French conditions here in Germany.'[13] Many of the arguments advanced in favour of the 'politicisation of literature', like the events behind it, lent themselves obviously, if paradoxically, to the view that there were better ways of making a political effect than writing books. The 'politicisation of literature' was in fact poorly supported by direct practical examples, apart from a certain amount of *agitprop* poetry and 'songs' (neither of which was new), some 'street theatre' plays (like Johannes Schenk's *Produktiva. Ein Agitationsstück* (1967) and Peter Schütt's *Kampnagel lehrt euch: Arbeiter wehrt euch!* (1969) and othe examples mentioned elsewhere) and, as we shall see, certain developments leading to the formation of Werkkreis 70. (Schütt, incidentally, was one of the founders of Werkkreis 70, and also of the literary activist group Hamburg linksliterarisch and, also in Hamburg, of the Schule schreibender Arbeiter.)

Nor is it hard to understand why on the whole the response of younger writers was more clear-cut and activistic than was the case with those rather older. It had been true earlier in the decade, and to a not insignificant extent it remained the case, that writers 'at the time of their greatest self-confidence, around the beginning of the sixties, were never particularly political or particularly left-wing. Rather, they had been moralists.'[14] This was reflected in the difficulties surrounding the 1966 meeting of Gruppe 47, when, supported by the Ford Foundation, it held its conference that year in Princeton. There were a number of important absentees, including Böll, Walser and Hildesheimer. The last-mentioned spoke of his dislike of going to America at the time of the escalation of the Vietnam war and of accepting money from the Ford Foundation, associated as it was with American industry, which was heavily involved in the war. The nature of the response defines it as primarily a moral one, though it may well be true that political activities of the kind referred to had helped to alert these writers to problems thus presented to them. In 1966 Walser spoke in defence of political protest at a meeting in Munich about Vietnam and in a directly political tone. He had, he said, 'swallowed a lot of the political tranquillisers offered. I took the SPD very seriously, I adjusted . . . to an age in which American freedom was spread around. I found that life was more comfortable if you didn't put up too much resistance. But since America has been openly engaged in its man-hunt in Vietnam, I no longer respond to the drugs of justification.' For him, therefore, protest had 'become as necessary as war for the generals'. In the same year, also in Munich, he said that he wanted to rouse and unify opinion in the Federal Republic as 'probably the only West European State (with the exception of Portugal and Spain) in which criticism of the American war has found no political expression'. What he suggested, however, was not so much political action as a policy of enlightenment. His idea was to set up an organisation which would 'collect and circulate information, document developments, and prepare a petition that everyone opposing the American war in Vietnam could sign'.[15] This is fully in line with his radio talk on

'Engagement als Pflichtfach für Schriftsteller',[16] where he insisted
that the writer can influence opinion by making information available
about the political situation. At the same time he betrayed some
scepticism about the practical effects of political action: 'the climate
merely becomes more bearable; the Victorian qualities of the Federal
Republic become visible, and the laughable nature of its claim to
power recognisable. Things start to stir. Since nothing really alters,
one might say that in this way a charming, entertaining game begins.
The appearance of movement within what is actually mere lethargy.'

The stress on literature as, economically speaking, 'production'
was in large measure due to Walter Benjamin who, after a period of
relative neglect, began in the sixties to exercise an influence as never
before. One of his most important texts in this connection was his
essay entitled 'Der Autor als Produzent', originally given as a lecture
in Paris in 1934, and now at last published. He was here concerned
to show that the notion of the writer as autonomous, free 'to write
away at whatever he liked', identified him with specific class
interests, with the capitalists against the proletariat. His aim was to
help bring about a situation in which art was taken out of the capitalists' control and placed in the hands of the working class. Taking as
his text a quotation from Aragon, he requires from the writer and
intellectual a 'behaviour that transforms him from a supplier of the
apparatus of production into an engineer, who sees it as his job to
fit in with the aims of the proletarian revolution'. What he must do
is to 'further the nationalisation of the intellectual means of production', which means seeing ways of 'organising intellectual workers
in the actual process of production' and of having practical proposals
'for changing the function of the novel, the drama, and of poetry'.
The better 'he can direct his activities towards this task', the 'more
correct' will be the 'slant', and the 'higher will the technical quality
of his work necessarily be'. The 'more precisely in this way he
becomes aware of his job in the process of production, the less is he
likely to think of wanting to appear as an "intellectual" '. The other
essay of Benjamin important in this context, one of his most famous,
is that entitled *Das Kunstwerk im Zeitalter seiner technischen
Reproduzierbarkeit*. It is a work of brilliant insights in many
respects; distorted, however, in others by its too close proximity to
the phenomenon of National Socialism and from over-generalisation
from the relatively new arts of the cinema and photography. The
relevant feature here is the argument that the 'reproducibility' of

art shows with exceptional clarity its setting in a material process of production and the alleged results.

Again and again the appeal was made in the sixties to 'Der Autor als Produzent', and at the close of the decade it figures yet again in Hans Christoph Buch's important essay 'Von der möglichen Funktion der Literatur'.[17] Benjamin, he says, 'measures the critical potential of literature by its ability not only to feed the apparatuses of production but also—in a socialist sense—to change them'. Publishing houses, theatre and journals 'must change from being apparatuses of alien capitalist control' into instruments 'for the self-determination of their producers' and thus within the existing conditions 'anticipate one aspect of socialist utopia'. About the same time appeared Michael Scharang's *Zur Emanzipation der Kunst* (1971), which draws systematically on Benjamin's thinking, selectively turning his ideas to account along rather the same lines. Scharang, an Austrian, had made his début with the collection of texts *Verfahren eines Verfahrens* (1969), with a foreword by Heissenbüttel. It is a collection of sophisticated and sometimes obscure prose texts, 'progressive', as one might say, in formal respects, open to criticism, one would think, from a radical point of view for not directly enough coming to grips with real political issues. In his next volume, *Schluss mit dem Erzählen und andere Erzählungen* (1970), the verbal structures have a more direct and more political content and purpose. The first piece ('Ein Verantwortlicher entlässt einen Unverantwortlichen') begins: 'and for this reason delivers a speech / which is here / reconstrued and construed and reproduced and / produced in order / to fire / the anger of all who've had enough of their superiors'. 'Die Ausbreitung des Unglaubens' revolves around themes of power and authority, and language is arranged in such a way as to expose different types and attitudes. The literary effects predominate over the political ones, and it would be easy to use against Scharang his own criticism of Hubert Fichte's novel *Die Palette* (1968), on the theme of Hamburg's 'underground', which he censured for a 'literary stylisation' which is in reality 'an impotent defence mechanism against the language of the ruling class', a 'poetic transformation ... of sociological phenomena'. This has 'always been the affirmative function of a type of art that sees itself at one with the established society'.[18]

All the more striking, therefore, is the way Scharang in *Zur Emanzipation der Kunst* espouses Benjamin's ideas and the use to which he puts them. Taking as his point of departure *Das Kunstwerk im*

Zeitalter seiner technischen Reproduzierbarkeit, he briefly recapitu-
lates the argument thus: 'the new concept of art that Benjamin
creates is a technical one or, in other words, is determined by a technical concept of production'. It is 'political' because 'the technical
is understood socially, in its importance for production'. The theme
of 'production' then quickly establishes itself in *Zur Emanzipation
der Kunst* as the central one. The writer's work as 'Produktion', the
writer as 'Kunstproduzent', culture as located in a 'Produktionsbereich', culture itself as 'Kulturproduktion', 'Überbauproduktion',
the university as the students' 'eigener Produktionsbereich'—the
concept is put to varied use. If art has now to be seen just as one kind
of 'production', the question arises as to its place in the overall
bourgeois system of production. The answer runs as follows: 'art as
a productive force was useless to the capitalist process of production,
at least in the sense that it could not determine and further production in the capitalist sense'. Therefore in bourgeois society art was
no more than an 'ideology for purposes of justification', and the
writer was not free. Benjamin's argument thus becomes the basis of
the case for the 'emancipation' of art, not meaning merely 'being
made equal to what exists', but something 'qualitatively different',
namely 'liberation'. As to how this can be achieved, Scharang com-
pares the masses in capitalist society ('who have no right of access
to the means of production and no right of control over production')
with 'those who produce art'. These 'seem to be less aware of their
situation because they have failed to recognise the technical means
of production, such as they themselves have developed . . . in the
mass media, as their own means of production'. They are left with two
alternatives. One is acceptance, as a compensation for their loneliness and isolation, of a privileged position, and the sense of being the
last defenders of culture. The other 'would be directly political',
namely, the 'disappropriation by producers of art of the technical
means of production necessary for an up-to-date kind of art-
production', and this alone would make 'a free development of
artistic productive forces possible'. The conclusion is 'that emancipation of art cannot take place without the emancipation of its
producers', and this is 'a revolutionary need, because it would
challenge the existing arrangements of property ownership'.

On the one hand, the argument, reinforced by references to
China, makes the fullest possible use of Benjamin's thesis about
literature as bound within the context of 'production', the aim being

to give the writer a revolutionary political role. On the other, it seems anxious to assure the writer that, if he follows this advice, he really will be free. Especially in conjunction with the evidence of Scharang's literary work, the contradiction might be taken to suggest a guilty social conscience seeking the consolation of a declared interest in political involvement—reflected in the horrific jargon of the essay—but reserving its position in the final analysis as regards the specific social and political realities, their limitations and their obligations, and whatever might follow from them. The poles of the argument are marked at the one extreme by a generalised and abstract image of power ('Herrschaft'), at the other by emphasis on 'liberation' and 'emancipation'. The one has to be demolished in the interests of the other, and in the context of the time the latter has to be seen with implications beyond institutionalised political solutions.

The 'politicisation of literature' implies, then, among other things, enrolling literature as a means, grandiosely and vaguely, of undermining 'Herrschaft'. Equally involved, and not likely to be satisfied in terms of political solutions other than those of an anarchistic kind, is a motivation directed more inwards than outwards, interested in politics because the restraints of the existing political system—of any political system, one is tempted to say—are necessarily obstacles in its way. To this extent the motivation is political only in a very partial and diluted sense. The extremes, theoretically at least, are held in balance, in a statement of Yaak Karsunke, a writer of radical political conviction and intention. 'Topical polemics,' he says, 'are more my field than eternity and art, in which I am not interested at all', but mere 'agitatory poetry' is something in which 'I am frequently aware of the lack of sensuous qualities': 'a successful fusion of the sensuous, emotional and spontaneous qualities of the beat and post-beat generation with the historical and critcal awareness of Brecht and his socially radical intentions would be ideal'.[19] In practice such a balance was difficult to sustain.

For if at the one extreme the 'politicisation of literature' meant subordination of literature to the need to change society, at the other, in a way prefigured in the writers of the Vienna Group, it was represented by a radical subjectivity, enthroning spontaneity and the expansion of the self. In the 'Statement' introducing *März Texte* 1 (1969), from a publishing house closely associated with the 'politicisation of literature', we read that the aim of the volume is 'to provide evidence of, and stimulus for, new modes of behaviour that have freed themselves from the constrictions of traditional evaluative categories, and stand for subjectivity and spontaneity'. Another anthology, of the same year, contains, as we have noted, Helmut Salzinger's poem 'Das lange Gedicht'. At the one pole it uses motifs associated with the political organisation and institutions of revolution; at the other, revolution begins 'within yourselves' and through it 'the wonderful, unique EGO' comes to feel itself 'eternal'. Thus the 'politicisation of literature' brings us back to the question of identity, and links this once again to the phenomenon of the public demonstration.

Demonstrations, we learn, are fieldwork in practical sociology, educating those who participate in the way society works, represented by the forces of law and order. But at the same time the 'learning process of the protest movements'[20] provides euphoric occasions for the release of an emotional energy by which the restraints of the *status quo* can be measured and the more passionately combated and rejected, and the self rewarded with a sense of reinvigoration and revitalisation. Literature and the demonstration can be compared in other ways too. The novelist and critic Reinhart Baumgart, using the idea of literature as 'symbolic action' and the demonstration as making politics something 'able to be sensuously grasped and experienced', describes the demonstration as 'literary also as far as its method is concerned'. Literature had now come to be 'no longer written, but demonstrated', from which fact he derives a category of 'what one might call demonstration-authors'.[21] This puts us in a better position to appreciate the special role played by Marcuse in moulding awareness at this stage through his rejection of the idea of revolution as able any longer to come from a single class, and through highlighting the role of small and scattered groups, lacking though they may be in real economic or political power. The class struggle in 'late capitalist' society, says Scharang, will be one 'that does not follow a historical model, and which . . . will acquire completely new features'.

Any general account therefore of the culture of the sixties in West Germany, to do justice to the mood of the younger generation in particular as an important element within it, must treat the urge for change not just in terms of a political logic facing outwards towards the institutionalisation of values and ideals but at the same time in relation to inward-directed instincts and impulses, to reasons more of the heart than of the head. The interplay is familiar, and is bound to figure in the motivation for political and social change at any time and in any circumstances. The distinguishing features in West Germany in the sixties were the force of the subjective impulse, the intensity of the interplay, and the revolutionary verve generated by it. The mixture is reflected in this description by a close observer of the scene: 'the idea of change captured people's imagination and brought into being a whole range of oppositional concepts: utopias of modes of existence free of domination, proposals for the humanisation of an alien technological environment, for the liberation of sexuality and creativity, for the development of the suppressed potential of man, of all men'.[22]

The extent to which, nourished by so insistent a subjectivism, utopian perspectives governing the drive for fulfilment now came to dominate the radical imagination is the corollary of weakened belief in the idea of the class struggle as any longer following an historical model, and this in the context of a weakened sense of the force and relevance of memory and history. Writers who view 'their production as totally political', it was stated in 1969 over the signatures of Michael Krüger and Klaus Wagenbach in *Tintenfisch*, an influential journal in the context of the 'politicisation of literature', are those whose aim is 'through language to help create a utopia'. Enzensberger's 'Gemeinplätze, die Neueste Literatur betreffend' reflects this aspect, written as it is, as one commentator very shrewdly remarked, from a sort of 'bird's eye view' from which historical, political and geographical determinants are cancelled out by being merged into some higher unit. As a result, the concept of revolution is made to appear 'new and endowed with futuristic qualities'.[23] Part of the theme of Böll's *Gruppenbild mit Dame* is the way of life adopted by those who, rejecting the competitive efficiency of modern capitalist society, move towards what the protagonists of capitalism in the novel contemptuously regard as a 'utopian idyll', as 'paradisism' (*Paradiesismus*). In previous works Böll's resort to the happy ending may sometimes seem incongruous. Here the happy ending rounds off the underlying concept more naturally than it did, for example, in the case of *Billard um halbzehn*. His predisposition to the happy ending on earlier occasions, one is now prompted to reflect, seems to indicate a pull of his imagination all the time in the direction of the position thus reached in *Gruppenbild mit Dame*. The happy ending is of the essence of Walser's *Die Gallistl'sche*

Krankheit (1972). This is the story of a person who, devastated by
the pressures of capitalist society, turns towards the alternative offered
by socialism. But this is vaguely in the future, and in any case the
novel points rather away from the sphere of politics towards a situation in which politics as such seems almost to be in abeyance.

Whereas in *Halbzeit* and *Das Einhorn* play-acting as a mode of
existence had been seen in a positive light, as the diversification of
the self in conditions making it necessary and productive, in *Die
Gallistl'sche Krankheit* it figures as symptomatic of the emptying of
self. A reference to an episode in Gallistl's life, when he was for a
time an actor and made a mess of a particular assignment, recalls,
and, as it were, takes leave of, the world of Anselm Kristlein: 'After
that I never again tried to find work as an actor. Although acting was
for me still the loveliest thing of all. Not to live oneself, but only to live
the lives of others.' In another remark this predilection is related to
the sense of the weakened self: 'successfully capturing the gesture of
someone else not only sticks in my mind. I have to repeat it . . . Even
if it isn't at all suitable. From that I conclude that I have a minimal
life of my own.' This occurs in the first section of the book ('Sym-
biose'), when Gallistl is aware of the symptoms of his 'disease' caused
by the overstrain of life in a competitive and alienating society, without as yet being able properly to diagnose the source of the trouble,
still less to do anything about it. In the next section ('Zuspitzung')
the symptoms and their results are more marked. He is now obviously
in a worse condition—lethargic, afflicted with 'total immobility',
and morosely introspective. By the beginning of the third part he is
both clearer about where the trouble lies and more determined to
put it right: 'it's a case of . . . separation from oneself, which for
me has led to an impotence *vis-à-vis* myself and to a certain ignorance, perhaps even to incompetence'. But 'I'll take myself in
hand again. I'll fight for myself.' He knows that he cannot get better
'in these conditions', but, motivating his will to recovery, he has
vague ideas of a warm and cosy world where his troubles will end
and, in a blissful state of non-alienation, he will be reunited again
with himself: 'I dream of a better world: dryness, warmth, hardly
any disturbance. People who are glad to do something.' It is then
that he meets his socialist friends, whereafter he can say: 'I'm becoming myself again. Things will get moving then. I see that quite
clearly. I have the good fortune to serve the future.'

Thus in what has sometimes been thought of as Walser's most

political novel Gallistl's utopia appears to be a society, simple and idyllic, so lacking in complexity and tension as to make politics in any ordinary sense unnecessary. In the real world this sounds more like regression than progress, yet the way to this state of bliss is presented as through the politicisation of awareness. There could hardly be a better definition of one basic aspect of the 'politicisation of literature' than the passage in which, talking about those corrupted in infancy and prepared for capitalist society by love too much based on a system of rewards, Walser writes: 'now, however, more and more of those who have been pampered—and I believe they'll increase as time goes on—see through themselves and their position, and they become political, i.e. they try to understand the relationship that caused their very unhappy experiences as a socially determined one and to draw the conclusions'. So, if it is not really a political novel its context is undeniably the 'politicisation of literature', and it demonstrates the utopianism so often part of it. The 'that's how it used to be' of an earlier phase of the novel becomes the 'that's how it's going to be' which provides the title of the final part. The language often sounds the tonality of the fairy-tale. The names of Gallistl's socialist friends—they appear unannounced, as in the guise of saving angels—are, in contrast to the bleak system of reference (by letters of the alphabet only) to his earlier acquaintances in the competitive society, suggestive of an archaic, provincial world, and at the end Gallistl is driven off in an old car into a romantic future. If the touches of red rust are anything to go by (especially coming just after a reference to stars), he is on his way to the German Democratic Republic. It is a trip to socialism all right, but the destination is as full of unreality as it is of hope. The novel might easily be taken as a joke at the expense of naively romantic idealism. That obviously is not the intention. Or should the interpretation be that, presenting with such apparently ironic effect what he believes in, Walser catches up with the obligations of the 'politicisation of literature', but with such reservations about the prospects of the utopia in the actual world as to make his case seem as much fairy-tale fiction as reality? It is improbable that Walser would agree with that either. A more likely suggestion—and this is how the protagonists of the new 'utopianism' would put it—is that in present circumstances, for one imprisoned in habits of awareness conditioned by capitalist society, it is only as a fairy-tale that such happiness and fulfilment are conceivable.

If, then, at the one extreme the 'politicisation of literature' signifies the idea that literature must be made to bring about swift and radical social change, at the other it embodies such sensitivity to what is felt as the repressive rigidity of organised political society as to amount to something like a desire to escape from politics altogether, while using the terminology of socialism to indicate the hopes for the future. This is most obviously the case the more the stress is laid on the dynamism of subjective experience, and, matching an ahistorical awareness in the present with a sort of ahistorical view of the future, the more the solutions are orientated in remotely utopian directions. Then we move in the direction of attitudes 'characterised by the destruction, as a matter of principle, of the old in order to clear the ground for a radical new start, i.e. one beginning at the roots . . . The aims . . . are predominantly only markers along the path towards a future that is never defined any more precisely than that.' For 'if the prevailing conditions are only fit to be criticised, no new conditions can be allowed to prevail'. Therefore 'there is logically no final goal, but just goals, i.e. markers along the path to an ever open future'.[24]

What place in our discussion, then, should writers have who, working through the established channels of party political practice, were all the time pursuing aims seen as attainable only in organised form and as constituting a political programme for a government that might actually come to power? The hopes for the future of those associated with Gruppe 61 could only be realised in terms of economic and political organisation more specific than abstract talk about the abolition of authority and vague, grandiose optimism about socialism as the alternative to capitalism, and Grass was directing his political energy towards objectives to be attained by a practical programme of reform through parliament and the SPD. Then there were those, like Weiss, operating on the basis of traditional Marxism and so bowing to the authority inherent in its intended results. Weiss and Grass are good examples of what should be called committed writers, a term familiar long before the 'politicisation of literature' was ever heard of. Without that distinction how can it be thought, as the term implies, that, becoming politicised, something was being done to German literature that had not happened before?

There remains to be considered a type of literature directed to political ends in a way specific to the sixties, but associated with circumstances at a particular juncture, when in the Federal Republic

the revolution had not materialised and the objectives of the Paris
students too had been frustrated. Only a few months after the failure
of the student riots in Paris Enzensberger, though by this time he
must have been working on *Das Verhör von Habanna*, wrote in
Kursbuch regarding left-wing literature: 'its claim to enlightenment, its utopian excess, and its critical potential have withered to
a hollow shine'. 'Marx put off all problems till after the revolution,'
it is said in Brinkmann's novel *Keiner weiss mehr* (1968), 'but it is
after the revolution now.' It was not long before, looking back on
the recent past, Wolf Wondratschek could observe, 'one could almost
say that what was a reason for demonstrating in '68 is in '71 a
demonstration of the impotence of those who still go out on the
streets and shake their fists in anger'.[25] This was the phase dominated by the idea of 'cultural revolution'—not a substitute for revolution but a preparation for it, aiming to liberate the masses from the
'false consciousness' generated by the 'consciousness industry'.

Wondratschek's sudden rise to prominence at this point was symptomatic. His problem was that of communicating effectively with a
public who, as events seemed now to have shown, had been so
manipulated to 'false consciousness' as not to be adequately responsive through political awareness. The implication is that otherwise
they would have been roused by a politically orientated literature and
things might have turned out differently. The problem he faced in
Früher begann der Tag mit einer Schusswunde (1969) and particularly *Ein Bauer zeugt mit einer Bäuerin einen Bauernjungen, der
unbedingt Knecht werden will* (1970) can be seen from his essay
'Über den grösseren Teil und den kleineren Teil einer Gesamtbevöl-
kerung. Zugedacht dem grösseren Teil':[26] 'To whom can we say
something he'll understand? How can we say something to this someone that he'll understand, since it's no longer enough just to understand . . . How can we write down what they've forgotten?' Since
from his point of view false consciousness is characterised by the
desire always to see things—the existing reality, that is to say—as a
meaningful whole, Wondratschek's task became that of so using language as to disrupt this experience.

This he set about doing by consistently avoiding writing in such
a way that the result makes sense, at least in the same easy and
natural way as a structured and continuing story. Language is reduced to its smallest unit, the sentence, and, despising those 'bourgeois extravaganzas called stories', he will have nothing to do with

straightforward sequences of narrative. The reader, denied the usual aids to understanding, has to complete what the author has begun, and his awareness is put to work as part of his political education. Hence Wondratschek's interest in films and in particular the effects to be gained by 'cutting' them: 'the only right films are those that destroy order'. He challenges the medium as a means of challenging the reader's awareness and of provoking it into different habits. He uses the radio play similarly, and *Paul*, the play for which he was awarded the Hörspielpreis der Kriegsblinden for 1969, has the subtitle, 'oder die Zerstörung eines Hörbeispiels'. Thus, in an article asking whether the radio drama of the fifties was reactionary,[27] he answers in the affirmative, attacking Ingeborg Bachmann's *Der Gute Gott von Manhatten* (1958) because she 'concentrated entirely on the no-man's-land of pure feeling', and for the reasons that led one reviewer, quoted by him, to praise her 'mystic and orphic expression of ecstatic longing'. An obvious comparison outside Germany would be with the Tel Quel group in France, to the activities of which *Alternative* devoted a number in 1969. One of its spokesmen is there on record with what could be a commentary on Wondratschek's work: 'each class develops its own means of absorbing language. For the bourgeoisie, for example, this is rhetoric and the novel. To reject the rhetorical system or narrative forms is immediately to question the bourgeois ideology and the bourgeois Weltanschauung (as a cumulative hierarchy and "meaning-full").' The striking success achieved by Wondratschek's first book, repeated by his second, can be appreciated only in the light of their place in the context of the 'politicisation of literature' at that particular phase. *Früher begann der Tag mit einer Schusswunde* appeared just about at the point at which for all practical purposes the students were abandoning their method of confrontation in the streets and public places, drawing the conclusion from the failure of their immediate objectives that more theoretical work was needed, and the New Left withdrew from the streets to rethink the situation.

By the end of the decade the unity of the students' movement was breaking up, and the result was to heighten and polarise the implications present within the category of the 'politicisation of literature'. One faction, at the opposite extreme to the anarchist tendencies on the Marcusian model, veered towards a rigid view of communism as an organised system of government. The body representing it was, and still is, Spartakus. In other circles there was a revulsion against politics altogether. Brinkmann and his co-editor of the anthology *ACID* would have no truck with anything having 'political content' on the grounds that politics were 'not as relevant as is commonly assumed'. There was no doubt, Baumgart wrote in *Tintenfisch* in 1969, that after the failure of the great demonstrations and of the French riots one could no longer 'talk enthusiastically about demonstrations as symbolic actions'. This 'phase of the new opposition seems to be over. It is in a state of crisis.'

What then, he asks, are the choices facing oppositional literature? One is to try out the idea of itself as an 'instrument of information about society', offering 'critical reflections of bourgeois society', but 'enriched, made enjoyable, through montage techniques'. But then it would merely move 'in the footsteps of bourgeois realism', with nothing more to offer than the 'depressing logic of past experience'. Or it could accept what circumstances had proved, namely its 'sublime dispensability as far as the attainment of political objectives is concerned'. In this case it would 'make up by becoming once again belles lettres, more so than it had for a long time dared to be'. It would forget its 'aesthetic modesty' and resort once again to 'fantasy and the sensuous'. Then, 'in line with the ideas of Ernst Bloch or Marcuse', its function would be to articulate 'unfulfilled hopes, emancipatory needs, anticipatory dreams'.[28] The reference, as far as Bloch is concerned, is primarily to *Prinzip Hoffnung*, and as regards Marcuse a relevant work would be *Eros and Civilisation*, with an argument which can be summarised by saying that it is in fantasy 'that our allegiance to the pleasure principle is preserved, in play, in dream, in day-dreaming, and that it is works of the imagination that we find the most visible "return of the repressed" and the anticipation of new forms of human life in which it is not only the case that our sexuality has been transformed, but that libido informs all our human and work relations'.[29]

Baumgart, in line with Marcuse's idea of 'humane sensuality' as a 'political factor', thus recommends the idea of literature as awakening subjective needs and expectations in advance of their practical realisation by its appeal to the senses and the imagination. This to some extent was the purpose of the symposium *Trivialmythen*, published by the März Verlag in 1970. It accepts J. G. Ballard's notion that, with reality so fantastic as to seem tantamount to fiction, the writer does not need to invent fiction any more. It sees itself 'as proof that literature is also possible, and especially possible, when

the general fictionalisation of the world challenges its claim to have
a monopoly of imagination': 'the "pictures" of consumer society
with which television, film, magazines, newspapers, fashion, sport or
pop concerts feed our minds continually drain the energy of literature, but at the same time supply it with new material'. The volume
was to represent a kind of writing which 'uses the waste from the
media stored on the fringes of consciousness' and tries 'to develop a
new relationship with it', and the imagination, 'normally goal-orien-
tated within the given material', 'manoeuvres itself into freedom'.

This raises once again the question of the association, increasingly
asserted towards the end of the decade, between the 'politicisation
of literature' and the utopian orientation of literature. Trends
apparent in the early seventies in West Germany, and reflected in
an important article by Karl Heinz Bohrer entitled 'Die lädierte
Utopie und die Dichter' (1972),[30] have served to increase rather than
diminish its significance. Bohrer draws particularly on the work of Urs
Widmer and Nicolas Born. The former, earlier the author of some
shorter prose texts (*Alois*, 1968, and *Die Amsel im Regen im Garten*,
1971), has recently published an essay of special relevance in this
connection on 'Das Normale und die Sehnsucht'.[31] The latter is the
author, apart from one novel (*Der zweite Tag*, 1965), of two volumes
of poetry, *Wo mir der Kopf steht* (1970) and *Das Auge des Entdeckers* (1972), both supported by theoretical reflections on aim and
method.

Widmer states his position in the form of a long series of questions,
tantamount to statements of opinion. The essential points are that
what we take to be 'normal' is merely an 'arrangement' with reality,
that language is an 'anchor with which we secure our position in the
outside world', and that with the 'acceptance of language' we indicate our readiness 'to accept realities and its rules'. Thus far the
argument reads rather like a straightforward gloss on Handke's
Kaspar, but the difference is that Kaspar's situation does not take
him in the direction of the revolt implicit in Widmer's further remark
about 'longings' which 'clash with reality'. Widmer is concerned to
see literature as a means of making man aware of the extent to which
'human imagination and reality diverge', expressing thereby the
'crazy hope of closing the gap between desire and reality', of 'doing
away with alienation'. Nicolas Born's obvious point of contact with
thinking of this kind is in his observation, 'just as utopia is contained
within reality, so is reality contained within utopia. The need for

liberation is not liberation, but it is its precondition. It is the same with literature. It produces an idea of things that hitherto were merely the ignorant goal of longing.' A comment by Reinhart Baumgart about the same time can serve to make the connection between ideas of this kind and the principles underlying the volume *Trivialmythen*, with Widmer among the contributors. Nothing is more important for literature, Baumgart said, than 'to shatter the apparent rationality of society by provoking the imagination by, above all, developing and intensifying vulgar myths: Red Indian stories, science fiction and pornography'.[32]

We are brought back to the question raised earlier in this chapter about the 'politicisation of literature' carrying implications rather apolitical than political in any ordinary sense of the term. We want now to add the case of Enzensberger's book about the Spanish anarchists of the thirties, *Der kurze Sommer der Anarchie* (1972), with what Bohrer rightly calls its 'absolute ideal of unmanipulated man'. We agree with him when, talking about contemporary 'forms and themes of utopian discourse', he stresses in recent literature the way 'concrete utopian content of social and political origin is drained away in favour of the utopian expectation of a new psychic disposition of man', and when he notes that, while the 'new utopians' do not necessarily cut themselves off in artistic reserves', they 'argue above all as artists', going back 'indirectly to Schiller's idea of the "aesthetic education of man" '. Their utopia 'involuntarily becomes an aesthetic utopia'. Round the corner there is a familiar feature of German literature which in the past has always been seen as a hindrance to real political energy, the inwardness of what Thomas Mann called 'non-political man'. Also the nearness of the 'new utopianism', as it might seem, to consumer-society ideals on the lines of 'taking the waiting out of wanting' and 'giving wings to your dreams' is not easily compatible with the so frequently declared rejection of bourgeois values and capitalism.

The limitations, illusions and contradictions of many of the ideas, and their implications, sailing under the flag of the 'politicisation of literature' may now be apparent, and, whatever may be its merits, it is important that these should not go unnoticed. Also, this paid virtually no attention, except of a mainly hostile kind, to certain aspects of West German literature in the sixties which can be recognised as embodying a type of political awareness. These include the work of Heissenbüttel and in some respects concrete poetry.

Eugen Gomringer's beginnings date back to the fifties and the
same applies to Georg Rühm and the Vienna Group. Interest in
the theory and practice of concrete poetry increased considerably
during the sixties, and representative editions were published of
Gomringer (*worte sind schatten*), with an introduction by Heissenbüttel, of Rühm (*Fenster*) and of the Vienna writers. Gomringer said
of concrete poetry that it is 'a reality in itself, not a poem about
one', 'not a valve for the release of all kinds of feelings and thoughts,
but an area of linguistic construction'.[33] This might seem to rule out
concrete poetry from our present context, but its relevance is apparent from Heissenbüttel's relationship to Gomringer's texts or
konstellationen, and the way he interpreted them. In his introduction to *worte sind schatten* he singled out for praise the way they
'break the impact of authority in society', and affirmed the manner
in which Gomringer, in the 'reduction of language to words and
word combinations', destroyed the 'status structure' by which, in the
form of 'linguistic grades of rank' (*Über-, Unter-, und Beiordnun-
gen*), social values had stamped themselves on the language—what
Rühm, in his introduction to the anthology *Die Wiener Gruppe*,[34]
called the 'hierarchical principle of the sentence'. Others responded
to his work no less politically, but in a different way. Gomringer
talked about the need for 'a new, universal concept of human relations', the necessity 'of bringing economic productivity and human
relations into harmonious correlation', and of human relations to be
'universally rationalised, i.e. organised'.[35] For this reason he was
accused of a 'thoroughgoing positivism' which, ignoring 'all criticism of a technological society', is a 'reflex of the . . . semi-fascist
glorification of technological rationality'.[36]

If in one sense, therefore, concrete poetry has no 'content', in
another it clearly has. Franz Mon's cult of concrete poetry, and of
'language games', can be seen in conjunction with his contemptuous
thoughts about the 'incessant and inescapable torrent of talk and
speech-making that runs through our world—the endless babble of
science, of advertisements, of politics, of information offices, of the
press, of the radio, of conferences and movements',[37] or with his
comment, acknowledging a debt to Karl Kraus, about all the 'verbal
communications, which we have to pick up and process every day',
making society appear as 'a reality weatherproofed with linguistic
stereotypes'.[38] The 'content' of poetry without content can be a
message about a world burdened with too much content, from which,

'released for a moment from the general network of functions', man frees himself through 'play'. Poetry, Ludwig Harig states in the programmatic foreword to the texts in his *im men see* (1969) is 'playing', 'experimenting with chance', has 'its own self-sufficient meaning', does not serve 'extraneous goals'. It is, he says, to be compared with the activities of children, and with children's games, whose incantatory features are reflected in the character of some of his texts. They 'constitute a world in themselves', they 'play with themselves alone', 'express nothing but their own wondrous nature'. These are more than statements about poetry. They are polemical assertions about society. 'Permutational art' is the 'watermark inscribed on the era of technology'.

This might be taken in conjunction with what Heissenbüttel has said[39] about its being characteristic of modern movements—Les Fauves, Cubism, Expressionism, Dadaism, Surrealism, Concrete Art —to turn against the 'traditional idealistic assumptions', thus breaking out of an older cultural role of art as the bearer of 'Bildung'. As a result, he says, literature acquires a wider basis and a new freedom. It is 'thrown back on itself' and becomes 'independent of any of the rules'. It is liberated from the 'factors governing it in the social and economic sphere, and in that of ideas and politics'. Art is transformed 'into something that is intended for all and which . . . can be practised by all'. Herein resides the 'immanent political significance' of art; 'that, and only that, today denotes the political element immanent in art'. It was thus that Heissenbüttel could speak of the liberating experience for him of Gomringer's poetry: 'the art of liberation which I recognised in Gomringer's texts means that I could do whatever I could and whatever I wanted. I could try anything . . .'. Literature ceased to be a 'bearer of ideas'. It acquired instead a new 'material intensity', of 'images, conceptions, associations'. His own practice as a writer on this basis is best defined in terms in which he characterises as the task of modern literature that of 'multiplying reality in language'.

This is Heissenbüttel's method in his *Textbuch* sequence, beginning in 1960. A good example—not of concrete poetry, however—is 'Deutschland 1944', which Mon talks about in a way not dissimilar to that in which Heissenbüttel speaks of Gomringer's work. What it does is to 'break through the illusionistic web of language and to expose one to the harshness of reality'.[40] This, too, has political implications, though what Heissenbüttel does not do is to seek to put this experience to the service of an ideology of social or political change. Hence he found himself on a collision course with those most wedded to the notion of a direct relationship between literature and political results. From their point of view he does no more than 'copy the world through quotation', without changing anything. This is the gist of Karl Markus Michel's criticism in *Kursbuch* 15. Another critic censured him for his 'feeling of impotence in face of a reality which . . . conceals its real structure', for representing a modernism which 'conforms to the deformation of "reality" ', for the 'static character' of his 'linguistic constructions'.[41]

However, Heissenbüttel and writers of the left have one important thing in common. The latter, rejecting the bourgeois system of values, stand firmly opposed to any idealisation of the 'creative personality' as the voice of reality and truth. For Heissenbüttel, too, this tradition is now superseded; crucial to his theory of literature is the 'dissolution of the subjective point of reference' and the disintegration of the 'unity of subjective self-awareness'.[42] This is for him an unalterable fact of life, and in all his work he uncompromisingly adjusts himself to what seem to him the consequences. He may even be more consistent in this regard than some of those in the same camp as his critics, taking account of evidence already noted on the radical wing of the desire to redress the weakening of identity. This is reflected in the summary, in part quoted above, of a characteristic criticism of Heissenbüttel: in his work there is lack of 'resistance' to the social pressure which 'destroys the subject'. 'The self and its possibilities of development' are 'reduced' to a 'cluster of familiar verbal habits', and so trivialised.

So our discussion touches once again on the problem of the two extremes represented in the 'politicisation of literature', and any definition of this must embrace both in their dialectical relationship. One is the insistence that literature must be politicised in order to change society. The other is the ultimate incompatibility of what the institutionalisation of values can ever offer, since ultimately the dynamic of the inner demands motivating the politicisation cannot find satisfaction beyond the destruction of what exists. The more radical these demands, the more do organisations and institutions, and the obligations arising from them, suggest alienation and repression. 'Herrschaft', authority, is the enemy, the point on which all the discussions in the sixties in favour of the 'politicisation of literature' finally converge. Important from this point of view is the fact that the neo-Marxism involved took its cue from the discovery of Marx's early manuscripts and so represented Marx with emphasis more on the subjective and romantic aspects of alienation than with regard for his maturer view that the way forward lay through a changed system of power, but a system of power all the same.

The effects of this were felt in many different ways. The general result may well be to make one wonder at the extremes to which it was possible to go in discovering, or claiming to discover, oppression at work in culture and society. Even literature itself was charged with being an instrument of authority, which is why so much energy was devoted to attacking it and why the campaign against it could become a paramount feature of the decade.

Notes

1 In *Erfahrungen und Leseerfahrungen.*
2 K. H. Bohrer, in his review in *Frankfurter Allgemeine Zeitung*, 28 September 1968.
3 Cf. 'Peter Weiss und Hans Magnus Enzensberger. Eine Kontroverse', *Kursbuch*, 6, 1966, pp. 165–76.
4 *Ibid.*
5 'Grass oder Gruppe?', *konkret*, November 1967.
6 In *ibid.*, February 1969.
7 *Ibid.*, October 1967.
8 'Journalismus als Menschenjagd', *Kursbuch*, 7, 1966.
9 *Kursbuch*, 20, p. 19.
10 Cf. Lothar Baier, 'Literatur im Schaukasten', *Die Zeit*, 11 November 1966, and the account in *Der Spiegel*, 14 November 1966.
11 *Speak Out!* London, 1968, p. 62. This consists largely of a translation of texts originally published under the title *Über das Selbstverständliche*, Neuwied, 1968.
12 K. H. Bohrer, *Die gefährdete Phantasie*, Munich, 1970, p. 90.
13 'Notstand', in *Tintenfisch*, 2, 1969 ('Jahrbuch für Literatur', published by the Wagenbach Verlag). Enzensberger's speech was delivered in 1968 in Frankfurt am Main.
14 Bohrer, *op. cit.*, p. 90.
15 *Kursbuch*, 9, p. 176.
16 In *Heimatkunde. Aufsätze und Reden*, Frankfurt a. M., 1968.
17 *Kursbuch*, 20, 1970.
18 *Literatur und Kritik*, 38, 1969, pp. 506 ff.
19 Cf. Renate Matthaei (ed.), *Grenzverschiebung. Neue Tendenzen in der Literatur der 60. Jahre*, Cologne and Berlin, 1970, p. 233.
20 H. P. Piwitt, *Das Bein des Bergmanns Wu*, Frankfurt a. M., 1971, p. 127.
21 'Sechs Thesen über Literatur und Politik', *Tintenfisch*, 3, 1970, p. 34.

22 Matthaei, *op. cit.*, p. 16.
23 Bohrer, *op. cit.*, p. 58.
24 Andreas von Weiss, *Die Neue Linke*, Boppard, 1969, p. 39.
25 *Omnibus*, Munich, 1972, p. 152.
26 *Ibid.*, pp. 150 ff.
27 *Merkur*, 262, February 1970.
28 *Tintenfisch*, 3, pp. 29 ff.
29 A. MacIntyre, *Marcuse*, London, 1970, p. 53.
30 In a volume of that title, Zürich, 1972.
31 In a volume of that title, also Zürich, 1972.
32 *Merkur*, 268, 1970, p. 746.
33 *worte sind schatten*, Reinbek, 1969, pp. 281, 286.
34 Reinbek, 1967.
35 *Op. cit.*, pp. 289–90.
36 Matthaei, *op. cit.*, p. 27.
37 *Akzente*, 1, 1961, p. 29.
38 *prinzip collage*, Neuwied, 1968, pp. 50–1.
39 'Die Irrelevanz des Erfolgs in der Beziehung zwischen Literatur und Leser, Kunst und Publikum', in Georg Ramseger (ed.), *Das Buch zwischen Gestern und Morgen*, Stuttgart, 1969.
40 *prinzip collage*, p. 52.
41 Matthaei, *op. cit.*, pp. 22 ff.
42 *Über Literatur*, Olten, 1966, p. 202.

Chapter 3

Literature and the 'end of literature'

The debate in the sixties about the validity and function of literature is, as will soon become apparent, closely connected with the question of the 'politicisation of literature'. It also overlaps with the issue of identity, and for this reason we have to look again at aspects of German culture in the eighteenth century. It was then that, on the basis of belief in the firm identity of the self, the work of art came to be idealised as a 'self-sufficient whole', the product of a mind characterised by harmony and wholeness. The 'beautiful totality' of art was an expression of the 'highest beauty of nature', uniting the 'disparate objects in one'. It was in such terms that Goethe and Schiller formulated their views.

Trust of so high an order in the organic unity of personality implies distinctions between people, between the quality of their individuality. It is more consistent with ideas of hierarchic authority than egalitarian principles, and opinion will not take kindly to it in a period dominated by radical theories of democracy. Also, and especially against the German cultural background, it presents problems at a time when, as in advanced industrial society, the reality of life is not easily grasped in images giving pride of place to qualities of balance and synthesis. In West Germany in the sixties both factors were felt to an extreme extent, and this is the fundamental reason why in this phase literature, so long accustomed to a different situation, could be called so drastically to account.

Already Heine had spoken of the 'end of that artistic age (*Kunstperiode*) that began at Goethe's cradle and will end at his grave'. For Hegel art was no longer to be regarded as necessarily the supreme mediation of truth. In ages governed more by scarcity in material goods as well as in social opportunity the imagination could more easily and more naturally be felt to enrich the reality. Increasing industrialisation, in fact and in prospect, brought conditions favourable to the idea that it falsified reality or lagged behind it— hence ultimately Marcuse's theory relating the 'conquest of nature' and the 'progressing conquest of scarcity' to the 'liquidation of high culture'.[1] Reflecting, too, the diminishing spiritual rewards of scarcity in a materially advancing society, those able naturally to enjoy the pleasures of ordinary life could become, like Hans Hansen to Tonio Kröger, objects of envy. It was the developing crisis of identity that had some of the most important consequences. Nietzsche, profoundly aware of the limits set in modern life to 'character' and 'personality', saw art as hard pressed to preserve its dignity and self-respect. One Expressionist writer (Wilhelm Klemm, in a poem in *Menschheitsdämmerung*) juxtaposes the motif of the 'shrivelling' and fragmentation of the soul and the decay of art: 'Die Seele schrumpft zu winzigen Komplexen. / Tot ist die Kunst . . .' In *Tubutsch* Alfred Ehrenstein occupies himself with much the same problem. 'Around me, and within me, there is emptiness and desolation, I've been worn away,' comments the narrator. 'I notice that my soul has lost its equilibrium, that something in it has broken, that the inner springs have dried up.' He has become one of those people whose 'focus' lies 'outside themselves', who must 'constantly feed their senses' in order 'to overcome the gaping void', who 'submit to every impression' and become 'like wax'. 'If it becomes too dreary to be "me",' he reflects, 'I am forced to become someone else.' He has therefore given up writing, for a poet is just a 'beggar', lacking a 'voice of his own'.

The sixties opened without any such doubts and difficulties about literature. The writer was unaffected by any uncertainty about the importance of his role and function. A few years later Enzensberger was to criticise this in his 'Gemeinplätze, die Neueste Literatur betreffend'. Literature, he said, was at that time 'supposed to stand for a genuinely political life, something that did not exist in the Federal Republic', and so the 'restoration' was 'fought as if it were a literary phenomenon, namely with literary methods'. Opposition could be 'shoved into the literary supplement'. Changes in poetics 'had to stand for the revolutionising of the social structure that had never come about, and the artistic avant-garde had 'to veil political regression'. The more 'West German society settled down into stability', the greater 'was the need for social criticism in literature'. The more ineffective the political commitment of writers became, 'the more loudly people demanded it'. Literature, Karl Markus Michel commented in 'Ein Kranz für die Literatur', 'captivated and satisfied intellectual interests as if they were directly social and political ones', and thus 'blocked their view'. It 'trapped the discontent and unrest, which it nurtured, in a cage where mock fights took place and mock victories were won, while business carried on as usual'.

Enzensberger's and Michel's essays appeared in 1968 in *Kursbuch* 15. This included, too, a broadsheet by Walter Boehlich, for some time hitherto the leading editorial figure at Suhrkamp, and as such himself actively involved in the promotion of literature. Until this point the 'end of literature' had not been an issue in the public literary life of the sixties. It became one only when, above all through this particular number of *Kursbuch*, the debate was lifted beyond the confines of discussion groups in and around the universities, and when, amid the clamour about the 'politicisation of literature' as an aid to revolution, literature could the more easily be made to appear as a distraction of time and energy. Particularly Enzensberger's contribution gave courage to this belief, and to the idea that literature, as ordinarily and traditionally understood, was on the way out.

His essay is prefaced with a motto quotation from Kafka's story *Josefine die Sängerin oder Das Volk der Mäuse* concluding with the lines: 'but Josefine will have to start going downhill. The time will soon come when her last note is heard, and people will get over the loss.' Enzensberger interprets this as a contribution to his theme of literature's 'pompes funèbres', the title of one section of the essay. Sometimes, however, a slightly cynical tone is heard: 'we hear the dear old death knell of literature being sounded yet again ... and everyone is being invited to the funeral . . . The mourners do not seem particularly depressed', and there is a 'sense of wild jollification, of frenzied exhilaration'. Or again: 'the whole affair beautifies itself with the name of cultural revolution, but it looks desperately like a fair. The moments when things become serious are few and quickly fade. The rest is provided by television, organised public discussions about The Role of the Writer in Society.' Much of it, he is saying, has been heard before, and in any case it will be turned by the media into entertainment and rendered harmless. The anti-literary enthusiasts find themselves critically admonished. Revolutionary excitement, seeking 'in the liquidation of literature relief from its own impotence', is useless; 'a political movement, which, instead of setting about the power of the State, went for the established poets, would only expose its own cowardice'. Efforts to find an answer by 'forcing one's way out of the ghetto of cultural life . . .

with the help, for example, of agitprop-songs or street-theatre' have obviously failed, proving 'irrelevant as literature and ineffective', and passing all too easily 'into the consumer sphere'. In short, a 'revolutionary literature does not exist, except in an empty sense of the term'. As to how such a literature might come about, he has little to offer with confidence, and in any case he does not go all the way with the prosecution's case against literature—the final section is affirmatively entitled 'Yes, Writing and Reading'. Writers, he says, need in the first place a 'fitting estimate of our own importance', and nothing is to be gained if, 'troubled by doubt . . . we swop our traditional immodesty for a newly rehearsed humility'. They can still discover from themselves 'limited, but useful occupations'. He instances the reportage texts of writers like Günter Wallraff, but not without criticism of what they actually achieved in literary terms, and of weaknesses which he attributed to reliance on the form of the book for publication, on the resources of the capitalist market for distribution, and on the failure to combine theory with practice.

Michel's essay is concerned with points also touched on by Enzensberger. Like Enzensberger he is cautionary in some respects. In others he is more militant. The Paris students, he commented, had euphorically proclaimed the end of literature. But their slogans were false since, in fact, art 'is busily alive, even though now a corpse, as commodity, as fetish, and pretends to offer a zone of freedom and autonomy', and 'this has to be unmasked as a swindle'. Nor were they original. Borrowings and references included Mao and Che Guevara, Heraclitus, Nietzsche, Peguy, Camus, Rimbaud, movements like Dadaism and Surrealism: 'in short, this is all the familiar "Western civilisation", and even the talk about the death of art has, for at least 150 years, been a sacred part of the very culture that it is now turned against . . .'. What the Paris students opposed to the traditional culture—liberation of feeling, imagination, passion—is 'at the heart of this culture', and their revolutionary zeal has 'pumped new blood' into an existing culture 'always in need of new stimulus, however shocking in the first place its effect may be'. He praises the contributions of particular writers, and attributes the limitations of their impact to the fact that their medium was the printed book, with its involvement in the capitalist cultural market. The graffiti of the Paris students, to be properly appreciated, have to be read as other than literary texts. What matters about them is not what they say, but the situation which made people chalk them up, their message consisting 'in this provocative writing-on-the-wall'. In book form they would be 'different', their information value would have been 'minimal, their power to provoke nil'. He is concerned to defend the Paris students against the charge that their action in painting slogans amounted to 'infantile self-deception', confusing symbolic actions with real ones. They were 'real actions' which 'offend social taboos', and as such have to be seen as 'potentially *political* actions', but aiming 'at a kind of politics that does not exist'. As to the future, Michel has little more specific to offer than Enzensberger, mainly the conviction that 'our world can no longer be made poetic, it can only be changed'. This, he says, has been shown most obviously in the streets, and 'so poetry and theory have virtually entered a new stage, and this has still to find its language'. Traditionally, Michel observes, the writer was seen as one who 'bore responsibility for society and its morality', a person 'called to hold on high values and truths', the 'conscience of society', whereas nowadays literature has become mere 'luxury', 'something reserved for Sunday, for the literary supplement, the evening radio programme, the literary seminar'. The writer's 'stock stands high', but he 'has nothing to say', and, as soon as he expresses himself on contemporary affairs, it is seen 'how puffed up is the authoritarian voice of this conscience'.

The style of the third of this group of pieces, Boehlich's 'Autodafé', is strikingly dissimilar to that of Enzensberger or Michel. Hardly amounting to an argument, it comprises a sequence of hard-hitting, polemical assertions. Bourgeois literary criticism is dead, it died with the 'bourgeois God' of the bourgeois world. There are no 'great critics' left, only 'Grosskritiker', the intended parallel with 'Grossunternehmer' implying the exercise of power on the analogy of managerial authority in capitalist society. In the interests of authority the bourgeois critic seeks to isolate culture from politics, blinding himself to the fact that 'there is no longer a sphere free of politics', that even 'Geist' is political, and so he idealises the work of art as autonomous, self-sufficient and self-justifying. Boehlich calls for another kind of criticism based on different assumptions, one which 'finally understands that the decisive function of all literature is a social one, and so recognises its artistic function as incidental'.

Oversimplified, the arguments presented in these articles could easily encourage in those ideologically predisposed in that direction the view that literature is a waste of time and that politics is all that matters; that art, as Peter Hamm said, is merely 'compensation', 'drugs', a 'means by which one evades the provocation of reality. If you cannot do anything, you do art.'[2] In the situation as it was at the time, this was often how they were received, and it is why voices were heard on the left warning against some of the implications. In 1968, for example, Yaak Karsunke, attacking Peter Hamm's presuppositions, and also commenting on those who were so enthusiastically declaring their intention of giving up writing, said in an essay called 'Vom Singen in finsteren Zeiten' ('Making poetry in dark times'): 'in reality this is to grant victory to bourgeois art without a fight, and after dark those who have stopped writing will return and in the pale light of the moon turn the pages of new volumes of lyrical poetry'.[3] Wolfgang Heise, writing on the theme 'Warum Poesie?' ('Why poetry?') commented that the idea that 'poetry is dead or impracticable' is a 'gift to the bourgeoisie'. What it means 'is that revolutionary poetry is impracticable'.[4] The confusion was in part a terminological one. What was really at issue was bourgeois literature. This does not mean that as such its image was not distorted by its detractors. The important question here is why they were now so much, and so militantly, to the fore.

We have, first of all, to bear in mind the impact of a politically awakened younger generation. For all its revolutionary fervour, and frequently against its conscious image of itself, it was often still bourgeois in its attitudes. The most perceptive comment about this comes from Hermann Peter Piwitt, himself a left-wing writer, and anxious always to safeguard the literary left by criticising it constructively. He nicely characterises a person precisely in this situation: 'but perhaps he is seized by a feeling of disgust about literature, he devotes himself entirely to political work, and only proves thereby to what extent he himself has internalised the bourgeois distinction between the private (literary) and the public (political) sphere'.[5] Enzensberger, about forty at this juncture, is also interesting in the same connection. An early poem of his is about the temptation to want to withdraw from the pressures of civilisation ('lasst mich allein unter treuen kristallen / in der hut der sonne in der pflege des windes'). Then there followed in due course his shift to a position more political than literary and declarations of disbelief in literature—which, as one was to discover, had not stopped him writing poetry on the quiet. The tension in his case between the two spheres—the 'private' and the 'public'—is obvious enough, and it is reflected in a poem like 'lachesis lapponica' (in *Blindenschrift*). There are many other by-products of the relationship between the theme of the 'end of literature' and the demand for the 'politicisation of literature'. One affects the attitude to the avant-garde. Already in *Einzelheiten* Enzensberger had argued that its importance tended to be exaggerated. Michel now advances to the position that the only effective avant-garde is in the political sphere —is, specifically, the students' movement.

Common to both areas of debate, and central to each, was the question of authority, with implications involving reference back to aspects under discussion in the first chapter and revived at the beginning of this one. They are made more explicit in an essay, also of 1968, by Peter Hamm, in the use which, like Boehlich, he makes of the idea of the 'Grosskritiker'. Those belonging to an older generation, he says, presuppose the autonomy of art and of criticism, for reasons associated with an individualistic view of art, with its terminology of 'character' and 'genius'. People of the younger generation stress the material context of art, 'economic determinants', 'division of labour', 'laws of the market'. The 'Grosskritiker' treats all art as 'timeless', 'original' (*ursprünglich*), the fruit of an inner and inherent capacity glorified as 'creativity' (*das Schöpferische*). As a living model of the 'Grosskritiker' Emil Staiger, for many years now a respected German literary scholar at Zürich University, is instanced as one fond of talking 'about the "freedom of creativity" (*Freiheit des Schöpferischen*), which one has to concede without criticising, merely "experiencing" and confirming it, basically celebrating it'. The 'Grosskritiker', the spokesman of the principle of power, idealises the ego in conditions in which what it stands for—wholeness and synthesis—is anachronistic, championing the one because of his interest in the other. The 'Grosskritiker', runs the argument, 'evaluates literature, however, only in order to rescue those "values" which advanced art is concerned to liquidate. In short, to rescue his own value, his own supposed individuality, i.e. to make certain of his own claim to authority'. He imposes 'values on the work of art in order to confirm himself'.[6]

Striking here, as often, is a prickly reaction to the image of power, in direct conjunction with concern about belief in the creative individuality of the artist. This is not something that elsewhere people get worked up about. The explanation lies in circumstances peculiar to Germany. The background of National Socialism provided a

model in recent German history of power as evil and, with its glorification of the charismatic individual subserving a policy of repression and domination, it gave 'personality' associations with what is
bad. The force of Benjamin's essay *Das Kunstwerk im Zeitalter
seiner technischen Reproduzierbarkeit* is also clearly felt. The relevant part of Benjamin's argument rests on the theory that the tech-
nique of reproduction 'releases what is reproduced from the sphere
of tradition', and, multiplying the single and distinctive work of art,
makes it something not unique but available on a mass scale. In the
age of the 'reproducibility of art' the 'aura' of art is diminished. For
Benjamin, as communist and Jew writing in the strained situation
of the thirties, this was less a matter of regret than part of a politically intentioned argument directed against National Socialism,
hitting at it by way of the extremes to which, mobilising irrationalism in the service of brutal power, it went in exalting concepts like
'Schöpfertum' and 'Genialität'. These Benjamin accordingly sets
out to make 'useless for the purposes of fascism'.

This helps to explain why in the politicisation of awareness in the
sixties the debate about literature played so important a part, and
why within universities the native literary subject-area, namely
'Germanistik', provided a main forum for wide-ranging critical discussion, above all in the students' 'Basis-Gruppen', and particularly
after the younger university teachers of German had forced the
issues into the open at the Conference of Germanists in 1966. The
case against 'Germanistik' in its established form came to be its
association with nationalism in the past, culminating in its close
connection with National Socialism. Thereafter, ran the argument,
true to its conservative and authoritarian principles it concealed
what it really stood for behind high-falutin talk of literature as a
nobler and more refined alternative to the vulgar world of politics.
It continued to idealise in the writer precisely those attributions
which Benjamin had been so critical of and which he had associated
with fascism, and had made its teaching and research into a great
celebration of the past as a model for all time. Over broad sections of
the younger generation of intellectuals 'Kultur' came to be seen at
best as a hollow idealism furthering conservative interests, at worst
as an elegant alibi for the crimes of capitalism. 'Germanistik' served
as a representative issue in that it was accused of playing off, in its
image of society, art, and the individual, the organic principle
against the material forces of change. For the younger intellectual

generation this had been convincingly discredited by the lessons of National Socialism.

This was a principle that had for a long time played a distinguished and honourable part in German culture. By the twentieth century it appealed as a conservative counter-force to trends in modern industrial society disruptive of synthesis and stability. By contrast, the grotesque emphasises incongruity at the expense of integration and order. It is the enemy of consensus. A theory of literature determined by belief in consensus in the sphere of moral and social values is bound to be intolerant of the grotesque. It may well go so far as to maintain that literature characterised by the grotesque is not literature at all. This had been more or less the position of Emil Staiger, who came to serve in radical circles, especially in the case of people coming from the discipline of 'Germanistik', as a typical exponent of the values to be attacked. Michel names him in his essay; so does Hamm, and it is probable that, though Boehlich does not mention him, Staiger helped to provide him with his Aunt Sally, the 'Grosskritiker'.

In a famous, or notorious, speech in 1966 Staiger declared moral war on what is 'criminal' (*das Verbrecherische*) and 'vulgar' (*das Gemeine*) in society as interfering with the natural and the beautiful. At the same time he insisted on the supremacy of 'individuality' in conjunction with appeals to synthesis and continuity. His speech provoked a lively controversy, in which a number of German writers, overwhelmingly hostile to his argument, took part, and it was important enough to have a single number of a leading literary journal devoted to its documentation.[7] It brought out clearly the social and political assumptions underlying what had for some time been a central feature of Staiger's aesthetic doctrine, the concept of 'stylistic consistency' (*stilistische Einstimmigkeit*),[8] according to which all parts in the work of art must be at one with each other and with the whole. It is hardly to be wondered at that his speech idealised a more or less conservative image of society. This was reflected in his frequent recourse to the notion of 'Gemeinschaft', which made so positive a faith in 'individuality' so easy and so natural. Staiger's concept of society could be described as the 'centre–periphery model', with a 'clearly identified stable centre, diffusing a simple and uniform message to the peripheral parts of a unified system'.[9] This, too, is not a bad way of characterising the idea of the self within an intact order of identity.

Models of this kind were now heavily under attack, and not for the first time in German thought. All unity, Nietzsche said in *Der Wille zur Macht*, is 'unity only in terms of organisation and inter-action'. The ego 'enslaves and kills'; it is a 'thief, given to violence'. This was part of a radical critique of aspects of bourgeois values, such as we find also in the case of Carl Einstein, whose *Bebuquin* had appeared in 1912. For a long time relatively neglected, his work was now in the sixties attracting greater interest. The left-wing jour-nal *Alternative* devoted a whole number to it in 1970. Einstein objected particularly to the importance attached to the individual ego. Goethe, he said, in one of his essays, treated it as a matter of such importance as to overlook that 'we can only act in so far as the ego is destroyed'. Bourgeois man, glorifying ideals of balance and proportion, sustains his individuality only through the exercise of power whereas, as is said in *Bebuquin*, 'symmetry is as boring as the merely mechanical'. In the sixties arguments on similar lines were being mobilised against alleged social and political re-pression.

This is well illustrated in a book published in 1968 by Christian Enzensberger, brother of Hans Magnus. Here the idea of the beau-tiful comes under attack as resting on repressive structures and mediating corresponding values. The concept of purity appears as a 'concept of order', with an interest in maintaining authority and doing so by evaluative methods of correlation—of 'stilistische Ein-stimmigkeit' one is tempted to say—calculated to exclude anything in conflict with what it stands for, and by an idealisation of the 'pure' (one might substitute 'the beautiful') serving to define and protect a refined area of higher values and relegating others to a position of inferiority. Purity is 'clean' and 'good', it is 'the truth'; 'dirty' means what is 'below', what cannot be harmonised within the governing 'idea of structure and order', and which by its vulgar contact offends whatever sees itself as 'isolated, immune, unified, well formed, and in the singular'. The 'pure' validates itself by the 'impure'—and so, by analogy, the beautiful by its opposite. The more rigid a 'system of order', the greater 'amount of filth' it creates. To be able to 'make the other person dirty ... whether one is clean oneself or not' gives the feeling of being the 'boss'. 'Filth' is the regulator by which society defines itself 'at the cost of what is declared to be dirty ... One example: minorities.' The member of a minority is a typical 'fringe phenomenon of the social order', serving the 'cause of its strength and delimitation as a victim that by definition is forcibly excluded from it'.

Such, one might say, politicisation of the concept of the pure and the beautiful came to play a part of special importance in the sixties, above all through its association, as was claimed, with the maintenance of power and authority.

There was the argument that in a pluralistic society the individual writer could less than ever claim to have special and privileged view of the whole. To paraphrase a common type of argument, if the work of art was going to be a nicely balanced synthesis, it would omit too much. If it was going to find a place for everything that matters, it would not be what, as a work of art, it aspired to be. Walser, aware of the limitations of his own 'overall view of society and of ourselves', drew this conclusion: 'it is ridiculous to expect "free"-lance writers (*freie Schriftsteller*) in bourgeois society to be able, with the aid of some specious magic charm and so-called "creative" (*schöpferisch*) gift, to reproduce workers' existence in the aggregate of art or even be able to express it all'.[10] Brinkmann, introducing *Piloten*, a volume of his own poetry, and condemning the too exclusive notion of the 'true (*eigentlich*) poem', writes: 'there is no material other than what is available to us all and which we daily live with'. Then he lists a whole series of everyday experiences so fleeting and often incongruous that no 'aggregate of art', in Walser's sense, could possibly accommodate them all, least of all on equal terms. If this is what literature still insists on trying to be, Walser's argument would be that it will function as a repressive 'idea of structure and order', arbitrarily selecting and arranging things to the disadvantage of whatever is not to its taste and in its interest—the working class, let us say.

Walser's reaction was to give up imaginative writing altogether, or so it seemed, instead devoting his energy to instigating ordinary people, who would never have thought of themselves as authors, to recount their personal history and everyday experiences. We shall consider some of the results in the following chapter. At the same time, having eliminated the writer as an 'expert' and made everyone, potentially at least, a writer, he met the obligations of socialist theory by thus doing away, as far as literature was concerned, with the division of labour. He praises the achievement of one such person on the grounds that it does precisely what would normally be criticised in a work claiming the status of art: 'this is nothing but a report, just a report',[11] in the same way as Bazon Brock, describing himself as a 'writer without literature',[12] boasts that what he does as a writer is not to 'sublimate', but just to 'take what he finds'.[13]

Walser's change of course, in conjunction with the reasons given for it, raises the question whether ultimately it was not a problem of identity, and its consequences, that, however unconsciously, motivated the step which Walser announced with such an obvious sense of relief and release. The suggestion may appear to be of an existence so drained of self, and thus of the springs of 'creative' writing, that it was rationalising the excuse to look elsewhere than in himself. *Das Einhorn*, his last novel before he channelled his activity in the new direction, and at the same time his most extreme and differentiated treatment of the fragmentation of personality, contains a—for the moment ironic—remark directed against the 'transfiguring lies of memory' and in support of tape recordings and 'documentarism'. A more intimate aspect of Walser's psychology was also involved, bearing in mind in *Die Gallistl'sche Krankheit* the image of the bourgeois artist as a spoilt child, in later life driven to the need to attract attention to persuade himself that people still love him, and his reference to a type of person accustomed from childhood to being 'excessively rewarded' for good behaviour and always receiving 'more than he gives'. Made to depend on love, as a grown man he 'wants to force people to love him'. They must 'revere him, praise him, spoil him, and he becomes poet, composer, actor'. It is in this context that Walser then comes to speak, in a passage already quoted, about those who gain insight into the social factors conditioning such an attitude and so become 'political', as had happened to him. Crucial then is his ensuing comment on that observation: 'such a person simply withdraws from the competitive business of being efficient, he is not prepared to write poems or books or to compose symphonies, he wants love free, i.e. he looks for people of his own kind, he goes into a collective. He wants to be rewarded because he is himself and no other, he doesn't want to have to earn it. He is incapable of being alienated. He is not useful for competitive capitalist society.'

This amounts to the desublimation of the writer, and it was going on in other ways too. There was a desire also to desublimate the work of art. In his commentary on his poem 'Vanille' Brinkmann was keen to point out that it had been written very quickly, that he had stumbled on the theme while shopping the day before. The fact is, he says, that 'it is usually not "worth" spending long hours on a literary work'. The ' "long, difficult" hours of work on a series of prose or poetry texts' is a 'mystification forced upon the writer by society and which he does not see through'. There are better things to do than 'fiddle away at a poem for a long time—walking around town, reading the paper, going to the cinema, picking one's nose, listening to records, chatting to people about this and that'. The theme of any poem has to be entirely determined by the 'material presenting itself at the moment of writing'.[14] In the introduction to his *Piloten*, poems written in 1967–68 and published in the latter year, he says that 'one must forget that there is such a thing as art'. Formal problems 'have never interested me', they 'can remain the preoccupation of the professional literary athletes who sublimate their private scruples . . . in finely carved hocus-pocus. Let the dead admire the dead!' The view he represents, and for which he acknowledges his debt to Frank O'Hara, is that 'the poem is the most suitable form in which, like a snapshot, to catch the spontaneous effect of events and movements . . .'. Devices like the use of comic strips are used to cock a snoop at those conditioned to take poetry too seriously, though, curiously perhaps, the poems themselves, for all their touches of contrived banality in vocabulary, motifs and images, have often a well controlled and even self-conscious artistic structure which makes them genuinely and recognisably poems. What Brinkmann is aiming at is indicated in some remarks of his in praise of O'Hara's poetry, about 'the abandonment of a direction which makes the poem an exclusively literary product and so one that turns away from everyday, ordinary events', about a kind of poem, 'open on all sides', which does not reject 'the trivial and the banal, the daily images and headlines of the yellow press'. Brinkmann speaks of his poetry as if it was really rather shocking, but this could only be by the standards of so idealising a view of poetry that in this day and age one would hardly have thought it necessary any longer to tilt at it with such bravado.

There were in the sixties as many ways of being demonstrably banal as there were writers doing it—striking a blow at elitism, challenging the complacency of idealism, or ironising the consumer society. Brinkmann apart, examples would include Spoerri's *Anekdoten zu einer Topographie des Zufalls* (1968)[15] and Bienek's *Vorgefundene Gedichte* (1969). The result, a kind of literature which aspires to no more than to be quickly consumed and quickly disposed

of, looks more like a copy of the consumer society than a criticism
of it, even when allied to the idea that the best way of escaping from
and even undermining the world of commodities is to pretend to
affirm it—Bazon Brock's notion of the 'revolution of the yes'
(*Revolution des Ja*). Thus: 'eine, vielleicht heute die einzige Mög-
lichkeit der Warenwelt produktiv and konsumativ zu entgehen,
besteht in der Pseudo-Affirmation dieser Warenwelt and damit ihrer
Unterwanderung'.[16] Such intellectually pretentious language con-
fuses the issue. The concept is as dubious in practice as in theory,
even if that is what you want to do. Bazon Brock's *Theater der Position* (1966) calls for a huge display of consumer goods, but one production apparently roused the audience to such a frenzy of involvement that, like a lot of shop-lifters, people made off with whatever
they could lay hands on. 'Here on my desk,' says a critical voice from
the left, 'there are a few books which not by chance resemble each
other. *Ich, Urs Dickerhoff. Und so weiter, Eine Art Bilderbuch.*
And *Supergarde* . . . and *Pravda* by Guy Peelaert. And *Oh
Muvie*, a photo-novel. And Timm Ulrich's *Kunstpraxis*. And,
and, and . . . in a word, the most sensual, most attractive . . . and
most imaginative capitalism that ever was.'[17] Hence the warning:
'literature can be sensual only if it allows itself to have contact with
capitalist reality without succumbing to it'. Meysenbug's *Super-
Mädchen* (1968)—a comic-strip-type 'Bildungsroman' by a sociologist, pupil of Adorno and disciple of Marcuse, showing the development of a girl into a perfect saleswoman—did make a decisive impact
at least in one quarter, prompting the industrial executive from
whose book it drew quotations to consider having it withdrawn. The
nervous over-reaction makes this rather a special case; and one could
easily, if one did not appreciate its origins and intentions, respond
to the book as an amusing set of pictures about the world of selling;
certainly we seem to come pretty close to the common-or-garden
values of this kind of society when we find a man like Chotjewitz, in
Vom Leben und Lernen, idealising—under the label of 'Unkultur'—
'life lived sensuously', the making of things 'uglier', 'more worth-
less', 'more rejectable', 'gayer', 'nicer'. One senses a love–hate
relationship to the consumer society—capitalism, maybe, at its most
crude, corrupting and distracting, but generating within itself forces
of change by the desires it awakens and the instincts it sets on the
move in the way indicated by Walser in *Die Gallistl'sche Krankheit*:
'revolutions can happen only when the ruling class block the progress

created by still unfulfilled needs . . . Revolution serves the need to catch up.' Since, as Michel observed, the 'pleasure experience' serves the cause of 'offending conventions and taboos', 'sensuousness' and 'change' go hand in hand. The Wagenbach Verlag declared that its publications were not for readers 'with an idealistic relationship to history. Criticism from this point of view ("classical" prosody, old-fashioned theories of drama, treating the class struggle as if it were a relic of the Stone Age) does not count with us. What counts is wit, dialectics, sensuousness, materialism, change.'[18] This all points towards the desublimation of literature as a weapon against bourgeois authority and oppression. Hence in large part so ostentatious a cult of the banal and the ephemeral as an element in a general campaign against an image of literature made the easier to attack because it was parodied rather than described. There are comparisons in other aspects of life which at this time were claiming attention. One is with views being advanced at the time as regards the role of the doctor: 'health is no longer to be a gift of the magician in the white coat granted to the trusting patient, but the result of the joint work of doctor and patient together'. Another is with the idea that knowledge was not something to be proclaimed from on high but should 'emerge from a learning process in which both teachers and students take part'.[19] The equivalent in literature was the concept of making it more democratic by involving the participation of the reader in the process of its composition. To this idea a number of considerations contributed—the abolition in literature of division of labour, the removal of the barrier between writer and public, and the undermining of the writer's authority.

Franz Mon said of literary collage that 'it is the activity of the reader which ultimately creates the text. Whereas usually it is the intention behind a given meaning that directs the selection and structuring of the linguistic material, in the case of collage the meaning is retrospectively fashioned by the reader.'[20] Usually, however, the extremism of the arguments weakened confidence in their plausibility, and the implied alternative—the reader as a purely passive participant—is hardly credible at a serious level of discussion. In any case, the results of such extremism could easily look like a joke. Take the case of Chotjewitz's *Die Insel*, a novel partly about identity, as in the motif of Rottenkopf's many 'new lives', partly about time and memory, partly, in its constant ironisation of narrative procedures, about deflating the prestige of literature. At one point in the text the reader is instructed: 'you play with this book too, strike out sections and whole chapters if you don't like them, or tear the pages out. If the order is not to your taste, change it. The next reader of the book will be grateful to you.' The *Postversand-Roman* (1970) by Peter Faecke and Wolf Vostell—the former once a serious novelist (*Die Brandstifter*, 1963; *Der rote Milan*, 1965), the latter a protagonist and theorist of the Happening—requires the reader to arrange the parts by putting them together in his own way. The texts of Claus Bremer's *Anlässe* (1970), an extreme example, are, as he says in his own commentary, 'initial provocations to take the bits apart . . . to mix them up, to put them right, to change the emphasis, invitations . . . to a kind of reading which is not determined by me but by you'. Of one particular text he says: 'thus the movement of the text tempts the reader to abandon his usual passivity and suggests to him that he himself should become active . . .'. In the case of another he addresses the reader with this remark: 'let your own creative ability carry on'. The constant advice to this effect grows tiresome, and literature has never required of the reader such passivity as is here assumed. As if for political effect to rationalise a one-sided idea of reader-democracy, an extreme image of author-dictatorship has to be evoked. In the case of the poem 'das tier bekrönt mit blumen die sonne', the form of which varies the combinations of these words, the permutations are supposed to bring about this result: 'what gets lost is the element of the monumental, of the magical, and of the sense of grandeur—all that brings pressure on us. Every certainty is removed . . . The general validity of single perspectives is destroyed and every claim of principle broken.' There is a snide reference to the 'guardians of order' and a tribute to the principle of 'disobedience'. Excluding the 'organic' in favour of 'what has obviously been constructed', the texts are 'interchangeable', regarded just as objects to be used.

   The idea was to involve the reader and author in a mutual 'learning process' comparable to what was being campaigned for in the relation of pupil and teacher. Enzensberger, discussing at the end of his 'Gemeinplätze, die Neueste Literatur betreffend' on what lines literature might develop in furtherance of the 'education of Germans in political literacy', and describing this as a 'gigantic project' and a 'long-drawn-out and wearying process', talks about the 'principle of mutual relations': 'suitable for it is only the person who learns from those who learn from him'. The writer 'who is prepared to have this mutual relation with his public suddenly notices a critical cross-effect which the writer of belles lettres would never dream of'. Instead of merely receiving 'silly reviews, in which he is told that his development up to his third book was full of promise, whereas his fourth is a great disappointment', he 'has the benefit of being corrected, of writing something which has consequences'. Wondratschek, with ideas in mind close to Enzensberger's, likewise uses the term 'feedback'. His essay came a year or two after Enzensberger's, by which time, from the point of view of those setting their sights on the short-term political effect of literature, the outlook was disillusioning. 'Protests to start with,' Wondratschek wrote, 'later there were a few victories. That writers got out of the habit of writing poems was quite natural, no more than that': 'the feedback, which had been invoked, remained just a hope. It might as well be dropped. The acoustics of our cultural life are so full of echoes that references to politics fade away.' Writers are beginning 'to come to terms with their unimportance. That is the position.' Their 'influence remained lack of influence'. The 'death-rattle of the more serious literature' is 'absorbed' by the cultural market. As a 'revolutionary theme' it is made into something which can be sold. The conclusion: 'this is the point at which we now stand and, unless I am completely mistaken, we shall fall on our arses between the historical order of theory and practice'.[21]

As to how the disappointment felt after 1968 affected the debate about the 'end of literature', a point of reference is provided in an article by Peter Schneider entitled 'Die Phantasie im Spätkapitalismus und die Kulturrevolution', published in 1969. The idea of the death of art, he says, concerned only that kind of art which saw itself as existing above and beyond politics, 'and which dressed up the despair governing the existence of the majority of people' in 'beautiful form' and so 'concealed its social causes'—art which 'in the midst of abundance articulates only renunciation and ruination, and reveals to the masses their wretchedness in order to make them feel accustomed to it'. Such art, he says, is dead and ought to be buried. But he is contemptuous of the talk about the 'end of literature'. It has been a theme of bourgeois literature and it helps bourgeois society. Literature has a future in a revolutionary capacity, but not as another form of directly political activity. Its task will be to arouse the 'forces of desire in opposition to capitalism'. It will play off 'images of reality' against 'images of what is possible'. It will 'raise up suppressed desires' in order to 'put them at the disposal of revolution'.

There were, however, increasing signs of more passive types of inwardness, less the ally of serious political involvement than, in the long run, its enemy. Walser now found himself obliged to take up this question in his important *Kursbuch* essay 'Über die Neueste Stimmung im Westen', referring to what had been going on both in Germany and in America. He now felt it necessary to express his contempt for the idea of 'liberation on the road to inwardness'— its narcissism, its 'cry for pleasure'—and even praised Grass, not for the content of his political beliefs but for his contrasting position as a man party-politically engaged, his 'ability to draw practical conclusions', as a person who to the 'virtuosi of the trip to inwardness' must seem 'thoroughly corrupted by his practical work'. Quoting one statement ('the real job to be done is in your self') he comments on the many essays and 'ecstatic pronouncements' which regularly invoke Krishnamurti, Bodhisattva and 'all the other prophets of pure and beautiful inwardness', and he adds, in a reference to his current popularity, that 'Hermann Hesse comes as no surprise'. Indeed, he does not, and there are interesting correlations, particularly with the issue of identity.

Hesse's own 'path to inwardness' was now making its appeal as a signpost on the road to the recovery of self. This was how he would have wished it. His works, he said, can 'all be interpreted as a defence, even an SOS of the personality, of the individual self'.[22] His view of the type of person he most admired was one whose 'only living destiny is the silent, ungainsayable law in his own heart',[23] and this pointed, as he well knew, to existence lived out in a private sphere, above the vulgar *melée* of politics. 'When I call my articles "political",' Hesse remarked, 'it is always in quotation marks, for there is nothing political about them but the atmosphere in which they came into being.' In all other respects, he went on, 'they are the opposite of political', because 'I strive to guide the reader not into the world theatre with its political problems but into his innermost being'.[24] Hence the further aspect of Piwitt's criticism of works like *Ich, Urs Dickerhoff. Und so weiter, Supergarde* and *Oh Muvie*: 'never did such exhibitionism and self-advertisement so smack of self-realisation, never did a liberalistic restlessness look so like revolt'.[25] Into this category falls, too, Chotjewitz's exhibitionist self-exposure, with pictures, in his *Roman. Ein*

Anpassungsmuster (1968)—in collaboration with Günter Rambow—which otherwise might be assumed, from the illustrations, to be cheap pornography.

With the problem of identity and the 'politicisation of literature', and with features linking up with both of these, the debate around the issue of the validity of literature provides the third major focus in this section of our book. Here too the arguments involved could be naive, simplistic, absurd and downright philistine, exaggerating the contrary positions to make them easier to attack and demolish, or beating at at least half-open doors. Literature, however, continued to flourish, at least to outward appearance, the writer remained, in the wider public image, a respected or interesting figure whom a large public was anxious to know and ready to honour. When fame or notoriety came his way, he had, thanks to the media, every chance of appearing as a star before a mass public. The State rewarded him with grants and prizes, and the financial opportunities of the cultural market, which he might despise, made a career as a freelance writer a practical possibility for many who in earlier times might not have been able to afford it. The chances for new and unknown writers to make their way were vastly increased, and the road was more open than ever to experimentation and diversification. The reading public at large was not much touched by arguments that it was wasting its time.

It is true that after *Ende einer Dienstfahrt* (1966) Böll published no major work until *Gruppenbild mit Dame* (1971), Johnson none after *Zwei Ansichten* (1965) until the first volume of *Jahrestage* (1970), Walser none after *Das Einhorn* (1966) until *Fiction* (1970) and *Die Gallistl'sche Krankheit* (1972), Ingeborg Bachmann none until her return to the scene with *Malina* (1971). But a novel takes time to write, and silence does not necessarily denote inactivity. A certain symbolic significance did, however, come to be attached to this, all the more so because of the prestige normally associated with the novel, the rather special position it has played for the reading public, and the attention commonly given to it by the critics. The silence of a number of writers was welcomed by some as evidence that the 'end of literature' was at hand, their re-emergence by others as a sign that all was well after all. If the one view proved wrong the other was, in the short term at least, over-optimistic. For there had been a sense of shock and a loss of confidence. The work with which Günter Eich made his return (*Maulwürfe*, 1968) carried negative implications on the question of the role and function of the writer, and there is a tone of resignation in Ingeborg Bachmann's *Malina*. Whereas at the Frankfurt Book Fair in the first half of the sixties belles lettres were a main attraction, a change was felt around 1966–68 towards political material, and by 1970 towards books serving the purpose of information.

The decline and demise of Gruppe 47 is not irrelevant either. From the mid-sixties its image was becoming less prestigious. As far as the mood within the group is concerned, Handke's critical intervention at the last meeting but one (at Princeton) about the relevance of such literary activity struck, one is told, a sympathetic chord among a number of writers present. Michel contemptuously dismissed Gruppe 47 as 'not even a paper tiger, just a lap-dog', making no political contribution and unhelpful to the students' movement. Even before the events connected with the students' protest movement and the effect of this on the politicisation of attitudes had begun to affect its position, certain problems were making themselves felt which Hans Mayer has described in the light of practical experience within the group. An author would 'consciously produce a text with a good chance of being accepted by the group and so of being absorbed by the market'. Publishers were present, which meant buyers. Criticism within the group, originally comradely and unaffected by extraneous considerations, degenerated into 'market expertise'. Preoccupation with literature as belles lettres came to seem too exclusive, concentration on textual criticism too restricting. Widely differing points of view continued to be represented, but the 'pluralism' of Gruppe 47 had come to operate as a 'principle of integration'.[26]

There is an episode in Peter Weiss's *Der Schatten des Körpers des Kutschers* in which the narrator, hard put to it to give coherence to what he observes, is prevented from being able to do so by a self so reduced as to have no more than a fragmented and discontinuous awareness. He finds the effort of ordering his experience more than he cares to endure and there comes over him a feeling of 'extensive boredom'. Wolfgang Bauer, in whose play *Magic Afternoon* existence is made to seem futuous, life pointless and wretched, in *Das stille Schilf* (1969) (subtitled 'A bad masterpiece: bad texts with bad drawings and a bad disc', and described as embodying 'the worst of Wolfgang Bauer') satirically adopts as self-commentary the archaic stance of a 'Dichter', whose 'Dichtkunst' sets out to be 'lehrreich' and 'besinnlich' and whose poetry pretends to be a 'look into my inner self' and 'from there out on to the world'. This is a piece of fun, of course, but with a serious side. What it amounts to is heard in critical references, such as Heinrich Vormweg's to novels like Johnson's *Jahrestage* and Ingeborg Bachmann's *Malina*. They show, he said, that 'the idea of the creative personality and the traditional concept of the literary work are now merely dubious and flawed categories'[27]—a risky generalisation, despite the narrator's experience in *Malina*.

Her yearning, in this delicate and intimate book, is to be her true and natural self. This is what determines her relationship to Ivan. For him she does nothing 'just for the sake of appearance'. For that reason alone she would 'like to award Ivan the highest honours' and 'the highest of all for discovering me as I once was', uncovering the 'earliest strata of my being', releasing 'my buried self'. Now, having become a 'stranger' to herself in her own body, she feels 'how everything is turning inwards again'. She experiences a 'process of recovery', a 'purification'. But it is a struggle for identity against the odds. The name Ganz ('whole') disturbs her, 'causes me headaches'. Even to herself she is, as she often signs herself, 'an unknown person', and as she grows older one 'unknown person' in her will succeed another. Early in the novel there is an account of the hectic and scattered experience offered by town life, followed by a motion of intimate relationship with Ivan in which, alone together and in contrast to 'all that is schizoid in life', they find the way 'to come to be ourselves'. In an inner monologue, italicised to mark it off as such, her dream is of a world freed from technology and mechanisation, 'life whole and intact'. The theme of the novel, reminiscent of Christa Wolf's *Nachdenken über Christa T.*', is the problem in modern society facing, in the classical sense, the harmonious development of personality. It is also about a writer and one who for this reason fails as such. She has 'lost' the book she has been trying to write and she well knows why. 'I can no longer write the beautiful book. The beautiful will never come forth from me again.'

This is on the lines of Walser's generalisations about literature in modern society, and it was he who recommended to the Suhrkamp Verlag a young Austrian writer, Herbert Achternbusch, in whose work the main themes of this first part of our book are recapitulated.

Thus, on the subject of identity: 'Anyone who comes into this society is bound to be in a state of tension with the order of things, which is alien and hostile to life. He will revolt against norms dictated to him, and with all his energy will constantly and persistently endeavour to maintain his personality. But in the end no one can stick it out' (*Die Alexanderschlacht*, 1971). The debate about the problem of literature and politics is echoed in *Die Macht des Löwengebrülls* (1970), in the description of a person who, despite his 'respected duty to be a revolutionary', saw 'no possibility of realising this duty', but was unable 'to come to terms with a role which in this society would have granted him no influence as a revolutionary' —and he reaches the point 'where literature goes silent'. The destruction of literary form is a blow against reactionary political structures: 'anyone who cultivates any special literary form . . . serves the interests of the compact political system'. Every novel is a 'total institution', a place 'in which a great number of people, cut off from the rest, live an enclosed existence administered by literary form' (*Die Alexanderschlacht*). But the next remark promptly makes this look a bit like a joke: 'free space for the opinion of the reader', and this is followed by a blank page on which he is imagined exercising his democratic right to say what he thinks. In any case literature figures as a pretty hopeless undertaking, bullied by the realities of life: 'that was the end of art for me because such a marriage overwhelms art'. Just as one is 'having an idea to write about, the child has to be potted, and that's the end of that'.

The question is whether in Achternbusch's work these various issues are not beginning to turn into a play of wit and irony, into trendy motifs for literary effect. What remains is decoration, frills and motifs in a game with prose structure and language.

Achternbusch is one of a number of younger Austrian writers who came to prominence in the literature of the Federal Republic in the latter half of the sixties. Bernhard apart, they include also Handke, Scharang and Gert Friedrich Jonke. The explanation may be that 'the work of the younger Austrian writers . . . made its mark in West Germany just at the point when West German writers were becoming more and more involved in politics and when, with all the talk of "crises of literature" and "learning processes" there was a gap in the market to be filled'.[28] Typical of them all tends to be the way 'language is experienced as if it was something material, and the creative writer, aesthetically inclined, works with it as if it were substance, reality, life'.[29] Scharang's work *Verfahren eines Verfahrens* and *Schluss mit dem Erzählen* would fit this characterisation.

Handke's 'Sprechstücke', as he says, do not describe reality, but 'point at it . . . in the form of words'. The same might be said of Jonke's *Geometrischer Heimatroman* and *Glashausbesichtigung*.

A different sort of writing from this, however, was intended when right at the close of the sixties there were distinctive signs of a recovery of faith in literature. Compare, for example, *Kursbuch* 15 (1968) with *Kursbuch* 20 (1970). The latter contained the article by Peter Schneider already mentioned, as well as Hans Christoph Buch's essay 'Von der möglichen Funktion der Literatur'.

Against the idea of abolishing literature Buch directs Karl Korsch's criticism of the kind of Marxism amounting to 'an "economistic" contraction of Marx's revolutionary theory of society'. This results in the misguided view that all that matters, as far as proletarian revolution is concerned, is the 'economic struggle of the workers and the forms of social struggle arising out of it'. All else is dismissed as mere 'distraction of the workers from their revolutionary class objectives'. Buch censures those who see 'all work in the superstructure' as 'luxury'. He affirms art, and particularly literature, as a 'privileged place . . . in which mankind stores up its utopian dreams'. Instead of 'hawking their bad conscience around', intellectuals should see as their task the 'utopian promise' which lies buried in the great works of art, with the 'hopes held out of liberation' and the enrichment of the imagination. The 'portrayal of alienation, and making people aware of it through art', is the 'first step towards abolishing it'.

This is another version of the theory of literature as 'utopian utterance'. It is a simple theory, too simple to be very convincing in the absence of significant literary results. It was an easy way—too easy a way—out of the disappointment with what happened, or did not happen, in 1968. If, to quote Urs Widmer, the 'longings' could not be 'lived', they had to be 'written'. This, following the intentions of *Wie mir der Kopf steht* (1970), is also the direction marked by Nicolas Born's second volume of poetry *Das Auge des Entdeckers* (1972), each with a theoretical postscript. The former, in the same year as the essays of Schneider and Buch, contains a quiet and undramatic defence of poetry. Auschwitz, Vietnam and imperialism are 'reason enough to sit down in the streets and invest one's energy in extra-parliamentary activities' and 'reason enough to hang oneself', but 'no reason at all to become a hunger-artist'.

Notes

1 *One-dimensional Man*, p. 70.
2 In *kürbiskern*, 4, 1968, p. 383.
3 *Ibid.*, 4, p. 596.
4 *Ibid.*, 3, 1969, p. 486.
5 Piwitt, *op. cit.*, p. 123.
6 P. Hamm (ed.), *Kritik—von wem—für wen—wie*, Munich, 1968, pp. 20 ff.
7 *Sprache im technischen Zeitalter*, 22, 1967, in which the speech in question ('Literatur und Öffentlichkeit') was reprinted.
8 Cf. the essay 'Versuch über den Begriff des Schönen', *Trivium*, 3, 1945, p. 192.
9 D. A. Schon, *Beyond the Stable State*, London, 1971.
10 In his introduction to Erika Runge, *Bottroper Protokolle*, Frankfurt a. M., 1968, p. 9.
11 In his postscript to Ursula Trauberg, *Vorleben*, Frankfurt a. M., 1968, p. 270.
12 Cf. Matthaei, *op. cit.*, p. 111.
13 *Bazon Brock, was machen Sie jetzt so?*, Darmstadt, 1969, p. 391.
14 'Anmerkungen zu meinem Gedicht "Vanille"', *März Texte 1*, Darmstadt, 1969, pp. 141–44.
15 Originally published in French as *Topographie anecdotée du hasard*.
16 Baier (ed.), *Über Ror Wolf*, p. 104.
17 Piwitt, *op. cit.*, p. 10.
18 *Das schwarze Brett*, 7, Berlin, 1971, p. 45. This is the 'Almanach' of the Wagenbach Verlag.
19 Dietrich Bächler, 'Die Roten und ihre Zellen', *Die Zeit*, 5 February 1971.
20 *prinzip collage*, p. 50.
21 *Omnibus*, pp. 150 ff.
22 Quoted in Bernard Zeller, *Hermann Hesse*, London, 1972, p. 169. This was originally published in German as *Hermann Hesse in Selbstzeugnissen und Bilddokumenten*, Reinbek, 1963.
23 *If the War Goes On. Reflections on War and Politics*, London, 1972, p. 85. Originally in German as *Krieg und Frieden. Betrachtungen zu Krieg und Politik*, Zürich, 1946.
24 *Ibid.*, p. 5.
25 Piwitt, *op. cit.*, p. 11.
26 *Die Zeit*.
27 *Jahresring*, 1971–72, p. 283.
28 Piwitt, *op. cit.*, p. 73.
29 *Op. cit.*, p. 74.

Part II

Chapter 4

Literature and the documentary

The weakening of identity, the demythologisation of the writer, the denial of the claims of the work of literature to a special kind of insight and experience, these are all connected in their various ways, and logically related to the practice of documentary. Heissenbüttel in his theoretical pronouncements has made much of the limits now set, in the light of 'disintegrating subjectivity', to literature springing from a creative individual centre, and in his own work there are features inviting, superficially at least, comparison with documentary techniques. Walser's preoccupation at one stage with the dissolution of individual identity cannot be separated from his arguments at another against the concept of the writer as a person commanding respect by virtue of the privilege of creative imagination, and from his concern, arising from this, instead to encourage ordinary people simply to document their experience. What was being challenged as regards the creative imagination was the authenticity of its results. Documentary literature substituted the authenticity of the material.

It is therefore not surprising that documentary literature was a major feature of West German literature in the sixties. It was not peculiar to this period. Goethe's *Egmont*, Schiller's *Don Carlos*, Georg Büchner's *Dantons Tod* and *Woyzeck*, Gerhart Hauptmann's *Die Weber* and *Florian Geyer* all draw heavily on historical material, and the historical and documentary drama can be nearer to each other than their separate descriptions might suggest. The differences remain important. Writers drawing on historical evidence usually wanted to build up an imaginative structure of their own. Historical authenticity was not their aim. The typical documentary literature of the sixties stresses the documentary evidence as a means of authenticating the argument. In the Weimer Republic Piscator's productions were of at least a near-documentary kind. Friedrich Wolf's *Zyankali*, Peter Martin Lampel's *Revolte im Erziehungshaus* and Ernst Toller's *Feuer aus den Kesseln* rely on source material to such an extent as to correspond in some respects to the intentions of more recent documentary dramatists. For Thomas Mann at least, invention was not the 'criterion of being a writer'; 'very great writers (*Dichter*) have never invented anything, but have infused existing material with their soul and re-shaped it'.

The extent of the claim to objectivity can be used to distinguish the recent documentary of West Germany even from works of the preceding post-war years. These include Theodor Plievier's *Stalingrad* (1946), *Moskau* (1952) and *Berlin* (1954), or Erich Kuby's *Nur noch rauchende Trümmer* (1959). They all reveal a consciously individual response to their subject-matter. In the sixties this is still the case with Alexander Kluge's *Lebensläufe* (1962) and *Schlachtbeschreibung* (1964). The latter, on the theme of Stalingrad, deserves consideration in this connection.

Each section views the battle from a different point of view. 'Rechenschaftsbericht' is a bare, factual outline of events in a terse, matter-of-fact way, as in a military report. 'Pressemässige Behandlung' shows the way the progress of the battle was presented to reporters in official communiqués and, among other things, how the presentation of news was manipulated in order to boost morale. Other parts include instructions given to troops on how to cope with conditions at the front during the Russian winter, the sermons preached to the troops during the battle, and the views of officers and soldiers about the fighting. The later sections of the book have a different focus. 'Rekapitulation' is an historical look at the development of the code of the army and at the careers of the generals involved at Stalingrad. The concluding appendices examine the various plans put forward since the end of the last century for dealing with the Russians. They analyse the language of the officers and, in 'Formenwelt', deal with the military ethos, the criteria of status, factors affecting promotion, the generals' attitudes to Hitler, and the possibility of a successful officers' putsch to overthrow him. This section serves to question the traditions behind the officer corps, and ultimately its fitness to command.

Adopting a strong authorial stand, Kluge's intention is less to show the many facets of an historical event than to give his own interpretation of the reasons for the disaster. This rests on a few carefully chosen statements and extracts, and the result tends accordingly to be superficial, even sensationalist, a poor alternative to (in this case) the more appropriate form of a scholarly investigation. It is a fair point that the book is 'not a documentation but a fictional account that is particularly dubious because it continually tries to give the impression that what is being stated is factual'.[1] Where in the earlier sections of *Schlachtbeschreibung* various aspects of the battle are presented without comment, other than that implicit in the selection and presentation, the possibilities of the montage form within documentary literature become apparent. We are thereby made to see how the same event can be seen and understood in differing ways, and also how control of the channels of information can present the public with a systematically distorted view.

As to the factors accounting for the increasing prominence of documentary literature in the sixties, Walther Schmieding describes it as a response to an increasing distrust of power and authority, and as a reaction to the *Spiegel* affair of 1962. The argument is that writers now started to see themselves as the 'conscience of the nation', whose function was to keep watch against encroachments on the freedom of the individual: 'this moral function led to the assumption of the role of public prosecutor, who had to produce proof of his accusations, in other words, to use documentary material'. This, he says, affected views about the function of literature and made the writer better aware that he could 'expose links hitherto concealed, and ascribe guilt to individuals, institutions or States'.[2] This may be true up to a point, but what really provided the initial impetus for the growth of documentary literature in the sixties was the Eichmann trial of 1960 and the Frankfurt Auschwitz trials of 1962–64. The fifties having been a time of adjustment, when the Federal Republic was coming to terms with its new role in the Western alliance and was seeking to establish confidence, the Nazi past naturally figured prominently in the literature of that phase. The 'coming to terms with the past' (*Bewältigung der Vergangenheit*), as the phrase went, was dealt with rather more in private terms by a generation of writers who mainly grew up before the war. With the arrest and trial of Eichmann the problems of the recent past are taken up by a younger generation, with new directions of emphasis and new perceptives, and in connection with the question of the nature of modern military operations.

As Baumgart has said, the trench warfare of the first world war marked a qualitative change. The inhumanity of that war was its anonymity, with the individual eliminated in mass slaughter and deaths reduced to statistics: 'Verdum and Arras were bound to hit and shock the established bourgeois literature because it was used to focusing on the individual and his exemplary suffering and action. Its intention was individualisation.'[3] Karl Kraus had reflected this already in his play *Die letzten Tage der Menschheit*, where he says in the introduction:

> The play, which would last about ten evenings according to Earth time, is intended for production in a Martian theatre. Theatregoers from our own world could not stand up to it, for it is blood of their blood and the content is that of those unreal, inconceivable years, out of reach of the waking senses, inaccessible to memory, and only preserved in a bloody dream, when figures from an operetta played out the tragedy of mankind. The plot, going off into a hundred scenes and hell-holes, is impossible, full of yawning gaps, and as lacking in heroes as the acted events.

Even then conflict could sometimes be seen in personal terms, as in Ernst Jünger's war books. But the aspects highlighted by Baumgart do, in fact, find expression in most artistic treatments of the first world war, in literature as well as in the film (notably in Pabst's *Westfront 1918*). Baumgart sees an intensification of this phenomenon in the second world war. Writing of Auschwitz and Hiroshima, he says: 'behind the technical machinery of war guilty parties could no longer be identified. The comfortable causal links between deeds, guilt and atonement—which gave man his human dignity and which had been drawn for so long—were broken'.[4] What he fails to notice is the crucial distinction between Hiroshima, which he rightly sees as an extension of the features of modern warfare, and the Nazi extermination of the Jews, where in very large numbers of cases it is possible to name both the leading Nazi protagonists behind the undertaking and those who did the killing. The Eichmann trial showed how difficult was the question of the allocation of guilt. The documentary plays of the early sixties, which established the new quasi-genre, take up this question and try to reveal it in its full complexity.

The first literary response in West Germany, at least in documentary form, to the implications of the Eichmann trial was Rolf Hochhuth's *Der Stellvertreter*, first staged by Erwin Piscator at the Freie Volksbühne in Berlin in the autumn of 1962. Its central feature is the question of responsibility for the killing of the Jews. Piscator, the only person prepared to risk producing it, welcomed it on the grounds that it recognised and reflected the change of emphasis in society from the private to the public, from the individual to the

typical (first embodied, as he saw it, in Expressionist drama). The
new social realities are for him 'political, economic and social repression; political, economic and social struggle'. Piscator is thus in line
with Baumgart, but he is inconsistent in at the same time stressing
in the play's favour its adherence to the Schillerian idea of freedom:
'we must start from this freedom, which we all have, and which
everyone still had even during the Nazi regime, if we are to come
to terms with our past'.[5]

The idea of the freedom of individual action is clearly exemplified in the figures of Gerstein, the SS officer, and Riccardo, the
Jesuit. They do what they can to help the Jews, despite their differing allegiance. The struggles of Gerstein and Riccardo are seen as
being not merely against institutions but against individuals at the
head of them. Thus Gerstein stresses to Riccardo:

> For Hitler is not Germany,
> he is only her despoiler—the judgement
> of history will acquit us.[6]

At the end of his crucial interview with the Pope, Riccardo says:

> God will not forsake His Church
> simply because a Pope forsakes his office.

This point may appear to be contradicted by some implications of
Hochhuth's stage directions, about certain groups of figures being
played by the same actor: 'in an age of general conscription it is not
necessarily a question of merit or blame, or even a question of
character, whether a man puts on this or that uniform or is on the
side of the hangman or his victim'. But the stress on individual responsibility is strengthened by the parts of Riccardo and Gerstein
being excepted from this principle. Also, one actor is called upon to
play the roles of Pius XII and Baron Rutta of the Reichsvereinigung
Rüstung, another to play Ein Kardinal and Professor Hirt, of the
Reichsuniversität Strassburg. The effect of these particular pairings
is to intensify the impression, created by the dialogue, that the leading authorities in the Roman Catholic Church are grotesque characters, distinguished by their lack of humanity, little different from
members of the Nazi elite and those who backed the party.

There is a similar concern with the characteristics of individuals
in Hochhuth's depiction of the people immediately responsible for the
extermination of the Jews. They figure first in the Jägerkeller scene
in Act 1. 'The location of the bowling alley scene,' Hochhuth notes,

'is invented, but not the fact that the murderers discussed their atrocities over the table or in the mess, as if they were discussing farming.' This is a valid point, borne out by Eichmann's evidence at his trial—the Auschwitz killings were, indeed, carried out with an incredibly banal matter-of-factness, and it is in this that their true horror lies. But this is not the impact made by this particular scene, if only because of the prominence given to the grotesque figure of Professor Hirt, the notorious collector of the skulls of 'Jewish–Bolshevist commissars', or in Act 5 to the figure of the Doktor, an archetypal 'mad scientist', the 'beautiful devil', who behaves towards the Jewish children in Auschwitz with such a mask of kindness that Riccardo rounds on him with the words 'What sort of devil are you?' This personalised and melodramatic image is further heightened by his having the requisite liking for jokes in bad taste. He says to Riccardo:

> This afternoon, when that family you came with,
> is cooking in the crematorium—
> I shall be somewhat heated up myself
> between the legs of a nineteen-year-old.

He enjoys dilettante quasi-theological arguments with Riccardo, and can justify his extermination of the Jews within the terms of an absurd philosophy:

> I dispose of life, that is today's
> humanity—the sole salvation from the future.
> I am quite serious about it, even in private,
> out of pity I even buried my own children
> right from the start—in contraceptives.

The extent to which, in dealing with the phenomenon of Auschwitz on the stage, Hochhuth focuses on individual eccentricities and perversions sometimes has the consequence of turning the result into something not far removed from popular horror fiction, with the added difficulty that war can no longer, or at least not to this degree, be understood as the actions of individuals.

Hochhuth does not say that everything in his play is historically accurate, but he does claim that, as a whole, it is true to fact and, as such, revealing in a new way: 'the author . . . has only allowed free play to his imagination when it was necessary to transform the available historical material into a form suitable for the stage. The truth has always been respected, but the sediment has been removed.'

Again: 'to tie up the already available facts, intuitively, into an artistic and unified whole is the high and seldom attained goal of poetry'. Therefore in the printed edition of the play he includes detailed comments in the form of lengthy stage notes and a long postscript. The inner logic and structure of the play have thus to be substantiated by reference to extraneous material. This cannot be ignored because of the claim to present historical truth. That is to say, as a play *Der Stellvertreter* patiently fails in its own right to do what Hochhuth, in his notes as historian, presupposes, and in any case the question of its historical truth raises problems.

The most tricky part of the play from this point of view, and certainly its most sensational aspect, is Hochhuth's treatment of the attitude of the Roman Catholic Church to the extermination of the Jews. As he admits, there is no access to the Vatican files, and this is a major difficulty. There can be no doubt that the senior clergy, including the Pope, are presented as grotesque caricatures, as is apparent in Pius XII's opening speech:

> My good Fontana! We are delighted to receive you, brother—
> to hear your advice and also that of our honourable brother,
> filled, as we are with burning concern
> for our factories. Power stations,
> railway stations, dams
> *every undertaking* demands supervision and protection.
> We estimate, of course, the chance of finding a hearing
> on matters of industry and mining, realistically . . .

This impression of his being concerned only with running the Catholic Church as a vast commercial undertaking is constantly reinforced. For economic reasons he is generally pro-German and pro-Russian. Stalin is described as 'jolly good business / for the Society of Jesus'. When drafting a statement expressing his sympathy with the plight of the Jews he suddenly remembers certain financial implications of their situation, and breaks off to ask Fontana to be sure to sell some stocks in Hungarian railways. Blame, therefore, is attached to an uncharitable, rather absurd Pope, assisted by his faithful and equally perverted lieutenants—which, incidentally, could all too easily be interpreted as an attempt to transfer guilt for the death of Jews in Europe from the Germans to Pius XII. Also, remarks made by Gerstein allow the interpretation that Hochhuth is trying to exonerate the German people by shifting blame to individuals, such as the Doktor, and above all to Hitler:

You see, not every German has forgotten
his obligations to the name of Germany.
And there are monsters everywhere . . .
⠀⠀⠀⠀⠀⠀⠀⠀⠀⠀The Germans
are most to blame, it was their Führer's programme:
but as for the country itself,
the other countries are not much better.

In his introductory remarks to the play, Piscator states that Hochhuth had explained his use of free-rhythm verse as an attempt to
avoid the danger 'of being forced into a documentary naturalism as
devoid of style as the newsreel'. He wished, that is to say, to give his
play 'style'. But the real style of the bureaucratic war machine is
banality, as Hochhuth concedes in the remarks which preface the
Jägerkeller scene. To this extent the mood of classical tragedy which
is evoked is incongruous, as in the opening series of monologues in
Act 5, with Das Mädchen lamenting (with the classical tone stronger
in the original than in translation):

And the gods of old are as dead as their legends
and the antique rubble in the Vatican museum—
the charnel-house of art—or there might
still be a hope you would find me yet
as Orpheus, Eurydice.

But this truck is no boat to Hell,
the railway track to Poland, not the Styx.
Even the underworld has been snatched from the gods
and peopled with guardians whom no song will move.

While the point of the passage is that this is not the age of classical
tragedy, its verse form, tone and register evoke precisely that—
though to say the one in terms of the other might be allowed the
effect of irony. In Riccardo's efforts to persuade the dignitaries of
the Catholic Church to intercede on behalf of the Jews, the impression of his campaign as being the heroic struggle of one man against
a mercenary, unchristian Pope and his close supporters is intensified
through the period quality of the Schillerian language and metre.
In the case of the Doktor, too, the Mephistophelian image is brought
out much more markedly by the language.

Hochhuth, it is only fair to add, has never viewed his play as documentary theatre, and its mood and style are obviously much closer
to the older historical drama. What justifies its classification here
as a type of documentary drama is the author's rigorous claim to

historical authenticity, combined with the stress laid on documentary source material.

His second play, *Soldaten* (1967), belongs without a doubt in this category, and it is in many ways more satisfactory than its predecessor. The title, an allusion to J. M. R. Lenz's eighteenth-century play *Die Soldaten*, makes the point that Hochhuth's interest is not simply in the particular theme of the air offensives in the second world war; that he too is concerned with the military in general. The 'Vorspiel' and the 'Nachspiel'—the latter as a rule, unfortunately, omitted—set the main inner play as to be enacted in the ruins of Coventry Cathedral in 1964—in the year, that is to say, of the centenary of the signing of the Geneva Convention.

The fictional author of the inner play, Dorland, was a pilot in the bombing of Dresden, and has seen Belsen. His son, a NATO officer, cannot understand his father's assertion that he, as a soldier, is a 'potential professional criminal'. Against the background of this clash between father and son a dress rehearsal of the inner play takes place. This traces, primarily, the developments forcing Churchill to sanction the saturation bombing of German cities. Churchill is portrayed with some sympathy, and he emerges from the dramatically crucial debate on this question with the Bishop of Chichester clearly the victor. In the important 'Nachspiel', ending with the news that the National Theatre will not, after all, be allowed to perform the play, Dorland's son is shown as construing the play as an attack on the RAF and on Churchill. His father, however, leaves no doubt that he is not attacking Churchill, who in the situation of 1943–44 had no choice. The fault lay with the Geneva Convention, which had not been brought up to date to include aerial bombardment. Hence the sub-title 'Nekrolog auf Genf' ('Obituary of Geneva'). The use of a framework, in fact, sets a balance between the bombing of Dresden and Goering's policy of 'coventrieren', so that the play is not seen simply as an attack on Churchill's war-time policies.

By contrast with *Der Stellvertreter*, the language—prose, not verse—is happily never at variance with the subject-matter. In other respects, however, *Soldaten* has comparable weaknesses. The imputation of Churchill's connivance at the killing of Sikorski is not of central thematic importance, detracts from the main issue, and distorts the character of Churchill, just as the allegations about Pius XII damaged the earlier play. The professional playwright, with an eye on the box office, goes against the aims and intentions of the documentary dramatist. The play is more modern than *Der Stellvertreter* in its dramatic structure but is still conventional theatre in its concern for dramatic effect, particularly through the confrontation of dominant individuals: Churchill with Sikorski, for example, and, later, with Bishop Bell. The continued focus on the individual is seen also in the figure of Dorland himself, the enlightened prophet whose views are doomed to be rejected. He is fatally ill, and the play is to some extent his requiem. His cause remains a personal one, and in the final analysis the problem of the inner play remains personal to Churchill. Positioned in the highest arena of politics, he is, in fact, the main character. The framework attempts to make the central problems more general, but the historical and personal stature of Churchill stands in the way.

Despite the apparatus of documentation, *Soldaten*, like *Der Stellvertreter*, makes the impact of a modern historical drama. (Hochhuth's latest play, *Guerillas* (1970) cannot in any sense be called documentary.) Both plays are markedly similar in this respect to Tankred Dorst's *Toller* (1969). In its presentation of the fate of the Munich Räterepublik of 1919 and of Ernst Toller it draws on documentary evidence, but creates from this material what is really a personal dramatic statement: 'Dorst does not use the historical facts to produce a documentary play but as the concrete material for a fictional play, one that is admittedly indebted to history but does not just recapitulate it.'[7] This is equally true of Heinar Kipphardt's *Joel Brand* (1965), also on the theme of Auschwitz, whose claim to authenticity the author supports rather in the manner of Hochhuth: 'the material and the main characters are historical. For the purpose of writing the drama the author took the liberty of concentrating the action around those major political points he thought important.'[8] The material used is fully documented and accurate. Unlike Hochhuth, Kipphardt added nothing and invented no fictitious characters. What he did was simply to make the given material into a play.

It is concerned with the attempt by Joel Brand to meet the terms of an agreement with Eichmann by which a million Hungarian Jews are to be saved from the death camps in return for ten thousand new lorries and trailers equipped for winter use. Brand's task is to get the Allies to agree to this, which would mean supplying the enemy with war materials. The saving of the lives of the Jews is on

the level of a business deal, to be agreed with the official Jewish
organisation in Istanbul and the British authorities. Kipphardt
avoids the trap of trying to recreate Auschwitz on the stage. It is
a horrific background to the discussions, and while the negotiations
drag on we know that more Jews are being killed every day. Concerned less with the political than with the bureaucracy carrying out
the transportation, he is able to say effectively much more about
Auschwitz than Hochhuth could. As emerged in the Eichmann and
the Frankfurt trials, the extermination of the Jews was, for most of
those concerned, simply a matter of doing a job. Their characteristic
language was not the histrionics of Hochhuth's Doktor but of the
minor official under pressure, reducing human lives to mere statistics.
Thus Eichmann says, in the language of a dispatch clerk:

> I must ask for a feasible alternative that takes account of the load
> capacity of the trucks coming back from the Rumanian front.

The horror of the situation is heightened by the ironic fact that
those wishing to save the lives of the Jews are forced, because of the
vastness of their undertaking and the nature of the negotiations, to
talk the same language. Thus Berlasz of the Istanbul organisation,
who might have been expected to jump at the opportunity offered
him by Brand, can only reply:

> And the resultant contractual complications, have you thought of those?
> That you're endangering the entire legal immigration programme to
> Palestine? All our agreements!

Lord Moyne, the British delegate, is forced to adopt a similar tone:

> But I must ask you, Herr Brand, what can I do in our position with a
> million Jews? Where do I send them? Who will take them back?

Moyne has to talk like a salesman faced with a saturated market. His
hands are tied, regardless of his personal sympathies, because he is
one small part of an organisation, responsible to a government restricted in its turn by the state of negotiations with its allies:

> The very thought of supplying lorries in return for people is nauseating.
> No British government official can stoop to entering into negotiations
> with these mass-murderers. Quite apart from our agreements in Casa-
> blanca and Teheran, which do not allow separate negotiations.

In the face of these obstacles Brand's efforts to save the Jews are
bound to fail. Indeed, Eichmann has to commence deportations
whilst his negotiations are still going on; he has his job to do.

Joel Brand, says one critic, is a failure, able to provoke to thought only those unfamiliar with this particular historical incident. Kipphardt, however, is not attempting merely to recreate a particular episode of the second world war—better done in a film, one would think—but using the incident as a focus on the whole question of the extermination of the Jews at that time. He wants to illuminate the way people acted, and this he does, above all, in the dialogue. But the language used by Eichmann could be applied equally well to other situations, to other wars. The language of official reports of campaigns in Vietnam bears a haunting resemblance to that of this play. Although Kipphardt's model case, as one might call it, uses the most extreme instance of brutality, one sees it as throwing light also on the relationship of people in other situations, where they are reduced to statistics as parts of a bureaucratic machine. It is the language of the 'verwaltete Welt', a world dominated by administration.

Kipphardt's preceding play *In der Sache J. Robert Oppenheimer* (1964) is, along with Peter Weiss's *Die Ermittlung*, the most undisguisedly documentary of these early works, using for the most part the actual text of the Oppenheimer trial. Kipphardt has condensed above all by omission, and this is clearly stated at the beginning:

> The chronicler uses the records of the proceedings and other available documents. It is his intention to present a shortened version of those proceedings which does not distort the truth.
>
> He will add nothing that is untrue, even if this means sacrificing dramatic effect, and equally he will strive to the best of his ability not to distort the truth by selection.[9]

He is concerned 'to subordinate word-for-word accuracy to accuracy of meaning', and to this end found 'a number of additions and clarifications' necessary. Some of the ideas put forward by Teller to the commission in the play were taken from speeches and articles, and, as compared with the transcript, Kipphardt intensifies the expression of Oppenheimer's moral scruples over the atomic bomb by drawing on similar material.

The changes show that Kipphardt is not attempting merely to recreate the trial but, without falsifying Oppenheimer's position, to use it as a means of making a more general statement—in this case about the relationship between the scientist and the politicians. Some might think that, to achieve this, he would have been wiser to have used fictitious names: 'in this play of all plays not using real names would have shown that the focus of interest is not Oppenheimer the

man but the Oppenheimer case'.[10] But this would be to misunder-
stand the function and effect of a type of documentary literature
deriving its force from the fact that what is being shown did demonstrably happen as portrayed. It is at least arguable that on this basis
of fact it lends itself the better to indicating that the case is typical
of others. This is achieved particularly by the closing speech of
Oppenheimer—an instance, incidentally, of evidence taken from a
different source. By making the central character, representing also
the position of many others, express his views at this point the author
makes it clear that more than an individual standpoint is involved:

> I ask myself whether we, the physicists, have not sometimes given too
> great, too indiscriminate loyalty to our governments, against our better
> judgement—in my case not only in the matter of the hydrogen bomb.
> We have spent years of our lives doing the work of the military, and I
> feel it in my very bones that this was wrong.

This is all the more effective since, limiting the play to the hearing
in front of the commission, Kipphardt renounces the possibility of
creating out of the Oppenheimer story a melodramatic piece of
theatre. By localising it to one room, by minimising theatrical effect,
he focuses attention on the debate and its wider implications. The
audience cannot 'enjoy' the play in the way that one can *Der Stellvertreter*, and it is the better able to achieve its didactic purpose.

The theme of Auschwitz is taken up yet again in Peter Weiss's
Die Ermittlung (1965), drawing this time on the Frankfurt trials.
Avoiding, like Kipphardt, the dangers of actually trying to recreate
the reality on stage, he evokes it through the evidence of witnesses.
Basing his text too on the transcript of a trial, he goes further than
Kipphardt in the way he adapts it. Because of the emotional associations of Auschwitz, and recognising those being tried as only a few
of many who might well have been, he makes his figures impersonal.
As Counsel for the Prosecution, Counsel for the Defence, and Judge,
these have a generalised significance. The witnesses have numbers,
not names, and it is obvious that they represent more than themselves as individuals. The defendants are named when they first
appear, but thereafter they are referred to anonymously, and each
actor plays more than one. In this way, and also in his stage notes,
Weiss makes clear that he is not attempting to re-try particular
Frankfurt defendants but to use their evidence for wider purposes:
'they lend the author only their names, which stand here as symbols'.[11] The play, subtitled 'Oratorium in 11 Gesängen', is obviously

intended to some extent as a memorial to those who died in the death camp. That it is much more than this is indicated by the allusion to Dante's *Divine Comedy* in the structuring into cantos and in the movement down from the 'Gesang von der Rampe' to the final 'Gesang von den Feueröfen'. This, too, enhances the purpose of generalisation beyond the particular and extreme case of Auschwitz, and what emerges is a plea for critical self-examination affecting attitudes and values that may still be operative in society.

The defendants reject the charges and question the appropriateness of the trial itself, as in the statements of Defendant 1 in 'Gesang von den Feueröfen III', virtually amounting to the summing-up section of the play:

> We all
> I should like to emphasise again
> we did nothing but our duty
> even if it was often hard to do so
> even when we wanted to despair of it
> Today
> now that our nation
> has once again worked its way up
> to a leading position
> we should be concerned with other things
> than with recriminations
> These should long ago
> have been banished from the law books
> by the Statute of Limitations.

However, they are not presented entirely unsympathetically. In 'Gesang von der Rampe III' some understanding is shown for the fact that the common soldier had little choice but to obey orders. Defendant 4 describes his efforts to avoid work in the camp:

> I once lodged a complaint with the chief physician Dr Wirth
> The only answer I got was
> Camp Service is Front Service
> Refusal to serve
> will be punished as desertion.

This theme is followed through in the testimonies of various defendants, and their answers are responded to with some sympathy by the Judge and Counsel for the Prosecution. This idea of the individual being trapped in the situation, and having to accept it, is brought out most clearly in the statements of the witnesses. Witness

3 sees a common bond between guards and inmates, both caught in a system, and obliged to rest content with the roles ascribed to them:

> Many of those who had been chosen
> to play the role of prisoners
> were brought up with the same values
> as those
> who played the role of guards
> They had worked hard for the same nation
> and for the same incentives and rewards
> and if they hadn't been called prisoners
> they might just as easily have been guards
> ...
> We were familiar with this order
> from its very beginnings
> and so we could still find our way
> even in its final consequences.

Both groups take subordination to authority for granted. Each instinctively tries to adapt as well as possible to things as they are. At Auschwitz not only did the guards come to accept what was going on, but the inmates too found themselves evolving new standards of behaviour, substituting for the values of the outside world values befitting their new situation. Female Witness 5 describes this change:

> And we already began to live
> for new concepts
> and to find our places in a new world
> which for those of us
> who wanted to exist in it
> became the normal world.

She goes on to develop this idea of the way in Auschwitz normality became a very relative concept:

> It was perfectly normal
> that everything was stolen from us
> It was perfectly normal
> that we stole the same things back
> ...
> The dying away of our feelings
> was normal as was our indifference
> to finding corpses.

It would be easy and understandable to see the Frankfurt trials as the proper bringing to justice of war criminals. It is because this would be to beg the question as to why ordinary people were capable of committing horrific crimes that Weiss probes beyond the individual cases. He wants people to come to terms with Auschwitz, not to dismiss the problems with the sentencing of individuals, because the guilty are seen to some extent as victims of social attitudes not peculiar to the time. His sense of the subliminal presence of the attitudes and values underlying Auschwitz in his own society explains the presentation of the Counsel for the Defence, with his strictly legalistic mind, and, when Witness 3 describes in horrendous detail the torture he had to endure, the callousness of his response:

> Then it was possible after all
> to survive this treatment.

The defence refuses to countenance the wider issues. The statements of Witness 3 on the common bond between guards and inmates are dismissed as 'a totally distorted view of society'. The inference by one of the witnesses that the German nation is on trial is rejected:

> This kind of general approach
> is trivial
> particularly reproaches
> against an entire nation
> which during the time under discussion
> was engaged
> in a hard and dedicated
> struggle.

The suggestion here that the witnesses are being unpatriotic is developed in a later speech, in which the Counsel for the Defence attempts to discredit them personally, suggesting even that the trial is a political conspiracy:

> Even if every one of us
> most deeply laments these victims
> it is nonetheless our duty here
> to counter the exaggerations
> and the muck-tossing
> we have been exposed to
> from a certain quarter
> Not even the total of 2 million dead
> can be confirmed
> in connection with this camp
> Only the killing of a few hundred thousand
> can be proved conclusively
> ...

It has become only too clear
to us during this trial
what political purposes
have been furthered by the statements
which the witnesses
have had the opportunity to devise
amongst themselves.

Not without good reason, therefore, the prosecution sees

the persistence
of that very sentiment
which inspired those actions
for which the Defendants
are here arraigned.

The defendants, like the witnesses, were victims of an ideological system.

The play, then, is more than merely a requiem for those killed in Auschwitz. If, differently from Hochhuth in *Der Stellvertreter*, Weiss chose verse, it was in order often to force the actors to project their lines dispassionately, with more generalising effect. In the speech of the Counsel for the Defence quoted above, for example, the stress falls on words embodying attitudes intended to be seen as still persisting—the case against those who murdered Jews as 'exaggerations', 'muck-tossing', the notion that 'only a few hundred thousand' were put to death, the evasive reference to what had happened as merely 'killing'. The descriptions of the use of torture by Defendant 2 have a similar matter-of-fact tone, as if he were talking of something ordinary and everyday:

Often they were more intensive interrogations
they were carried out according to the prevailing
regulations
. . .
In the interests of camp security
strong measures had to be taken
against traitors and other vermin.

Through language, and more effectively than merely by listing the atrocities, Weiss reveals the attitudes behind them, and, using it so consciously and deliberately, makes it part of a documentary record embracing both past and present, linking the one with the other. The relationship is sometimes made more directly explicit, as when Witness 3 says:

> the defendants in this trial
> are here only as underlings
> Others more important
> than those
> standing before this court
> have never had to justify themselves
> Some we have met here
> as witnesses
> They live without shame
> They enjoy high office
> They multiply their possessions
> and continue those works
> for which the prisoners were formerly employed.

Other sections of the play accuse sections of German industry still in existence of having been involved in the extermination. At one point the Counsel for the Defence bursts out:

> industrial concerns are not
> on trial here[12]

but this is, in part, what Weiss is doing, sharing the view of Witness 3 that there are people still in bureaucracy and industry who benefited from the Nazi era and go unpunished, the inference being that fascism in Germany is now merely less overt.

Die Ermittlung thus marks the change coming over documentary literature in Germany from the middle of the sixties, away from issues of the past to a greater concern with the present, together with a more marked political engagement. In an interview at the time of *Die Ermittlung* Weiss surprisingly revealed what is really a non-political view of the social function of literature. It should influence people for the better, make them aware of the inadequacies of the present situation, but 'what is questionable about my situation' is the inability to see any clear alternative: 'since I do not believe in political forms of society, as they exist today, I do not dare to suggest any other kind'.[13] Rather different is then his position as reflected in a statement about his views on the proposed Verlag der Autoren in 1969: 'the great task of helping to change society is more important to me than achieving political results little by little, than compromises and utopias in publishing . . . Since I . . . want to carry out my attacks on capitalism and imperialism on the broadest front, I shall stay with the publishers who have so far given me the chance to do just that.'[14] By this time he had identified himself firmly with a socialist viewpoint: 'the guidelines of socialism contain for me the

ultimate truth . . . So I say: my work can become productive only
when it has a direct relationship to those forces which for me represent the positive forces of this world.'[15] This shift to a committed
concept of literature is reflected in the works which Weiss published
after *Die Ermittlung—Gesang vom Lusitanischen Popanz* (1967)
(against Portuguese imperialism), *Diskurs über die Vorgeschichte
und den Verlauf des lang andauernden Befreiungskrieges in Vietnam als Beispiel für die Notwendigkeit des bewaffneten Kampfes
der Unterdrückten sowie über die Versuche der Vereinigten Staaten
von Amerika, die Grundlagen der Revolution zu vernichten* (1968),
and *Notizen zum kulturellen Leben in der Demokratischen Republik
Viet Nam* (1969). All deal with the Third World. The first, although
drawing on factual information, is not a documentary drama in
style or intention, but rather a piece of agitprop. The second, as its
full title indicates, is declaredly documentary. It follows through the
history of the struggle of the Vietnamese people against occupying
powers from 500 B.C. to the present day, setting the contemporary
American campaign in an historical process, before going on to
examine the intentions of the United States to North Vietnam.

The best example of the treatment in documentary drama of the
Third World is Enzensberger's *Das Verhör von Habana* (1970). In
a way reminiscent of Kipphardt's *In der Sache J. Robert Oppenheimer* and Weiss's *Die Ermittlung*, he draws on the material of a
public hearing. He selects a representative sample, while remaining
essentially true to the transcript of the hearings in Cuba in 1961 involving people captured during the Bay of Pigs invasion. This was
not a trial and so allowed greater frankness. The people voluntarily
gave their views to journalists on radio and television. For Enzensberger their testimonies are the more revealing for being by people
who have lost their position of dominance: 'the ruling class can be
made to talk only fully when it is in the position of being the defeated counter-revolution'. The phraseology reflects Enzensberger's
intention, typical of the politically committed documentary, to make
a statement drawing its validity from a particular situation, but with
more general implications, especially about the nature of the ruling
class. The Third World has for him also the advantage of presenting
things in a clearer light than would be the case in the more complex
European situation. He sees his play as 'an exemplary case study'
whose 'importance goes beyond the reasons for writing it', and in
which the social structure revealed 'recurs, in fact, in every class-

society . . . The Habana hearing is a heuristic stroke of luck, to which I can find no counterpart in Europe.' Thus it is not just a dramatisation of the Cuban revolution, rather a sort of parable illuminating the class structure of contemporary Western society.

This is why in the introduction Enzensberger expounds at some length his views on the way the social reality is obscured by the ruling class through language, 'not only from those it exploits, but also from itself'. He cites the Cuban capitalists, whose prosperity had in reality been based on the exploitation of the peasantry, justifying their position in their own eyes by claiming that they had created jobs. Another instance is the excuse for the Bay of Pigs invasion under the guise of nationalism, although, as what they say also reveals, they, like the Americans who assisted them, only wanted the return of their own property. The difficulty is that in the flow of dramatic narrative the linguistic niceties are too obscured to be properly effective. At the same time, so Enzensberger claims, the Americans actually owned most of the best land in the country, and shipped out vast profits. The patriotism of the invaders was on this showing very much class-based, with a large percentage of the refugees in Miami in 1961 coming from the bourgeoisie, and the majority of the soldiers in the attacking force from rich families. The invasion, one is given to understand, was inspired by the CIA, for Enzensberger the most reactionary element in American capitalism. Its intention was to install a puppet regime, which would then ask for 'help' from the American government.

The play is made up of ten interviews with a series of representative members of the invasion force—including sons of dispossessed land owners and factory owners, a man put under pressure by the CIA, another who has been misled as to the nature of the invasion and the mood of the Cuban people *vis-à-vis* Fidel Castro, a priest, and a former police torturer from the Batista regime. There follows a discussion between the prisoners and Castro, and a postscript containing details of the punishment meted out to the prisoners at the later trials. To underpin the basic idea of the play, no attempt should be made, we are told, to recreate the locality. In the interests of typicality the prisoners should be played by one actor in different masks. The stage directions also call for the use of banners bearing slogans associated with the Castro regime, and the prisoners wear the familiar camouflage suits. The text deals with individuals, and is full of references to real situations and political persons. Reactions to the first stage production show that interest was aroused on the local issue of Cuba rather than, as Enzensberger wished, on the wider issue of the nature of capitalism. The printed version of the play, with Enzensberger's introduction, comments, and analysis of the language of the prisoners, is far more effective than the actual play in setting the hearing in its wider context.

Whilst in *Das Verhör von Habana* Enzensberger tries to analyse and expose the nature of capitalism by looking at a model outside the Western world, Günter Wallraff's *Nachspiele* (1968), a 'szenische Dokumentation', first performed in the Ruhrfestspiele Junges Forum in Recklinghausen as a 'project on Article 1 of the Basic Law: Human Dignity', is a literary attempt of the 'extra-parliamentary opposition' to focus directly on injustice in the Federal Republic. The techniques used in the three parts are reminiscent of those of the political theatre of the Weimar Republic. In the first section ('Demonstranten oder der Druck der Strasse') Wallraff operates mainly with quotations from newspaper articles, letters to the press and speeches by politicians, read out or flashed on a screen. The montage is designed to show the antipathy of sections of the public to students, and, with the chorus reflecting its dissemination over a wider public, to illustrate the language used in the press and in political speeches to encourage such an attitude. The second section ('Verfassungsfeinde oder wie das Gesetz es befiehlt: Politische Justiz') employs similar techniques, drawing this time on court verdicts and statements of judges, to illustrate the official attitude to the illegal Communist Party and the way this amounts to harassment of people holding a particular political view. The last section ('Sozialpartner oder die Überwindung des Klassenkampfes') contrasts public statements of the employers' federation, other organisations and individual firms about their concern for the welfare of workers, particularly of redundant miners, supported by case histories. The aim here is to show the weak position of many individual workers, and the way in which firms are supposed to use contacts with the authorities to act against strike leaders and people felt to be potential trouble-makers. The picture that emerges is—and this is the point—at variance with the public statements.

If *Nachspiele* makes particularly effective political use of the documentary theatre, it is not least because of the limits of its theme. Restricted to the situation in the Federal Republic, there is less danger, by comparison with the Third World plays, of the audience becoming involved in matters remote from their own situation, and the way the montage is used concentrates attention on specific examples of language without its being diffused in the flow of dialogue, as in the case of *Das Verhör von Habana*. There are parallels, therefore, as far as language is concerned, with F. C. Delius's *Wir Unternehmer* (1966), subtitled 'Über Arbeitgeber, Pinscher und das Volksganze; eine Dokumentar-Polemik'.

This, we think, is the most successful of the documentary literature under consideration. Not a play, but rather a verse text, it nevertheless invites comparison with documentary theatre. The material is selectively taken from the proceedings of the Economics Conference of the CDU/CSU in Düsseldorf in 1965, and the claim is that the result is true to the spirit of the occasion. Delius sets out to expose the nature of the concept of the 'formierte Gesellschaft', starting from the premise that the political attitudes of the speakers are best revealed in their use of language. He takes as his motto a comment from Martin Walser: 'even people who try to use language for concealment betray what it is they are trying to conceal. No one controls the language he speaks.' He illustrates his case by reference to the slogan 'die Funktion des Eigentumsbegriffs vor Verfälschungen schützen' ('protect the concept of ownership from distortion'), representing for him a desire to preserve property for the privileged few behind what claims to be a crusade on behalf of truth. The idea of property ownership is constantly reinforced, and that it is a basic principle of social order that responsibility and risk should fall solely on the entrepreneur:

> Wir Unternehmer, die wir als einzelne Verantwortung und Risiko
> tragen müssen, sehen diese Gefahr einer
> Verformung der Gesellschaft vielleicht klarer als viele andere.
> Wir brauchen mehr Unternehmer.
> Das unternehmerische Element in unserer Gesellschaft
> muss verstärkt, es darf nicht geschwächt werden.

Characteristic, too, it is made to appear, is the rejection of opposing views by bold generalisations that are the harder to refute:

> Der Intellektuelle kommt vom Rationalen her,
> die Sphäre der Wirtschaft ist
> in hohem Masse
> irrational . . .
> Die erschreckende Fehlbeurteilung junger, evangelischer Pfarrer,
> welche die Fabrik als furchtbare, bedrückende Welt hinstellten,

> hat letzten Endes ihre Ursache in einem rationalen Akt,
> weniger in ethisch-religiöser Verpflichtung.

Effects such as these are achieved not by simply selecting key speeches but also by arranging them into a free-verse pattern. This, as Delius says in the introduction, makes the text easier to read and prevents crucial statements from being too easily forgotten. Re-styling the original material in this way, he is the better able to make the reader aware of the way in which language is being used, as when the verse pattern is devised to go against the syntax, breaking up the easy rhythm of a sentence, or making the stress fall on the key words, at the beginning of a line or elsewhere. As was rightly said, this 'goes against the intentions of the person responsible for the content of the speech, and as such is manipulation. This robs the speech of the primary polemical effect aimed at by the speaker. The graphic form ironises the spoken word.'[16]

In the same year as *Wir Unternehmer* had appeared Wallraff's first book *Wir brauchen Dich*, marking a new form of documentary prose literature, characterised by the more direct way in which it uses the day-to-day experience of the author as a person researching his material on the spot. It is, that is to say, a 'reportage', a term that is more naturally at home in the German than in the English vocabulary, and this in itself tells us something about the reasons for its role in the latter half of the sixties. With a large proportion of the country's newspapers owned by a single and widely hated concern (Springer), party allegiance had been a far greater controlling editorial factor in the press, radio and television than in England, where quality journalism provides greater opportunities for a wider spread of opinion, as is illustrated by both the role of a number of leading papers and journals as forums of debate and the diversity of contributors. The need for a critical 'alternative' literature in West Germany was correspondingly strengthened. To obtain the material for *Wir brauchen Dich* (1966), to be looked at more closely in our next chapter, Wallraff took a series of jobs in German industry, and all these 'Reportagen' consist of a personal record of the work done, conversations held with management and workers, and descriptions of the working conditions. There is no analysis of these experiences, but each piece is by intention a critique of capitalist industry as exploitation of the workers.

In the subsequent *13 unerwünschte Reportagen* (1969) the charge is against 'the ruling class' in general, not just against employers. Masquerading under disguised identities, Wallraff was able to collect material designed to expose the attitudes and conditions of various institutions and social groups—a Hamburg doss-house, welfare workers, Catholic Bundeswehr padres discussing the role of the Christian soldier, the police in their different attitude to the extra-parliamentary opposition and the Communist Party. (When Wallraff offered himself as a spy on the Socialist Students' Association the police were interested, we are told, but none of the departments contacted with regard to the Nationalist Party saw any reason to keep a watch on them.) He also looked at the alleged hypocrisy of municipal officials in Paderborn over the treatment by the Nazis of the Jews in their town, at the hounding of a half-Jew by a Württemberg rural community, and the advice given by Catholic clergy over the morality of making a profit out of the manufacture of napalm. The most controversial of these pieces ('Wehe, wenn sie losgelassen!'), is concerned with the secret establishment and training of para-military groups in private firms, encouraged, it is said, by Bonn Ministries as part of the Emergency Laws. This was publicly denied, but it led to Wallraff's trial and subsequent acquittal on a charge of 'Amtsanmassung', i.e. pretending to hold public office.

Reflecting the sharpening politicisation of awareness, the aim is to expose to a wider public the real attitudes of powerful groups and institutions: 'the individual's strong line of defence against an organisation is his chance of bringing things to the attention of the public'. Although his pieces are all based on personal experience, Wallraff does not see them as presenting his particular viewpoint. They are, he says, increasingly objective accounts. He began by noting 'everything according to my subjective response, and only what happened to me'. But 'that gradually changed' and 'I noted down what happened to the others. I became an involved observer.'[17] This claim to objectivity goes hand in hand with a belief in the political effect of printed reportage: 'the captive, written word lends distance, draws you to get hold of and to communicate the spoken word, and, if it has been adequately checked, possibly with a few things added, brings authority into doubt, and is the first step towards a later analysis'.[18]

Wallraff's work is the more persuasive in political terms the higher his artistic achievement. *Wir brauchen Dich* had been characterised by a rather naive faith in language and in the objectivity of the narrator. There is a certain irony in the fact that the bourgeois literature that Wallraff dismisses was more aware than he at this stage of the problem of language and narration. *Wir brauchen Dich* is really a highly subjective, personal account of experience, unlikely to convince the sceptic. In *Nachspiele* he seems to have realised as much. Its use of language is more critical and, with its application of montage, it is more sophisticated. In *13 unerwünschte Reportagen* Wallraff as narrator is less naively and directly in evidence. Here, in a way comparable to Delius, he sees to it that people damn themselves in their own words. Juxtaposing public statements either with those made to him in one of his assumed roles, or with documentary evidence to the contrary, he shows the hollowness of the 'facts' presented to the public. A case in point is 'Vergangenheitsbewältigungen', where he contrasts the statements made to him by the Bürgermeister of Paderborn—Wallraff was here pretending to be a member of an Israeli friendship mission—with the man's war-time record as a member of the SS, and with his attempts apparently to prevent the publication of an accurate record of the treatment of the Jews in Paderborn under the Nazis. In 'Wehe, wenn sie losgelassen!' the statements about the arming of security guards made to Wallraff's direct and open enquiries are contrasted with those made to him *alias* 'Ministerialrat Kröver'. However, when he forgoes montage there is little to distinguish his 'Reportagen' from the journalism of the popular press, with its appeal to the 'facts' and its claimed authenticity.

In *13 unerwünschte Reportagen* he no longer narrates experiences but, with the help of a tape recorder, orders and arranges material he has collected, linked by his own comments and explanations. This change in the role of the author is typical of prose documentary literature in West Germany in the later sixties. Retreating as narrator, the author tends more than ever to become a compiler, an editor—like Walser when he makes it his business to induce other people to document their experiences. It is a method that very soon, and not necessarily by chance, Böll was to turn to fictional account in *Gruppenbild mit Dame*, giving himself, incidentally, the advantage of combining what overall makes the effect of a pretty radical position with a fictional narrator who, if pressed, could offer the excuse that he is merely the arranger of diverse, even contradictory material, and who as such all the better allows the real narrator—Böll himself—an alibi for any definitive and precise commitment. An opposite case is that of Grass's *Aus dem Tagebuch einer Schnecke* (1972). It also makes extensive use of documentary material—in this instance Grass's election campaigning for the SPD —but here the material is directly derived from what really happened. The result is a strong authorial presence, far more marked than in any other of Grass's works.

This development in documentary prose writing is sometimes assumed to have been stimulated above all by Danilo Dolci's *To feed the hungry* (1956) and Oscar Lewis's *The children of Sanchez. Self-portrait of a Mexican family* (1961), which share the same feeling of bitterness at social injustice. The most significant works of this 'literature of non-authors', as Reinhard Baumgart called it, are Erika Runge's *Bottroper Protokolle* (1968) and *Frauen Versuche zur Emanzipation* (1970), Ursula Trauberg's *Vorleben* (1968), Wolfgang Werner's *Vom Waisenhaus ins Zuchthaus* (1969) and Rosalie Rother's *Rosalka oder Wie es eben so ist* (1969). Of these only the last-named book can be said to owe nothing to the influence of Martin Walser. It was he who persuaded Erika Runge to undertake her first book, and wrote the preface to it, and he who encouraged, edited and arranged to have published *Vorleben* and *Vom Waisenhaus ins Zuchthaus*. The relevant circumstances of Walser's own development having been discussed in previous chapters, we can proceed to a closer look at these particular works.

Wolfgang Werner, in describing his childhood and youth in orphanages, his lapse, along with so many orphans he knew, into crime, and the impossibility, as he felt, of living a normal life, feels society to be responsible for his predicament. He puts over convincingly his fear of the various authorities. He comes into close contact with authority—police, orphanage officials, and so on—and the law treats him increasingly unsympathetically with each offence. Referring to one friend who had just been imprisoned, he says: 'the State reaped what it had sown', and of others: 'they were all going the same way as me. From orphanage to prison.' However, although there are inconsistent features about his experience, his accusations are not fully substantiated, and they ignore the considerable influence of his mother's behaviour. Even taking all these environmental factors into account, it is still difficult for the reader to see why he continues his life of crime. The book often reads as if Werner, knowing that he has a readership and that his story is being presented as a critical indictment of the system, sees a chance to excuse his past. It is hard to accept his claim to intrinsic moral uprightness as a person led astray only because of the ethos of the homes, when he lives cynically off the earnings of several women. He abandons one in Paris after he has had a good time on her money, commits incest with his sister on innumerable occasions, and indulges in group sex, not to mention his constant car thefts and petty pilfering.

Werner's character fluctuates and so, therefore, does the focus of the book. It is not so much a documentation of the path of crime as of his personal uncertainty and his almost schizophrenic state of mind. This comes out clearly in his language, with its vacillation in tone and register. Thus, on the question of sex, he oscillates between a very bourgeois code of moral values and complete amorality. On one occasion he describes the scene at his mother's house as a 'hell of madness and sexual degradation' but then can write: 'later, when the children had gone and were playing in the living room, I climbed into my sister Marion's bed, and, when I saw how Gustav was screwing my mother, I began to screw Erika as well, so there was a right old screwing session'. Masturbation is described coyly ('on each occasion I induced sleep in an ugly way'), whereas his first pimping is introduced without any ado: 'she had no objection and that's how I got my first tart to go out on the job for me'. Against this can be set in turn the stilted description of the first act of intercourse with his sister: 'in einer noch im Rohbau befindlichen Garage kam es zum ersten Verkehr, welcher von beiden Seiten bis zum Orgasmus vollendet wurde' ('the first intercourse took place in a garage still in the process of construction and orgasm was achieved by both parties'). Similar attempts at writing in a more elevated style are seen in the cliché image of the judge as a 'Pilatus der Neuzeit' ('latter-day Pilate') and, most grotesquely, in Werner's description of his efforts to switch off a car's windscreen-wipers, where he 'fand aber nicht sogleich den Knopf wieder, um deren Tätigkeit Einhalt zu gebieten' ('he didn't find the knob again straight away, so that he could put a stop to their activity'). The pompous tone, with the ludicrous inappropriateness of the last phrase, shows both his linguistic uncertainty and his attempt to sound intellectual. Walser claims that Werner's language is the product of his upbringing in homes and in institutions and that it brings an additional dimension to the social criticism inherent in his story. In fact, however, Werner unwittingly reveals himself, through his language, as someone trying to conform, to leave behind the sort of milieu in which he has grown up. He does not succeed. He has internalised that milieu's values and code of behaviour more than he realises. In Werner's language one sees, too, his desire to be 'respectable', to find acceptance by the society from which he claims to feel estranged. So, *pace* Walser, the book is less protest against society than acceptance of its values.

A similar attempt by an editor to make a political statement through a piece of documentary literature is to be found in *Rosalka oder Wie es eben so ist*, edited by Bernhard Schütze. Rosalie Rother narrates her experiences of childhood in German-speaking Poland, her life up to and including the second world war, in which she lost everything, life in refugee camps, and finally her attempt then to drink herself to death. Her life is marked throughout by a series of personal tragedies, and she cannot face rebuilding her life again from nothing:

> I couldn't go on, I'd lost everything, been through every camp, lost everything in Poland, fitted out a new flat, it all went up the spout, I lost everything again in Berlin, I'd fled there earlier, lived there, lost everything, left it behind, would you want to do anything when you've seen your daughter, your eldest one, seen the bomb slice into her, everything had gone, was ruined, cocked up, carted off, buggered up . . . so I said, Dad, we'll drink ourselves to death, to hell with it, we've had enough, let's put an end to it, oh, bugger everything, I can't take it any more.[19]

Her story is moving and tragic, but Schütze sees it as more than that. For him her experiences are a powerful 'critique of the inhumanity of class society', with her final breakdown the result of inability to keep up the struggle for the personal achievement which she feels is expected of her. Her tragedy is precipitated by what in fearful jargon Schütze calls her 'internalisation of the principle that perpetuates class domination, namely the reduction of all collective understanding to the principle of achievement'. To underpin this view from within the text, he arranged the taped material so that the final section consists of Rosalka's views on political and social questions. These correspond to his own left-wing position. But there is nothing within the main body of the text that accords with these views, and this section consequently reads like a mannered coda.

Schütze supports his interpretation of Rosalka's story by claiming that her language reveals her impotence before the 'system'. True, referring to incidents in her childhood, Rosalka had felt herself at times trapped between the Polish and German worlds, accepted by neither. However, the general impression of her that emerges is of a real 'character', proud, sly and resourceful, with a raciness of expression that marks her as a natural story-teller. Only in her account of the decision to take to drink and in her concluding remarks is her story linguistically unconvincing. Her remarks about Willy Brandt's rumoured drinking habits, her critical comments about students, her stress that 'there's got to be a leader, you can't do things any old how, there's got to be order, that's right enough'— all these are recognisable clichés and would appear to support Schütze's views. But against this must be set the fact that her statements supporting the left-wing position are equally stereotyped and derivative. She feels, for example, that 'little people like me always get shat upon by the big ones', and that 'everyone's got to have a say, all us little folk ought to be able to have our say, they ought to ask us, but we're not asked, the bosses at the top do everything just as they want to'. Rosalka has no consistent political views, just a series of phrases she has picked up.

All this 'literature of the non-authors', as a documentation of social injustice, rests ultimately on its claim, directly or indirectly, to authenticity. Thus Walser, writing of *Vorleben*, states that 'artificial authenticity is no longer to our taste. We no longer believe that anyone can know all about someone else.' Ursula Trauberg's book has a 'credibility that can only be achieved when it is not intentional'. However, there are contradictions in her various testimonies, and Walser has to admit to 'corrections of her original statements'. The crucial event in Ursula's life, her killing of her lover's wife, is not illuminated at all, and Walser has to comment that 'this grim part of the twenty-four-year-old's path needs further explanation'.[20] In *Vom Waisenhaus ins Zuchthaus*, as we have seen, the basic thesis is weakened by the language Werner uses, and in *Rosalka* contradictions in her statements throw doubt on the evidence. She herself draws attention to such as appear in the book, but one questions the truth of all she writes, not least because she reveals herself to have so fertile an imagination. The editors of these works present them as typical case studies supporting their own view of society, but they turn out to be highly personal accounts. They are interesting as such, but there is nothing in them that supports the claim of factual accuracy and general applicability. The value of Erika Runge's *Bottroper Protokolle* is that it produces not one view but several, in some cases directly contradictory ones. Thus the portrayal by the chairman of a factory council, Clemens K., of the situation in Bottrop immediately after the war contrasts with that by the clergyman Johannes L. Erika Runge's achievement in both her books, is to have presented a variety of views on an area of common experience, showing how age, sex, social background and other factors colour experience, and that, contrary to Walser's assumption, one individual's account need not be authentic, however familiar he may be with what he is talking about.

Walser's position on documentary literature is ambiguous. He assents to it, on the one hand, because he sees here a chance for literature to break away from pure 'language games' (which in a sense he himself had been cultivating in sections of *Halbzeit* and *Das Einhorn*) and expose and document features of society that he deplores. He welcomes *Vom Waisenhaus ins Zuchthaus* and *Bottroper Protokolle* because, as with *Vorleben*, the author merely 'reports' . On the other hand, he sees in such texts the possibility of 'narration', which he feels to be no longer possible in bourgeois literature (though he was soon to indulge in it again in *Die Gallistl'sche Krankheit*). Both *Vom Waisenhaus ins Zuchthaus* and *Vorleben* are marred in their narrative by attempts to produce too self-conscious, too 'literary' a style, resulting in linguistic inconsistency. The taped texts—both *Bottroper Protokolle* and *Rosalka*—substantiate Walser's point much better, frequently characterised as they are by the racy quality of the language spoken (and then written down). Their weakness is that their editors reshape the verbal material. The *Bottroper Protokolle* were 'written down just as they were said and then shortened—they were tightened up and arranged with a mind to the dramatic effect'. This helps continuity and the flow of narrative, and undeniably imparts a certain 'literary' quality. But this is of a rather conventional kind and it militates against the intended socio-critical impact. The 'literature of the non-authors', moreover, reveals rather too naive a faith in documentation to make its case, in conditions in which 'facts' can hardly do justice any longer to the complexity of situations. It reflects an inadequately differentiated view of society and a too simplistic ideology, and the selection of facts, and the language in which they are presented, easily become merely tendentious.

Heissenbüttel might well have been commenting on these weaknesses when outlining his own position: 'what people call reality, facticity, including the social and psychological conditions under which it appears, is now beyond the reach of any simplifying ideology (and most particularly of this ideology)'.[21] The alternative position would be one more fully aware of the density and opacity of the material reality, seeking to deal with it by a sort of collage of language elements, as through a juxtaposition of quotations: 'only by *quoting* the relationship to things stored in words can we get anywhere near what, outside language, could be called the world'.[22]

Franz Mon appropriately cites Heissenbüttel's text 'Deutschland 1944' as a good example of the effectiveness of this method. It is an impression of Germany in the later stages of the war, drawing on speeches made by Hitler and Himmler, on orders, reports and Nazi poetry. One section consists almost entirely of a Wehrmacht report of 20 July 1944; there are also quotations from a paper on atomic fission, and extracts from the diary of an unnamed observer. A typical example is provided by this passage:

> sie hörte wie der Todesschweiss plätscherte das Uranatom dessen Auf-
> spaltung den Physikern gelang lässt die Möglichkeit ins Auge fassen
> durch fortgesetztes Aufprallen von Neutronen auf Uranatome in sich
> multiplizierenden Wirkungen soviel Energien freizumachen dass die
> Planeten in Katastrophen verwickelt werden können es trat an uns die
> Frage heran wie ist es mit den Frauen und Kindern ich habe mich ent-
> schlossen auch hier eine ganz klare Lösung zu finden ich hielt mich
> nämlich nicht für berechtigt die Männer auszurotten sprich also um-
> zubringen oder umbringen zu lassen und die Rächer in Gestalt der
> Kinder für unsere Söhne und Enkel gross werden zu lassen es musste
> der schwere Entschluss gefasst werden dieses Volk von der Erde ver-
> schwinden zu lassen sie hörte wie der Todesschweiss plätscherte sie
> hörte wie der Todesschweiss plätscherte[23]

The statement which opens and closes this final section ('sie hörte wie der Todesschweiss plätscherte' ('she heard the dripping of the sweat of death'), used as a sort of leitmotif throughout the whole collage, conveys the horror of the death camps. The next segment 'das Uranatom ... verwickelt werden können' opens up the prospect of an even greater catastrophe for mankind than the second world war. The next 'es trat an uns ... gross werden zu lassen' gives the personal dilemma of the observer, possibly a camp guard, in the face of the extermination campaign. The last statement 'es musste der schwere Entschluss gefasst werden dieses Volk von der Erde ver-schwinden zu lassen' might be an extract from a speech or a newspaper article giving the official Nazi Party position in a way which avoids mention of the horrors of the actual processes necessary to make the Jews 'disappear'. Thus in this section, as in the others, the reader is presented with various partial views of the situation which, with their different registers, build up a kaleidoscopic image of Germany in 1944. Unlike collages utilising a random selection of words and phrases to convey an impression, in 'Deutschland 1944' Heissenbüttel carefully plans repetitions and juxtapositions to bring out his view of the reality, taking sentences out of their expected syntax and context to expose them linguistically to the light. The cool language of the scientist contrasts with the struggle for personal clarity, which in turn highlights the coldness of the formal statement on the policy of extermination. The way we read the section is relativised by its incapsulation within the statement 'sie hörte wie der Todesschweiss plätscherte', which is then repeated at the end. What dominates is fear of imminent death, the inexorability of the camp deaths, and the horror of being amongst people afraid of the death that awaits them.

Heinrich Vormweg, a champion of Heissenbüttel's work, says of the use of quotation and collage that it provokes the reader 'to see what is concretely experienced as it really is and to exclude the false assumptions about it embodied in language'. This obviously works best, as in 'Deutschland 1944', when a subject is being treated (with hindsight) on which there is now a general consensus. Whether it always necessarily makes the individual aware of the 'need to find one's bearings amid processes of perception and information that totally lack any valid pattern of assessment'[24] is another question.

Heissenbüttel's most recent and extended work *Projekt Nr. 1: D'Alemberts Ende* makes intensive use of quotations, this time more within a montage than a collage. It depicts the events of an apparently arbitrarily chosen day, 26 July 1968, in Hamburg, within a circle of friends, mainly reporters and radio correspondents. They come together in bars, have discussions in their offices about various projects, meet in the evening in a flat and discuss events of the day. Later d'Alembert is found dead. The cause of his death is unknown, and he is without his toupé, which is discovered going round and round on the turntable of a record-player. The plot, such as it is, is of no great importance: 'the bit of story that was recognisable has a linking function, it is without significance'. What really matters is the continual talk.

The book comprises ritualised conversations in which names and quotations from many different sources in place and time proliferate. One section is a 'Conversation about students and similar matters'. The discussion consists for the most part of an exchange of views, represented by quotations from Marcuse, Enzensberger, Habermas, and various pamphlets and leaflets. This section is undoubtedly successful in demonstrating how such a debate can become just a social ritual, instead of being a real interchange of ideas. There is the danger, however, of the reader being drawn into a game of trying to recognise the unacknowledged quotations, and Heissenbüttel seems to be encouraging him to play it. We read that Frau d'Alembert does not find 'the picture of a naked woman exposing her pubic hair' obscene, but rather 'one of a general exhibiting his medals', and this view crops up again. A little later we are told that 'Ottilie Wildermuth finally responds with a quotation from Herbert Marcuse', and 'even Dr Johnson now quotes Marcuse'. The statement on obscenity is, however, a quotation from Marcuse's *An Essay on Liberation*; the discussion in the section 'Gespräch über die eigene Lage' about the individual and the crowd has quotations from E. T. A. Hoffmann and Edgar Allan Poe, but the argument is taken from Benjamin's essay 'Baudelaire, ein Lyriker im Zeitalter des Hochkapitalismus'.

Heissenbüttel is not turning his use of quotations into a game, but his characters are making conversation into one. For a feature of the book is to expose what goes on among littérateurs and intellectuals in a society in which endless and sterile gossip about culture usurps the place of real and creative culture. Another, connected with this, is to follow through Heissenbüttel's thesis, expounded in his essays (and featured in this novel), about the weakened significance of the individual as the creative centre. This he does to the point at which the figures, creative only of talk, and each no more than a collection of more or less interchangeable units, have no real individuality left. A past in which the individual self had reality and substance is, as it were, evoked in a long initial quotation, virtually intact, though not referred to as a quotation, from the opening of Goethe's *Die Wahlverwandtschaften*. But the conclusion of that episode finds Eduard and Ottilie—the names as in Goethe's novel, the figures themselves work for television—moved to ironic laughter as they turn their gaze over the expanse of a modern city.

This being so, with *D'Alembert Ende* we reach an aspect of Heissenbüttel's work not dissimilar from parts of the *Textbuch* sequence, but pushing features in those texts to a stage at which it is no longer appropriate to speak of a documentary element at all. What might superficially be taken as such is material used not for its own authenticity but as ingredients in the, as it were, borrowed existence of people who, in Heidegger's sense, themselves lack 'authenticity'. Heissenbüttel, that is to say, comes into our discussion more by virtue of what distinguishes his work from documentary literature than of what might on a surface view seem to lend itself to comparison with it.

It remains now only to say something about the prospects of documentary literature. It has established a market and, so long as this lasts, there will no doubt be works to fill it. It is not, after all, necessarily difficult to write, and in a climate of opinion calling for the discussion of social problems it has obvious attractions, whether as a means of focusing attention on particular situations for purposes of information or—a function to which it easily lends itself at the same time—providing information. As to the factors favouring it in the sixties, one was undoubtedly the much publicised belief in the demise of 'literature', in the loss of relevance and value—that is to say, of the formalised structures of the imagination. This belief came to be challenged by counter-arguments which, holding fast to the need for radical social change and to the idea of literature's part in it, attributed a decisive formative role to the imagination and so to literature. The future of documentary literature will not be unaffected by the extent to which this position consolidates itself.

It is not by chance that in a volume of essays Hans Christoph Buch, whom earlier we singled out as representing this attitude (*Kritische Wälder*, 1972), immediately follows the reprint of his article 'Von der möglichen Funktion der Literatur' with a harsh critique of documentary literature. 'Forms of literary fiction', he says (with reference at the same time to older arguments about socialist realism), were dismissed as 'bourgeois luxury', distracting people 'from the political content'. The theory of the 'death of literature' was a 'still-birth'. But theories replacing it have been no less dogmatic, 'such as the assertion that you can now only write documentary literature, that the raw material of reality has to be worked into literature in its crudest possible form'. 'Formalism was replaced by mechanical "content-ism"', and 'for the reader or spectator there remained only resignation about the underprivileged or sympathy with them'. The point at issue as not the rightness or wrongness of these charges but the bearing on the prospects of documentary literature. These will be influenced by whether the trust thus placed in 'fantasy' as an aid to literature's 'utopian potential' establishes itself as a significant factor on the intellectual scene. It is too early to say. By the end of the sixties this had come to provide the most direct challenge in radical circles to the simple cause-and-effect view of the relationship between literature and political change and to the idea of the imaginative writer as a useless scribbler. At the end of his essay, without renouncing his hopes of literature as in the end politically effective, Buch's case against documentary literature becomes a return to the argument in favour of 'aesthetic autonomy'. This looks a bit like wanting the best of both worlds, but in any case his final sentence is one that we can all agree with: 'Therefore we should be on our guard against over-hasty simplifications of whatever political colour.'

Notes

1 Marcel Reich-Ranicki, *Literatur der kleinen Schritte*, Munich, 1967, p. 62.
2 'Der lange Marsch. Aspekte der deutschen Kultur seit 1945', in K. D. Bracher (ed.), *Nach 25 Jahren*, Munich, 1970, p. 200.
3 'Unmenschlichkeit beschreiben', in *Literatur für Zeitgenossen*, Frankfurt a.M., 1966, p. 12.
4 *Ibid.*, p. 13.
5 In his introduction to the original German edition.
6 All quotations from this play are given in the translation by R. D. Macdonald, *The Representative*, London, 1963.
7 *Toller*, Frankfurt a. M., 1969, p. 2.
8 *Op. cit.*, Frankfurt a. M., 1965, p. 141.
9 This and other quotations are taken from *In the matter of J. Robert Oppenheimer*, trans. Ruth Speirs, London, 1967.
10 Marcel Reich-Ranicki, *Literarisches Leben in Deutschland*, Munich, 1965 p. 249.
11 All quotations from this play, with one or two minor changes, are from *The Investigation*, trans. Alexander Gross, London, 1966.
12 These lines were contained only in the pre-publication edition of the play in *Theater 1965*, Velber bei Hannover, 1965, p. 86.
13 'Dramatiker ohne Alternativen. Ein Gespräch mit Peter Weiss', in *Theater 1965*, p. 89.
14 'Erklärung I', *Die Zeit*, 28 February 1969, p. 13.
15 Quoted by Helmut Salzinger in 'Zwei, drei, viele Standpunkte: Der lange Marsch des Peter Weiss', *Die Zeit*, 3 May 1969, pp. 21–2.
16 Alois Brandstetter, 'Lyrik als Inszensierung der Grammatik', *Literatur und Kritik*, 38, Salzburg, 1969, p. 479.

17 *Von einem der auszog und das Fürchten lernte*, Munich, 1970, p. 38.
18 'Wirkungen in der Praxis', *Akzente*, 4, 1970, p. 316.
19 *Op. cit.*, Frankfurt a. M., 1969, pp. 136–7.
20 In the postscript to *Vorleben*, Frankfurt a. M., 1968.
21 Helmut Heissenbüttel and Heinrich Vormweg, *Briefwechsel über Literatur*, Neuwied and Berlin, 1969, p. 93.
22 *Ibid.*, p. 29.
23 *Das Textbuch*, Neuwied and Berlin, 1970, p. 272.
24 Heinrich Vormweg, 'Literatur und Lebenshilfe, neue Version', *Merkur*, 268, 1970, p. 785.

Chapter 5

Literature and the industrial world

A distinguishing feature of the sixties was the emergence of a group of writers concerned to portray adequately the world of industrial labour. They were largely of working-class origins, with present or past experience as manual workers. This was a notable development and new in the post-war context.

The relationship of German literature to the sphere of industry and the worker has never proved easy. There has always tended to be something strained about it. Even in the sixties this still remained the case. Advanced industrialisation came late to Germany and, when it did come, it took place very quickly. It happened in conditions in which capitalism, with confusing intellectual and ideological results, was developing under the paternalistic aegis of a State structured on a quasi-feudal pattern. English literature has a background of longer experience of industrial society and found less difficulty in coming to terms with the world of the factory, the worker and the city. The German Naturalists declared the need to face up to the new industrial society. They often wrote sympathetically about the workers, but, as it were, at a distance, and they revealed a profound distaste for the factory.

The particular features of the post-war situation created problems of their own. The virtual suspension of the German economy in the circumstances prevailing after 1945 meant that for the time being conditions did not encourage class antagonisms. The growth of prosperity in the fifties also militated against them, and so, in middle-class or working-class circles alike, against the sense of any urgent need for literature to tackle the question of the industrial world with special regard to a working-class point of view. Apart from this, there was the discrediting effect of the memory of National Socialism and the prominence it gave, for ideological and political reasons, to the figure of the worker in literature. Another factor was that, following the currency reform and the consequent economic development of the governing Christian Democratic Party away from its more progressive Ahlen programme of 1947, working-class writers with a class-conscious proletarian point of view tended, like Willi Bredel, to settle in East Germany. This developed a socialist realist literature linking up directly with the Bund proletarisch-revolutionärer Schriftsteller of the nineteen-twenties, whose leading members included J. R. Becher and Anna Seghers. (It was associated with the Communist Party and aimed at influencing the reading public towards an interest in the proletariat.) Important, too, is the disrepute into which Marxism fell through its association with Stalinism, with the result that in the tense political relationship between East and West in the period of the 'cold war' authors were disinclined to invite association with communism by writing in a manner that could be suspected of socialist realism, or could lend itself to use in East Germany for propaganda purposes. In Max von der Grün's auto-biographical story 'Etwas ausserhalb der Legalität', set at a slightly later date, one character expresses concern at a novel by another on the grounds that, with its attacks on West German industry, 'they'll crow in the East'. It was ridiculous, in other words, to attribute the relative absence of proletarian literature to a plot by Gruppe 47 to sterilise 'the official literary industry' against 'themes from the industrial world'.[1]

All the same, by the end of the fifties a number of critics and writers were coming forward with the view that West German literature was not doing justice to the theme of industrial work, this 'step-child of German literature', as Wolfgang Rothe put it. Walter Jens declared in 1960, 'The world in which we live still has not been firmly and truly captured in literature.' The world of labour 'does not seem to have entered the picture at all. Where is the portrait of a workman or the sketch of a bricklayer, where do we see girls at work in the factory or robots watching over red lights?' 'We describe the individual,' he went on, 'who can afford to have feelings: man in the state of an eternal day off, a gentleman of unlimited private means. Don't we ever work? Is our daily activity so unimportant?'[2] He returned to this theme in his opening address at the Frankfurt Book Fair in 1961, thinking also of the need for literature to reflect recent changes in the nature of industrial work: 'In Marl a lone man stands in front of the control panel, waiting for indicators to light up, a worker to whom the slogan "Workers of the world, unite" is as foreign as a saying from the age of Metternich—but does literature portray him?'[3]

Just about this time circumstances were leading to the creation in Dortmund of Gruppe 61. Its founder and chronicler, Fritz Hüser, tried to give the impression that the group was founded as a direct response to statements like that of Walter Jens. This is not so. None of those participating in that discussion aligned themselves with the Dortmund group; but it would be wrong to say, as has been alleged, that what they wanted was to 'extend the range of the literary market by the addition of exotic material'.[4] The reasons for the coming of Gruppe 61 were of a different kind, involving economic and regional factors. The technological changes that revolutionised the industrial world in the post-war years left the mining industry relatively untouched, and the miner's work as dangerous and exhausting as ever. In conjunction with the concentration of the industry in the Ruhr area, this meant that a sense of solidarity, eroded by affluence in other industries and in other regions, continued to exist among miners, on top of which came a recession in the industry in the late fifties. These factors, together with the strong popular tradition of literature about mining in that part of Germany and the sense there of a common bond through work, substantially explain why a body of literature with mining as one of its main themes came to the fore at this particular juncture. It was facilitated, too, by the encouragement given to would-be writers by Fritz Hüser, director of Dortmund Public Libraries and curator of his private Archiv für Arbeiterdichtung und soziale Literatur, and by Walter Köpping, a cultural official of IG Bergbau. Under their stimulus a number of writers and critics came together to form the Dortmunder Gruppe 61 (to give it its full name) in the spring of the year referred to in the title.

What, however, was to be the character and function of their work? Was it to be 'Kumpeldichtung'—by workers for workers—or not? These were among the questions that had been raised in earlier discussions in the area. It soon became clear that those who were to become the leading figures in Gruppe 61 were concerned not just with appealing to a working-class public but with presenting fundamental and general issues. This is clear from the stated aims of the group. One was 'the literary and artistic treatment of the contemporary world of industrial labour and its social problems', another 'intellectual concern with the technical age', and another 'critical involvement with the social literature of other countries'. That is to say, in Hüser's words, the authors of the Dortmunder Gruppe 61 did 'not write as workers for workers'. Their aim was 'to make a contribution to the literary portrayal of all the urgent questions and phenomena of our contemporary world, dominated as it is by technology and affluence', and 'neither the occupation nor the social status of the writer is decisive—the only important things are the theme and the power to deal with it artistically'.[5] This was why the group could view itself as responding to the appeals of Walter Jens. It was, and remained, concerned not only with the worker in his place of work but also with the general implications of the changes experienced in factory, mine, and leisure time. Also, it consciously aimed at literary respectability. By the mid-sixties it had abandoned the part of its original programme concerned with 'Arbeiterdichtung'—in the sense in which the term was applied to earlier writers like Heinrich Lersch, Gerrit Engelke, Karl Bröger and Paul Zech—and Fritz Hüser had come to reject the older writers as useful models for the new generation. So, if the views of Walter Jens had had any lasting effect on the group, it is in so far as his implicit rejection, by omission, of earlier literary efforts to tackle the theme of industrial society may have encouraged it not to set itself up as the heir of the twenties.

Thus, surveying the group's development, Hüser wrote: 'in this age of participation (*Mitbestimmung*) and automation, of cybernetics and atomic power, of workers' shares and the forty-hour week, the questions and problems that stand out are different from those of the earlier "Arbeiterdichtung" and agitatory literature'. All the same, the group did have a high regard for Bruno Gluchowski, whose best-known novel *Der Honigkotten* (1965) follows the fortunes of a miner in the Ruhr from the strike of 1912 up to 1925. The time in which it is set and the problems it deals with are anything but those to which Hüser refers. Thus to some extent Gruppe 61 *was* influenced by the earlier movement. As time passed and as younger writers came into it, its tendency was to move away. By 1966 Hüser was at pains to distance the work of Gruppe 61 from 'Arbeiterdichtung', and Max von der Grün rejected the notion of working-class literature altogether on the grounds that in conventional literary quarters it tended to have derogatory associations. Nevertheless, his first novel shows that so sweeping a generalisation was not without its problematical aspects.

Männer in zweifacher Nacht, published in 1962, portrays a mining disaster, with the scene shifting constantly between the men underground and those waiting for news at the pithead. The most striking motif in the first part of the novel is the sense of unity among the miners. The men's sense of comradeship owes a good deal to the feeling that their superiors will evade their responsibility if they think they can get coal more cheaply without adequate safety measures. Only an accident will force them into taking the necessary precautions, as Johannes, a theological student working in the pit during his vacation, rapidly comes to recognise. The place at which a roof fall does occur had been reported as unsafe on previous occasions, but without effect. Weigert, a former miner now on the management side, points out to his daughter that there are dangers inherent in mining that cannot be eradicated. The miner's lot is much the same as ever, he says. He may earn more, but danger will always be part of his life. She argues that amid the generally increasing prosperity the miner's wage is dropping, despite the arduous and hazardous nature of his work, whereas once he was relatively well paid.

This critical element in *Männer in zweifacher Nacht* helped to give it local notoriety when it appeared, though the accident is depicted as being caused just as much by a monster, wreaking some sort of vengeance on those who dare to work within it, as by negligence on the part of the management. The attitude of the miner to the mine is a divided one, a love–hate relationship:

> The pit, danger, the miner: a trinity of the dangerous everyday. The pit: a curse—a prayer! ... The miner is for ever exposed to the moods of this monster, whether he trusts it like a child or forces his way further into it like a burglar. The black coal is his bread, the sounds of the pit are his sole company, the roof is his sky, the roadway the one constant thing. And if the mountain were not like this, the miner would only be half alive.

In a manner familiar in many descriptions of mines in German literature, from the Romantics through to the 'Arbeiterdichtung' of the nineteen-twenties, the mine is depicted as a fascinatingly awesome being of terrible power. When Stacho, Sepp and Johannes are trapped by the fall, they feel, despite their earlier complaints about inadequate safety precautions, as if they have narrowly escaped a monster's clutches: 'The pit hadn't killed them. True, they were now sitting in its tentacles, but they were still alive. Life! Much better life, though imprisoned in this prison of a pit, than to be crushed by its angry rages.'

After the accident the situation is described from two perspectives —of those waiting for news on the surface or below ground, and of the men trapped beyond the rock fall. In the scenes underground both before and after the accident von der Grün graphically describes the exceptional life of the miner ('the everyday world has its norms, that of the miner has its own'), and the tensions that build up after the roof collapses. Still a miner when he wrote the book, he knew this world intimately, and, drawing on the racy quality of the miners' language, captures the drama of the accident and of the rescue attempt. The accident is the catalyst which brings about a basic confrontation of ideas. Stacho, an old miner, sees himself and his fellow miners as impotent before the two forces ruling their lives, the management and the mine. He does all that is necessary to keep them alive as long as possible, but he is doubtful about the prospects of rescue. He is being cheated, he feels, of the reasonably comfortable life that he regarded as his right and sinks into a state of resignation. Johannes cannot accept that the rescue will not succeed, nor can he passively accept the conditions in the mine. In the extraordinary conditions in which they find themselves the tension between the two grows, and they try to kill each other. Then Johannes, unable just to sit and wait for rescue, tries desperately to break through the wall of rock separating them from the rescuers, but breaks down with the effort, and has to be tended by Stacho. This reconciles them, and they re-define their positions. Stacho decides to have himself invalided out of his job and to settle for a degree of comfort in retirement. Johannes resolves to give up theology and study medicine, in order really to be able to help the miners. This newly-established friendship, engendered by shared adversity, gives a special significance to the bond of the 'Kumpel'.

These aspects provoked strong reactions from left-wing critics. Max von der Grün, said Hanno Möbius, 'evokes concepts of a primal, almost animal-like social unit on the one hand, and on the other he demonises the working conditions'. He 'archaises the relationship of the miners to the object of their work'.[6] The critical element in the book is, as von der Grün himself admits, not very substantial, and as Möbius points out, such criticism as there is is reduced in its effect by the narrator's propensity for metaphor, so used as to make the conditions underground appear an inevitable part of mining. It is in these narrative 'interventions' that the book reveals its major weakness. The depiction of the mine as a monster, rightly criticised by Möbius as archaic, is indicative of an attempt to elevate the style, but the result is often bathos:

> The prisoner breathes the earth's air, sees the sun—if not its fiery ball, at least the blue and grey of the sky—hears the song of the birds, sees the stars . . .
> But what of those who sit trapped down the pit, shut off from the world above ground? What do they breathe? What do they see, hope for, believe and think?
> How long and far that unbearable waiting can stretch out, how long anxious hope will hold out, how time drags out, until the lamps of the rescuers shine in their eyes, the first wave of fresh air making them shiver—all this uncertainty makes the soul despair.

It was von der Grün's next novel *Irrlicht und Feuer* (1963) that caught the attention of a wider public. This depicts phases in the life of a worker, Jürgen Fohrmann, searching for a sense of personal identity, for meaningful relationships and, above all, for satisfaction in his work. A crucial episode is a chance meeting with an unknown woman one night as he is on his way to the pit. He gets involved in a long conversation and misses his shift. For the first time he comes to realise the insecurity and the restrictions of his job, and his frustration expresses itself in increasing irritation with the administration both of the mine and of his union. The latter should represent the workers, but instead has come to add merely another dimension to 'those at the top' interested above all in defending their own position. His criticism has hardly any political slant. It expresses the dissatisfaction that he is coming to feel with his work. Only when at a union meeting he starts to talk of 'we' (the workers) instead of 'I' do we become aware of more openly political, and vaguely socialist, overtones.

The attacks on management and union are sparked off by the indifference to the workers as human beings. Fohrmann criticises the introduction of a new cutting machine—not to increase the mine's efficiency (in fact the men have already been informed of its imminent closure), but to try the machine out before it is put on sale in overseas markets. His fear of the new cutter proves justified. In an accident—the description of which led to an attempted injunction on the publishers by the manufacturers of the equipment—one man is decapitated and another has a leg crushed. Fohrmann, without having found a new job, immediately quits work, although his notice still has a fortnight to run. He loathes work in the pit, not because of the poorish level of pay but because he feels branded by it. He resents the fact that passers-by in the street immediately recognise him as a working man and seem to regard him as an inferior person. His hope is to find a job where his personal dignity is respected. He applies for a post in a porcelain factory in which he had worked as a clerk in his youth, and in which he senses a fundamental difference in the nature of work: 'yes, you can be a human being here, you can work here, be a human being with joy and pride even; not as before, surrounded by clouds of dust, boring and blasting your way into a subterranean world like a raving half-animal'. But he is only offered a manual post and instead takes a job in a steel stock-yard. He earns more money than down the pit, but is for some reason dissatisfied. Eventually, because the introduction of an electro-magnetic crane will mean that others will lose their jobs, he hands in his notice on the spur of the moment. He comes to see that he misses the close human bond that, as he can only appreciate with hindsight, had characterised work in the mine: 'there was friendship that money couldn't buy'.

Drifting from job to job, it becomes clear to him that the lack of a personal relationship with his mates is only one part of a general malaise. Unable to articulate it, he can express his feeling only in illogical actions. At one firm he asks for, and gets a holiday, but immediately gives in his notice. He moves on to a job that is not particularly arduous in a factory supplying parts for the electrical industry. He only has to bore a number of holes each day, though he has no idea what they are for. He now wears a white overall, this having always been for him the badge of a decent job. Even here, though, he is unsettled. Taking out his frustration on administrators at a works conference, he perversely votes for a proposal that runs counter to his mandate from his fellow workers. In all these jobs the common denominator, and so a major cause of his disorientation, is the sheer monotony of manual work. His marriage, without meaningful contact between man and wife, does not offer him any comfort. He cares little for money, rather despises it: 'we're selling our human dignity for prosperity and security amidst this prosperity'. His wife, however, is so adjusted to the consumer society mentality as to think only of keeping one step ahead of the neighbours. When she wins a lottery prize the money is not used, as Fohrmann wishes, to pay off debts, but to enable them to be the first in the street with a car. For his search for his 'second Adam' and his 'concern about the monotony of my life'—which she sarcastically calls the 'bees in his bonnet'—she has neither understanding nor sympathy. He hopes the birth of a child will save their relationship. This would give him some sense of purpose, but for her it would be a hindrance to their prosperity: 'Ingeborg says we've got so much left to buy, and a child would be the most expensive thing of all.'

Fohrmann's closest relationships are to people who stand somewhat outside society. He is the only person able to help Borowski, mentally disturbed as a result of maltreatment in a concentration camp during the war, when he has one of his fits. To Polenz, the one responsible for beating up Borowski in the concentration camp and now living in fear of discovery by the authorities, Fohrmann is strangely attracted. Above all he feels great sympathy for, even envies, Sillo, a young Italian fellow worker who always seems remarkably happy despite the monotony of his work, and invites him to spend Christmas at his home. He hopes to discover the secret of Sillo's contentment now that, through him, he himself has come to recognise what he wants from life. He longs for Sillo's sense of satisfaction, and envies the parson for the same reason: 'his life is devoid of monotony, there is no separation of hands and body; he and his work are one'. At last Fohrmann realises, and articulates, the cause of his frustration—the alienation of the worker from himself, from his work and from the prosperity around him. Hence the attraction outsiders have for him.

Like Gluchowski's *Der Honigkotten,* von der Grün's book was criticised for not offering 'perspectives and alternatives that could help the individual worker out of his tragic or grotesque isolation'.[7] More important is the objection that here, as in *Männer in zweifacher Nacht,* von der Grün 'does not generate a language to convey the reality, but obscures it with a battery of devalued symbols'.[8] It is true that there are too many stock metaphors and that the seductions of symbolism—Fohrmann's dream, for example, of a burning mounting of human bodies, the heat of which extinguishes the 'will-o'-the-wisps over the industrial landscape'—sometimes weaken its analytical force. But, unlike the earlier novel, *Irrlicht und Feuer* is in the main narrated in the first person. The language, whatever one may think about it, is Fohrmann's, not the author's, and it reflects Fohrmann's inability to understand or to articulate the reasons for a frustration intensified because he cannot properly express it. He resents the introduction of the new cutting machine, but when he talks about it, it is not in a practical sense as dangerous because it has not been sufficiently tested, but in quasi-mythological terms as a ferocious beast let loose. It is 'cold and slippery like a fish', 'always lying in wait'. It 'does not let itself be chained and forced into harness, but cry woe when it breaks out, for screams of pain and horror then mark its path'. The passages narrated in the third person are in marked contrast. They have the coolness, matter-of-factness and detachment of a report:

> Jürgen Fohrmann had thought that he would find not only work and a wage in the building trade, but also contentment. He found work and wages on the large building site between Unna and Dortmund where the Ruhr Expressway was being rebuilt and widened, but the days dragged by in as nondescript a way as before. The work certainly had variety—when it rained, for example, they all fled into the huts and chattered for an hour or two, or talked politics ... He met new faces, new voices, new ideas about work and money, but they were basically the same faces and the same views about money and work. Nevertheless he felt more at ease on the building site than he had in the metalworks and the work was more like that down the pit.

The difference of styles serves to bring out the inadequacy of Fohrmann's language, and it is a major achievement of the novel to reveal how it hampers him for so long from grappling meaningfully with the roots of his malaise. *Männer in zweifacher Nacht* had lacked a corresponding dimension.

After the promise of *Irrlicht und Feuer*, von der Grün's next novel, *Zwei Briefe an Pospischiel* (1968), is a disappointment, and this despite the fact that its main focus, the 'conflict between order and freedom, between the world of bureaucracy and the sovereign rights of the individual',[9] is as central to the problems of the industrial world as that of its predecessor.

Paul Pospischiel, working in the control room of a power station, leads a relatively comfortable life, although he cannot afford to be too blasé about money. There are recessions and unemployment in the district, and he is grateful for what security he has. For some time he has been feeling tired, and unresponsive to the sexual attraction of his wife. Then his mother writes to say that she has at last discovered who had denounced her husband to the Nazis in 1938 and wants her son to come and visit him. Pospischiel is less than keen to go, but confident that he could get time off. Eventually, under pressure from his wife, he agrees to ask for three days' unpaid leave and, to obtain permission, visits officials of the mine and of his union, only to be told in each case that he cannot be released from the work schedule, that he is 'verplant'. This apparent lack of understanding, he is told by his communist friend Fred Wördemann, is not the fault of the individual functionaries but of the 'system'; all are in the same boat. He goes off without permission, and one senses a desire on his part to test the consequences. He returns to find a dismissal notice waiting for him. The functionaries are all sympathetic, but the 'system' cannot take account of individual circumstances. Eventually, as a compromise, he is fired and then re-employed, but as a new recruit, with a corresponding loss of privileges. He is forced to realise that he has to accept the humiliating offer. His 'education' is now complete:

> It had taken a long time for me to realise what freedom means for the worker nowadays, and I began to envy the slaves of ancient Rome: they at least knew who their buyers and sellers were, knew who it was hitting them. Nowadays and in my case all this had gone, the sale took place on a duplicated sheet of paper and the blows were administered by an organisation.

There is also the lengthy episode of Pospischiel's trip to the Oberpfalz. On his journey he gives a lift to a young girl, Christl, who allows him to make love to her. This incident, reminiscent of the modish sex scenes of many popular novels, acquires added significance when we discover that she is the niece of Beierl, the man who had betrayed Pospischiel's father, now living a relatively secluded life, devoting his time to tending his mallows in his garden, to memories of his Nazi past—a past to which Max von der Grün attaches much importance for his analysis of the contemporary industrial world:

> This problem of the past is for me different than for other authors, because for me it is the present—the present, not in the sense of being a political factor, but subliminally there, and what people call fascism —just like that, fascism is Auschwitz—really starts in quite a different place, and I would say: whoever has had to earn his living in industry will agree with me that what happens there is pure fascism.[10]

It is difficult to see what relevance Beierl, now a gentle old man, has in the main framework of the book. The only link between him and the world of the Ruhr is with Pospischiel's friend Fred Wördemann, who had suffered in a concentration camp for his political ideals. Pospischiel and Christl for some reason cut down Beierl's mallows, and on his return Pospischiel finds that someone has also cut down

Wördemann's. The symbolism of the link is clear, but the implications are not. This is a protracted section and it damages the novel.

Thus far we have been referring to works viewing the industrial world predominantly in terms of manual labour. From an early stage, however, Gruppe 61 showed itself aware of the need to expand and diversify the image of industrial society to reflect the changes in the division of labour since the nineteen-twenties and to take account of office work and the service industries now becoming increasingly important. Only exceptionally and occasionally, as in the case of Ruth Rehmann, had they been dealt with by post-war German writers. Within a year or so of the founding of the group a significant number of its new members—Klas Ewert Everwyn, Matthias Mander, Wolfgang Körner—came from this tertiary sector.

Körner's first novel, *Versetzung* (1966), is the first from Gruppe 61 to deal with the world of bureaucracy. It is about the life of Rolf Hagen, a clerk in the welfare section of a social security office. He is a man ill at ease in this world of bureaucracy and resents the rigidity of the office hierarchy and the inflexibility of the administrative machine. When on one occasion he feels that instructions about the handling of a particular case are more than usually inhuman, he leaks details to the press. The result is a search for the person responsible, but not, as he had expected, a reappraisal of the case. The working of the bureaucratic mind is Körner's theme. It is best illustrated by Hagen's treatment when, presumably as a result of intelligent guesswork, he is held to be the one who leaked the information and, though never actually accused, is transferred to the debt-collecting division, the 'punishment section'. A replacement is not immediately forthcoming, and he is told to remain in his post for the time being. The implication seems to be that his superiors are content with his work and would like him to stay. His hopes are raised of the transfer being rescinded, but it soon turns out that the idea was merely to keep him working properly until a replacement was found. When the transfer comes through he is curtly told to move without delay.

Hagen is not in principle or consistently a critic of bureaucracy. The impression is rather of an intelligent man who has taken this particular job because of its security but is bored by the work and frustrated by its constraints. He genuinely believes that some cases are dealt with harshly, but his various protests against the machinery are also motivated by boredom and by resentment at the pettiness of less intelligent but senior colleagues. For much of the time, though, he seems to accept, however begrudgingly, the monotony of his work. The dust jacket claims that the 'movement of the plot corresponds to the monotonous pace of the bureaucratic machine', but Hagen's private life is equally arid and monotonous. Körner tries to convey this through very close observation of minutiae, with no attempt to isolate anything significant. The result is a book in a low key, without dramatic interest and filled out to make it a novel. Inevitably it is a dull one. It does not evoke sympathy for the monotony of Hagen's life. It irritates and repels.

The artistic weakness of this and most of the other novels from the group (with the exception of *Irrlicht und Feuer*) may suggest that the writers had not chosen the most appropriate medium. Perhaps the novel was not the most suitable genre for presenting a contemporary view of everyday life in industrial society. It can easily fall rather flat, as in *Versetzung*, or, if attempts are made to dramatise the interest, it can lead to distortion and a highlighting of the untypical. This is the case with *Männer in zweifacher Nacht*. Like most novels about mining, it deals with a catastrophe and so with a dramatic interruption of the daily routine.

How suitable, then, has poetry proved as a medium? In its early years Gruppe 61 showed an interest in this direction, but with markedly less success. The main reason is linguistic conservatism. Hildegard Brenner claims that this heightens solidarity between workers, and avoids the danger of absorption into the culture of the 'system'. But it has led to the poetry often becoming conspicuously derivative, falling back on outworn colloquial phrases and mannered imagery incongruously combined with the vocabulary of modern technology. The long-etablished Ruhr tradition of poetry about mining makes so many poems from the Gruppe 61 seem all the more epigonic. Thus Josef Büscher, whose poetry embodies most of the weaknesses, deals in 'Seilfahrt' with a theme that has long since become one of the topoi of literature about mining, and to which he can bring nothing new. The setting in the early morning is utterly conventional, and the result near kitsch: 'Durch Gitterstäbe sickert bleich / der frühen Stunde kaltes Licht.' The sensations experienced during the descent into the mine, with the bottom seeming to fall out of the cage, the pressure in the ears, the sudden braking, are all too familiar stereotypes, and the same applies to the initial reaction, on leaving the cage, of being trapped:

Ich steige ab. Das Tor schlägt zu.
Da überfällt mich jäh ein Bangen:
Achthundert Meter Felsgestein
vermauern Tag und Sonnenschein.

Der Korb zischt hoch. Ich bin gefangen.[11]

The world of the mine, as in 'Rauber rauben unter Tag', is portrayed
with rhetorical effect, in terms of a struggle with demonic forces:

Menschentier mit Menschenlist
sich mit den Gewalten misst.
—Aufgeschreckte Geister schrein
urwelthaft aus dem Gestein.

In 'Am Abbauhammer' the situation underground appears as a personal clash between the miner and the coal. His hammer has been
exchanged for a drill, but the battle remains the same, and the
'blessings of technology' pass him by. He figures as an 'Alter Kumpel
im modernen Streb' who sees modernisation all around him, but this
is simply an additional burden in an industry still essentially un-
changed from earlier times:

Ich bin jetzt Lakai, ein Hobelknecht
im Solde von Stahlgiganten.
Mich peitscht ihr technisches Gesetz.
Aber manchmal, wenn die alten Querulanten
hohnlachend rütteln an Kappen und Bau,
sie wie Röhricht zerbiegen und knicken,
erkenn ich wieder, Kampfgesell.
Ich ahne dein Tun und ich lauf um mein Fell
und höre die Uhr der Vergangenheit ticken.

By and large in the poetry the working conditions are not attacked
but resignedly tolerated and, as in the epigonic portrayal of a bitter,
personalised relationship between the worker and his tools in Artur
Granitzki's 'Lied der Arbeit' ('Hammerschlag du tust mir weh! /
Ich kann dein Lied nicht singen . . .'), ultimately accepted as inevitable. Yet this traditional love–hate relationship between the miner
and the pit, very evident in the anthology *Unter Tage—Über Tage*
(1966), is combined with a simple pride in being a miner, in being a
man:

Starke Vaterarme,
schöpferische Bergmannshände.
Tief unter der Erde
wuchs ihnen Brot und Wein,

bannten sie mutig
tödliche Schatten,
spannte sich mächtig
männliches Sehnen
nach friedvoller Heimstatt,
der braven Gefährtin,
und Mutter der Kinder.

Thus, in a way already familiar, the miner is seen as hero and victim, part of a distinct group of men who fight to win the coal and live close to tragedy. The Ruhr landscape is seen as littered with tips piled high with the suffering and anguish of their years of struggle, as in Hildegard Wohlgemuth's poem 'Berghalde'.

Conventional motifs of poetry dealing with mining are also to be found in the work of Günther Westerhoff. He has made a special effort to break out of the world well known to him in the mine and the industrial area of the Ruhr and to take as his theme wider features of the technological age. His poems, however, show how dominant the earlier models are and how difficult it is to portray the industrial world in a significantly new way. In his '100-kW-Station nachts', and above all in 'Anfahrt eines Turbokompressors', the close description of the operation of machinery, the sense of awe aroused by it, and of exultation in its power, are reminiscent of the poetry of Josef Winckler, or of Gerrit Engelke's 'Lokomotive':

Der Tachozeiger hebt sich an und steigt.
Bedächtig löst der Maschinist das Dampfventil.
Bei tausend Touren pfeift die Luft und geigt,
das Vakuum stellt sich ein und zieht den Lauf zuviel ...

Kommandozeichen kommt: Fertig, Maschine hat vollen Lauf!
Dreht Hähne, Ventile, die grossen Schieber auf!
Faustpaare greifen wild und fest in Räderrund und Speichen,
die heisse, gefangene Luft sucht zu entweichen,
stürmt in die mächtige Rohre, in die Tiefe fort,
zischt leise am Anschluss des Bohrhahns, in der Verlassenheit vor Ort.[12]

Even poets who, like Hildegard Wohlgemuth, seem consciously to resist the model of the Werkleute auf Haus Nyland and of writers like Lersch and Bröger, and strive to write a more critical verse, only rarely succeed in avoiding the same path as Engelke, Zech or Schönlank. Hüser has distanced himself from these writers, and it is true that the least satisfactory literary products are those that stand closest to the ethos of an earlier phase of industrial society. There is the additional difficulty that, the tradition of the various strands of the 'Arbeiterdichtung' of the nineteen-twenties being so dense and its language and imagery so well known, new poetry dealing with the industrial world has to show a very high degree of linguistic initiative to create something fresh, without the ideological overtones of a language debased in any case by the way the Nazis used it in their industrial poetry. Critics of the poetry of Gruppe 61 have, quite correctly, pointed to its 'worn-out metaphors, dubious images, hollow language and weak rhythms'.[13] Obviously these stem partly from the shortcomings of individual writers, but are also the inevitable outcome of a wrong choice of medium, a choice motivated by the desire to make the new industrial literature appear respectable.

The other possibility is the shorter prose form, and this is where the real literary strength of the group undoubtedly lay. In Max von der Grün's *Irrlicht und Feuer* the most successful passages are virtually independent stories. His short story 'Waldläufer und Brückensteher', describing the everyday life of invalid ex-miners, is effective, tightly structured, with a controlled, unsentimental use of language. His very real narrative talents are seen to their best advantage in prose of the more restricted kind. A good example is his semi-autobiographical 'Etwas ausserhalb der Legalität' (in *Fahrtunterbrechung*, 1966), portraying the attempt by the director of a firm to 'buy' an author–employee and thus effectively to censor the critical passages in his work. The same tends to be true of other writers from Gruppe 61. Consider, for example, the difference between the flaccid style of Körner's *Versetzung* and his terse, tightly structured 'Planstelle frei', which, in a series of very short scenes, shows the bitter and ruthless manoeuvrings by people in an office anxious to get promotion. Everwyn's 'Beschreibung eines Betriebsunfalls' describes how a worker's right hand is dragged between the rollers of a printing press in a matter-of-fact, emotion-free style well calculated to convey the horror of the situation:

> He merely cast an eye on the pile of sheets at the side of the machine that were waiting to be dispatched. The glance lasted not quite a second. It did, however, suffice to reduce the man's attention and alertness. His hand holding his rag consequently wandered too near the grippers, which suddenly no longer need to grab at air. They pull the object irresistibly with them.
> The man does not have a fraction of a second's chance of freeing himself. Instead, he has to stand and watch as his hand, clutching the rag, disappears between the upper and lower rollers in one revolution.[14]

Ewerwyn is here still concentrating on the dramatic, exceptional moment, but the dangers of the topic are avoided by the way in which the long, laborious process of freeing the man is depicted in dispassionate detail. The text works rather like an unedited piece of *cinéma vérité*. There is no gratuitous commentary and no attempt to create dramatic tension artificially. Close observation combined with linguistic economy is found in Angelika Mechtel's 'Im Glas-quadrat', about a team of women in a packing division of a toy factory, in a style terse to the point of reading rather like a telegram, almost devoid of adjectives. The contrast between the fulsome tone of the extracts from job advertisements scattered throughout the text and the monotonous, harsh routine of the working day is used with good effect:

> 'What a man,' says Herta. She has taken the band out of her hair. She always pulls the band off at break. The tables in the canteen are very close together. The room holds a hundred and fifty people. WITH BRIGHT WORKING CONDITIONS! GOOD AMENITIES. Two large windows. The coat-racks. Two cold drinks machines. Wash basins with water heaters. The men sit at the back of the room. The women at the front. More women than men. The four of them always sit in the middle. So that they're right next to one of the men's tables.[15]

Likewise, stories such as Matthias Mander's 'Das Dach' and 'Der Glühofen', by avoiding any stylistic features tending to romanticise and fictionalise the worker and his labour, penetrate all the better, often critically, to the reality of what is being described.

The shorter prose form did not solve all problems, however. One sees this from Bruno Gluchowski's 'Die Wasserkanone', portraying the successful prevention of a pit closure by strike action. The threat unleashes a spontaneous wave of support for direct action, leading to a sit-in at the pit bottom. The action by the miners, accompanied by the singing of workers' songs and an impromptu lecture on the development of the industrial revolution in England, gains the support of local organisations, of the local priest, of miners from other pits. The marches and demonstrations meet police truncheons, car-bines and a water cannon, but the workers resist as a collective hero. Mutter Heese, who triumphantly prevents a police charge on the crowd by exposing her matronly bosom to one of the policemen and suggesting that he needs breast-feeding, is, indeed, an 'earth-mother figure'. Cliff Morton dies the obligatory hero's death whilst blowing up the water cannon. The battle, and Cliff's death, are not in vain, and the government gives way to the pressure. The trouble is that the story is a 'series of naive clichés, somewhat in the style of a legend',[16] made all the worse by crudely jargonesque language.

The short stories of Everwyn, von der Grün, Angelika Mechtel and Matthias Mander, together with Wallraff's 'Reportagen', have widely, and rightly, been regarded as among the most promising prose works to emerge from the group by the middle of the decade. But the important difference between the stories and Wallraff's work has not always been appreciated. He joined the group in 1966 and helped to bring a new and critical stimulus to it, but it was he who effectively did most to bring about its virtual demise.

The finest achievements of the group were also more or less the end of the line as far as its original programme is concerned. They are 'literary' representations of single incidents from the industrial world. Wallraff was the first of the Dortmund writers to write 'Reportagen' as such, in which the 'literary' intent is of minimal importance, and which, although focusing on an individual occurrence, are not content, as Lukács said,

> simply to present facts; their portrayals always indicate wider connections, reveal causes, provoke conclusions ... The individual case presented, which may perhaps have been given literary shape, serves only as an example, as an illustration of the general context, which is shown more or less scientifically, or at least conceptually, is tied up (i.e. statistically underpinned) and logically proven.[17]

As to the function of 'Reportagen', Wallraff held that it was to show that what they describe is 'not just isolated instances, not flaws that can be simply patched up, but rather conditions inherent in the system'.[18] They are to be seen as referring to capitalist industry as a whole, and they marked the first step towards the dominance in the group of a socio-critical documentary literature.

To obtain the material for his first texts Wallraff worked in a number of firms—on the production line of a car factory, in a shipyard, in a steelworks, in a pipe works, and as a machinist on piecework. In his first published volume, *Wir brauchen Dich* (1966), he refers to firms and persons only by letters to emphasise the 'prototypicality' of his observations. He also introduces extraneous evidence, like the sociologist in 'Am Fliessband', quoted to show that the experience of production-line work having an adverse effect on leisure time is generally true. Mostly he draws either on the straightforward reporting of factual information, like the way piecework wages are calculated, and the 'cost' to a worker of a visit to the lavatory, or on the evidence of personal reactions. Conversations with or comments from temporary workmates are much utilised, though apparently only from memory. They could be inaccurate. At any rate they cannot be verified, and they are open to the charge of the possibility of distortion by selection. Wallraff's personal impressions being those of an outsider, they cannot necessarily be representative of those fully engaged in the industries he examines. He thought this an advantage. 'You go in as an outsider,' he said, 'and see things in an over-sensitive way,' which means that 'by being described from outside the situation is shown more sharply'.[19]

Wallraff's experiences, as recorded, are certainly in the main true of industrial labour as a whole—and not just under capitalism—but then, Wallraff is not reporting anything not already known. What he repeatedly says about alienation is familiar enough: 'work seems foreign and senseless to me because I don't know the finished "whole article" '. The worker has no idea of what other workers elsewhere in the factory are doing. When he stops being a 'little cog in the works of the production line' his free time has to be used to regain physical and nervous energy for the next shift instead of allowing him 'to be human again at last'. All this may be true, but it is no more than what Marx said and what has meanwhile been frequently confirmed by industrial psychologists. Moreover, Wallraff talks in such a stereotyped way about alienation as to suggest that he knew to start with what he could expect to find. Yet he reports, with a certain unspoken sympathy, the nostalgia of some older workers for the days when they were still 'masters of the production line'—one man, in fact, still builds models of older cars he himself once, in less automated conditions, helped to construct, and for which he still feels a certain fondness—though in the Marxist view all mechanical work in a factory alienates. Apart from the lack of new insights, the critical effect of these 'Reportagen' is hampered by their style. Narrated in the first person, they have a rather personal slant, and there is no proper documentation. Oddly enough, too, they are full of a familiar type of literary cliché. Work on the production line is 'like swimming against a strong current', and a factory is described as 'an insatiable octopus, reaching out with its tentacles into every street and forcing itself between blocks of flats and office buildings'. The description of an industrial town—uncannily like Gerd Gaiser's portrayal of Neu-Spuhl in *Schlussball*, the work of an essentially conservative writer—is the most striking example of such lapses:

> A city of smoke and soot, and the layer of grey dust on the facades is more real than the bricks underneath. The branches of the trees are bare and white as fog, as if they were covered with mildew. The faces of the people are colourless.
> There is no red sky here, only the reddish flickering against the clouds.

These 'Reportagen' may thus not always be consistent with Wallraff's aims, but they created a stir far greater than any of the previous publications of Gruppe 61. The paperback sales ran to over 70,000 copies, and they created such an impression outside Germany, especially in Eastern Europe, that Wallraff was accused by the political police in Cologne of 'treasonable connections'. Their impact in Germany was helped by the fact that the names of the firms in which he had worked were widely known, although he deliberately withheld them in *Wir brauchen Dich*. In fact the actual names had been given in those of the texts which were published in the union magazine *Metall* in 1965 and 1966. None of the other shorter prose texts of Gruppe 61 were so specific in their points of reference, and this is one thing that marks off Wallraff's first 'Reportagen'. 'Only through citing name, place, and time (i.e. by breaking out of the sphere of the fictional),' he was later to remark, 'is credibility built up.'[20]

Wallraff's emergence and the impact of his first publications helped to bring about a polarisation within Gruppe 61. Looking back, it had been latent from the start. From the earliest days left-wing commentators complained that its 'bourgeois-literary' direction dominated at the expense of the 'political-emancipatory'. It was said that, despite Hüser's disclaimers, the initial emphasis was on the tradition of the Werkleute auf Haus Nyland and Otto Wohlgemuth's Ruhrlandkreis (in which Wohlgemuth was himself active until his death in 1966) as models, not on the Arbeiterkorrespondentenbewegung and the Bund proletarisch-revolutionärer Schriftsteller. The striving for literary respectability was reflected in the removal from the group's programme of any reference to the earlier industrial literature, and, while it initially published mainly in the magazines of IG Bergbau und Energie and IG Metall, in daily newspapers (especially in the Ruhr) and in local journals, with the success of von der Grün's *Irrlicht und Feuer*, and also because of the hostile reaction of the unions (above all, IG Bergbau's refusal to publish further work by von der Grün), the trend came to be more and more towards publication in conventional quarters. The *Almanach* of the group, for instance, and Max von der Grün's *Zwei Briefe an Pospischiel* both appeared in the Luchterhand Verlag. There was also another change. The group had prided itself on differing from Gruppe 47 in not submitting the works of members to the same kind of institutionalised and often hard-hitting collective criticism. Informal discussion was the original aim. But in due course texts came to be criticised round the table—as Körner said, 'mercilessly, according to literary criteria'. The profile of the group, too, was shifting, with the majority of its leading writers no longer workers or ex-workers, and help not being offered to workers who wished to take up writing. It was felt by some to have become an 'agency for finished manuscripts', controlled by struggling bourgeois writers who saw membership as a backstairs way to success. The 'conformism to models of the bourgeois-literary avant-garde and the renunciation of a working-class public'[21] certainly helped to bring the problems of the world of industrial labour into the public eye, but this is one way of saying that the group had failed to reach the 'right' public. Views to this effect were sometimes expressed as criticism, but forgetting that the declared aim of the group was 'primarily to bring enlightenment not to the working class but to that part of the public to which the world of industrial labour still remains most closed—the bourgeois strata of society'.[22] In the light of this it could be said to the credit of Gruppe 61 that it tried to avoid the traditional danger of seeing the industrial world as a thing apart and attempted to make a wider public aware of it as an integral element in society.

The 'literary' nature of its programme, laid down by Fritz Hüser and Bernard Boie, prevailed in the mid-sixties mainly because there had been no one to challenge the achievement and authority of its dominant figure, Max von der Grün. With the rise of Wallraff, however, an alternative figure of some stature had emerged, embodying a completely different approach to the task of writing about the industrial world, and this coincided with the recession in West German industry, particularly the mining industry, of 1966–67. The situation of Gruppe 61 at this juncture is reflected in the fact that the most direct and forceful response to the recession and its implications did not come from the group, but from the radical political worker song movement, from writers such as Hannes Stütz and, above all, the Conrads from Düsseldorf. These songs were part of the 'extra-parliamentary opposition' and they deal with the problems facing workers in the phase 1967–69. Songs like 'Dein Standpunkt' and 'Streiklied der Fliesenleger', the fine Vietnam war songs, and those directed against the Nationalist Party are far more directly and specifically political than anything from within Gruppe 61 at that time.

Wallraff had been critical of Gruppe 61 when he joined it. His position was now strengthened by the upsurge of documentary literature in the latter sixties, by the impact of his own documentary works dealing with areas other than the world of industry, and by the influence now being exercised within the group by Erika Runge, editor of the *Bottroper Protokolle*. With the demand for the 'politicisation of literature' growing stronger, decisive support for him was also now coming from left-wing critics, notably Erasmus Schöfer and Peter Schütt. In 'Reportagen' like his they saw a chance for ordinary workers to start writing 'literature by workers for the education of workers', 'informative documentary writing' functioning as 'effective counter-information'. Together with Max von der Grün, who initially welcomed this new development, they set up in 1968 an informal Werkkreis Literatur der Arbeitswelt, and announced a competition for 'Reportagen' from workers. This produced some confusion in the group. A number of older leading members, led by Bernard Boie, clung resolutely to the idea of its aims as literary. Others were not so sure. Hüser publicly raised the question whether the group had not outlived its usefulness, and Körner, a little earlier adamant about the inviolability of literary criteria, came, with an agility smacking of opportunism, not only to doubt the group's future usefulness but to announce that 'artistic and literary methods' were not the appropriate ones for socio-critical writing. When, following the example of Erika Runge, he produced in 1969 a tape transcript, 'Christine und die Menschenfresser', he described it as no more literature than any rehearsed speech. Gruppe 61 decided officially not to recognise the new trend within its ranks; in the spring of 1970 the Werkkreis 70 was formally established.

This rejected the emphasis placed by Gruppe 61 on literary quality, 'this arrogant attitude to worker writers'. What mattered was accuracy and truth: 'formal originality is reached mainly at the cost of communication'.[23] The aim was to help workers in the course of their everyday experience to write 'in an unliterary, simple

language, from their own experience, true to life'.[24] The resulting
texts were intended for a reading public of workers, to promote
solidarity, and to impart political information. Political activity was
seen as a prerequisite of writing, and the aim was to bring about
social change:

> The works produced in the WERKKREIS LITERATUR DER ARBEITSWELT are
> directed above all at workers, and it is from their growing awareness
> of their class situation that they stem ... It [the Werkkreis] wishes to
> help to change social conditions in the interests of the workers. To this
> aim the Werkkreis links its work to the activities of all groups and
> forces that are actively seeking a democratic change of social conditions.

The Werkkreis was thus understood not as a 'political and literary
cadre organisation' but as a 'broadly based democratic movement
with unquestionably socialist aims'.[25] It is divided into seventeen
locally based workshops, with regular readings, discussions, and instruction sessions. Publication in book form is only part of the activity. Examples include *Ein Baukran stürzt um* (1970), *Lauter Arbeitgeber* (1971), *Schrauben haben Rechtsgeschwinde* (1971) and *Ihr
aber tragt das Risiko* (1971), and these illustrate the aim, as stated by
Wallraff, 'to provide a flow of counter-information on the broadest
possible basis'. They give, however, a slightly distorted picture of the
work producted. Despite the political aims, and the consequent rejection of Gruppe 61 by many members of the Werkkreis, the early texts
by workers in the Werkkreis were not 'Reportagen' so much as short
stories, satires or agitprop poems. They revealed the same sort of
weaknesses as many of the works from Gruppe 61. The Werkkreis
seemed therefore likewise to contain the seeds of polarisation. Erasmus Schöfer complained of this early 'Trend zur Literarisierung' and
of a lack of 'Reportagen' and montage texts, and Wallraff had a
remarkably unenthusiastic reception at an early session of the Werkkreis. Peter Schütt urged workers to write 'literature' on the model
of the nineteen-twenties and of the successes (if that is the right
word) of the 'Bitterfelder Weg' in East Germany.

So far most of the texts from the Werkkreis published as books
have been 'Reportagen', in the style, generally speaking, of Wallraff's *Wir brauchen Dich*, and with the same weaknesses. They are
reports of personal experiences, told in the first person. The authenticity of what is being narrated and the power of language to communicate it are taken for granted. They seem to have succeeded in
producing solidarity amongst workers sharing the same political

position, but not greatly in affecting the attitudes of those who accept the 'system' which the Werkkreis seeks to change. The 'Reportagen' purport to appear as objective accounts calculated to persuade uncommitted workers to become politically active, but they can easily seem highly personal, tendentious left-wing political statements, insisting on concepts of class structure too rigid to have much relevance in the circumstances and attitudes of workers in an affluent society. They assume a radical working-class consciousness, which does not correspond to Max von der Grün's reading of the situation: 'Where are the reactionary forces in our country? Amongst the working class. Where are the most conservative people? Amongst the working class. Where is the greatest hatred of minorities? Amongst the working class.'[26] Nor, for that matter, is the evidence produced in these texts—about the pressure of piecework, about a typical working day, about the unfair treatment of individual workers—so very novel: 'their only interest is the way in which they confirm what we already know. They contain no new information. And anyway, no one was in any doubt that there were so many bad bosses.'[27] Also, as was said of some 'Reportagen' of the nineteen-twenties, 'a hundred reports on a factory don't add up to the truth about the factory, but will always remain a hundred opinions about a factory'.[28]

When Wallraff does not limit himself to the narrowly industrial sphere, as in *Nachspiele* and *13 unerwünschte Reportagen*, he succeeds in moving beyond the incidental to the more general. Using montage techniques in a way comparable in certain respects to Heissenbüttel, he attempts 'to show up contradictions in society and in the system'. This is true also of his more recent industrial reportage, and this can properly be said to surpass anything else from the Werkkreis as far as 'effectiveness amongst the working class' (*basisorientierte Wirksamkeit*) is concerned. 'Ketten aus Kalthof' is a documentation of the August Thiele chain-making factory, consisting of extracts from the prospectus of the firm, glowing press tributes to Thiele, quotations from him and other directors, letters to employees, and reports of individual workers. The purpose is to expose the contrast between the image presented to the public and the actual working conditions. The firm's publicity boasts of 'welfare facilities which even today are still by no means commonplace', and of security of employment. This is contrasted with the case of the dismissal of a pregnant woman (infringing the Mutterschutzgesetz), unfair treatment of foreign workers, and intimidation of sick workers and a former shop steward. 'Brauner Sud im Filterwerk' is a critical examination of the firm of Melitta, and particularly of the owner, Horst Bentz. There is a carefully documented exposé of Bentz's alleged Nazi past, his support now of a certain strongly right-wing movement, the use of his financial power to block a television documentary critical of the alleged victimisation of 'troublesome' union members in the works, the ruthless treatment of workers in general behind a facade of collegiality, and Bentz's remorseless treatment of other firms:

> Former paper manufacturer Winkler: 'By now we've come to think Bentz capable of anything. What happened, for example, to the Brauer porcelain factory in Porta, which also used to work for Bentz? They too were first of all advised to install a larger kiln; then no more orders were placed. In the end Bentz was able to buy the whole plant at the bankruptcy sale. When it's a question of money he wouldn't even give you the time of day.' 'The history of the first fifty years of our firm shows that great success is achieved ultimately by something other than good luck, chance or sharp practice. The really decisive thing is that a firm has a concept ...' (Horst Bentz on the occasion of the firm's silver jubilee).[29]

As to the relative position now of Gruppe 61 and Werkkreis 70, it is notable that latterly the established members of Gruppe 61 have published virtually nothing. Max von der Grün came to concentrate his activity on journalism, television scripts and radio 'features', though a further novel (*Stellenweise Glatteis*) appeared in 1973. Bearing in mind also that he had by this time come to appear more as an independent figure than as a member of the group, in West Germany literature from the industrial world is today virtually synonymous with Werkkreis 70. Like Gruppe 61, the Werkkreis has been too hidebound by older models, and specifically it has instanced the example of the Arbeiterkorrespondentenbewegung and the Bund proletarisch-revolutionärer Schriftsteller. This has proved a corresponding limitation of the artistic sophistication necessary to meet the more complex demands of the present day. It may not be insignificant that it is Wallraff, not himself a worker, who has been most responsive in this respect and shown most initiative. So we have to agree with the view of the future of Gruppe 61 and Werkkreis 70 that 'for the moment, as far as future development is concerned, there is only Günter Wallraff and a few tentative beginnings'.[30]

Notes

1 Cf. W. Röhrer, H. Kammrad and H. Schmid, 'Es gibt sie halt, die schreibende "Fiktion",' in H. L. Arnold (ed.), *Gruppe 61: Arbeiterliteratur—Literatur der Arbeitswelt?*, Munich, 1971, p. 178.

2 'Gesicht der deutschen Literatur der Gegenwart', *Die Kultur*, 17, 1960, No. 155, p. 5.

3 'Plädoyer für das Positive in der modernen Literatur', in *Literatur und Politik*, Pfullingen, 1963, p. 23.

4 Röhrer, Kammard and Schmid, *loc. cit.*, p. 178.

5 In the preface to the 'Almanach der Gruppe 61 and ihrer Gäste', *Aus der Welt der Arbeit*, Neuwied and Berlin, 1966, p. 26.

6 *Arbeiterliteratur in der BRD*, Cologne, 1970, p. 64.

7 Peter Schütt, *Asphalt-Literatur*, Mainz, 1968, p. 38.

8 Lothar Romain, 'Die Arbeitswelt in der Literatur der Gruppe 61', *Frankfurter Hefte*, xxii, 12, 1967, p. 856.

9 Hans-Albert Walter, 'Mär von der Freiheit', *Die Zeit*, 20 September 1968, p. LIT 19.

10 In an interview with Keith Bullivant, Dortmund–Brechten, 4 January 1970.

11 This and other poems referred to are contained in Josef Büscher, *Gedichte*, Recklinghausen, 1965.

12 Günter Westerhoff, *Gedichte und Prosa*, Recklinghausen, 1966, p. 9.

13 Hans-Albert Walter, 'Die Literatur und die Welt der Arbeit', *Die Zeit*, 10 March 1967, p. viii.

14 This story, Angelika Mechtel's 'Im Glasquadrat' and Bruno Gluchowski's 'Die Wasserkanone', referred to in this section, are all contained in *Aus der Welt der Arbeit, ed. cit.*

15 In *Summa Bachzelt und andere Erzählungen*, Recklinghausen, 1966.

16 Dieter Wellershoff, 'Mal was hinkriegen', *Der Spiegel*, 53, 1966, p. 94.

17 'Reportage oder Gestaltung? Kritische Bemerkungen anlässlich des Romans von Ottwalt', in *Schriften zur Literatursoziologie*, fourth edition, Neuwied and Berlin, 1971, pp. 126–7.

18 'Wirkungen in der Praxis. Eine Gebrauchsanweisung', in T. Rother (ed.), *Schrauben haben Rechtsgeschwinde*, Düsseldorf, 1971, p. 15.

19 In discussion at the University of Mainz, 2 July 1971.

20 'Wirkungen in der Praxis', *loc. cit.*, p. 15.

21 Peter Kühne and Erasmus Schöfer, 'Schreiben für die Arbeitswelt', *Akzente*, 4, 1970, p. 322.

22 H. L. Arnold, 'Die Gruppe 61—Versuch einer Präsentation', in H. L. Arnold (ed.), *Gruppe 61: Arbeiterliteratur—Literatur der Arbeitswelt?*, *ed. cit.*, p. 36.

23 Erasmus Schöfer, in his introduction to *Ein Baukran stürzt um*, Munich, 1970, p. 19.

24 Kühne and Schöfer, *loc. cit.*, p. 333.

25 Erasmus Schöfer, 'Referat zur Eröffnung der Mannheimer Tagung des Werkkreises', printed in *Info*, 5, November 1970, p. 3.

26 Dortmund–Brechten, 4 January 1970.

26 Heinrich Vormweg, 'Im Interesse der Arbeiter', in *Eine andere Leseart*, Neuwied and Berlin, 1972, p. 51.
28 Siegfried Kracauer, *Die Angestellten* (1929), Frankfurt a. M., 1971, p. 16.
29 In *Von einem der auszog und das Fürchten lernte*, Munich, 1970, pp. 74–8.
30 'Woran krankt die Gruppe 61?', *Welt am Sonnt*ag 21–2 August 1971.

Chapter 6

Literature and sub-culture

The sixties, and most obviously from the middle of the decade, were internationally a time of protest, with anti-war demonstrator, protest singer, drop-out, hippie, yippie, acid-head and rocker among the hot-gospellers of the Marcusian 'Great Refusal'. Protest came to have close associations with the 'underground', and 'underground' culture with 'sub-culture'. In some respects this accepted and copied the existing society, in others it would have nothing to do with it. It is a mixed-up and contradictory phenomenon. It affirmed the pleasures of sensuous experience—colour, sound and sexual freedom—but rejected the industrialised, capitalist society that made these so readily available to be enjoyed. It was not as novel as its exponents liked to think. There are parallels with Bohème and Dada, and withdrawal into communes had been a feature of the German youth movement of the nineteen-twenties. Its place is in the context of a whole 'sub-culture of intellectuals'—'fringe groups' with 'expressly unbourgeois or anti-bourgeois attitudes and behaviour patterns'—in those 'industrial and partly industrialised societies in the nineteenth and twentieth centuries that accord scope to individual self-expression and tolerate symbolic aggression'.[1] Yet it is only in the second half of the sixties that one can speak in any specific sense of sub-culture as a widespread phenomenon in West Germany. The word 'underground' first cropped up there in 1967. By then it was of such importance in literary and intellectual life as to make any adequate discussion of the decade incomplete without discussion of it.

It can be described, with Diethart Kerbs, as the 'hedonistic left' or, with Brinkmann, as a 'confused but, despite this confusion, *homogeneous modern* sensibility',[2] conditioned by the sense of Europe in general, and West Germany in particular, clinging to sterile, old-fashioned notions of culture, with America freeing itself from their domination. The central role of the 'new sensibility' was highlighted in a policy statement of the März Verlag, and affirmed by Brinkmann. One of his principal concerns was to incorporate it in literature. This presupposed the 'breaking down of those authoritarian attitudes that are still constantly being reproduced today but which are now marked only by a hollow pathos and which have become more and more established as poetry has congealed into mere artistic form'. He wanted to get away from the formalistic preoccupations which he criticises in writers like Heissenbüttel and Jürgen Becker. His generation, he said, more than any other experiences things in visual terms, and literature should reflect this shift in perception. We live 'on the surface of pictures', and 'this surface must be accepted at long last and the visual qualities of daily life taken by directly using the world around us'. So he demands that literature should strive to reflect the trivial and the banal in a new 'open' type of writing better able to express the 'new sensibility'—which is why he could speak so affirmatively of Leslie Fiedler.

Brinkmann's introduction to his translation of Frank O'Hara's *Lunch Poems* meets Fiedler's requirements that the 'newest criticism must be aesthetic, poetic in form as well as in substance', but also 'comical, irreverent and vulgar'.[3] It satisfies his own call for literature to respond to a heightened sense of the visual, in the rather crude sense that the text is interspersed with pictures of Lana Turner, Marlon Brando, Greta Garbo, Errol Flynn, Marilyn Monroe in the nude, Elizabeth Taylor, Ginger Rogers and Marlene Dietrich. One of the few poems of his own that fits his theory is 'Vanille', to which we have already referred, a collage of ready-mades (newspaper headlines, letters, extracts from poems, diary entries, references to advertisements, details of films on at the cinema, the instruction on his wife's Pill packet, cosmetics labels, a funeral announcement), together with an illustrated description of intercourse. It is a cataloguing of things Brinkmann read while sitting at his desk one morning with nothing in particular to do. Another of his attempts 'to simulate life as accurately as possible' is his text 'Flickermaschine', the action of which takes place in a room on the Rudolfsplatz between 00.48 a.m. and 00.49 a.m. This is a collage of observations from the window, of thoughts that flash into his mind, of quotations from various books (especially Hedda Hopper's Hollywood reminiscences and the biography of Marilyn Monroe), of pictures of Elvis Presley, Gina Lollobrigida, Alfred Hitchcock, Marilyn Monroe, and of naked women, including two in orgasm. He said here that he 'only mixes the same old pictures up again in a concrete-mixer and puts them together again in a slightly different way. *That's all.*'

There is a similarity in the close tabulation of experiences and sensations to the Naturalist 'Sekundenstil'—and in other ways, too, Brinkmann's theory suggests comparison with Naturalism. Or to the stream-of-consciousness techniques, particularly as developed in the film, with its flash-back and jump-cutting. The formative influence of the cinema is evident from Brinkmann's choice of pictures of film stars and in his emphasis on the visual in literature. This is seen in its most extreme form in 'Wie ich lebe und warum' (1970), a 'text' consisting entirely of pictures of his flat, the street, his wife and his children, the effect being that of a short, silent documentary. In one of his critical essays, significantly called 'Der Film in Worten', he justifies the use of techniques familiar from the cinema. The 'system of associations inherent in words', he says, and 'which is active in conventional grammatical patterns' no longer corresponds to the 'sensory experiences we have day by day. Jerry Lee Lewis bending over the piano keys—an old photo covered with associations and images of tomorrow . . .' His interest in the film goes hand in hand with a scepticism about 'literature'—a word that he is known not to like. Literature depends on language, and he has no great confidence in the power of language any longer to mediate reality adequately—and in sub-culture circles literature is suspect as elitist. However, neither Brinkmann's own writings nor those of the American literature which he and his close associate, Ralf-Rainer Rygulla, have offered to the German public in translation (*Fuck you*, 1968, *Silver-screen*, 1969, and *ACID*, 1969) have done anything at all to make literature any less socially exclusive. They have themselves simply become fashionable in some trendy intellectual circles.

Brinkmann's stress on the need for literature to turn its attention to the ephemera of the everyday, to the trivialities of the consumer society, to pop and Hollywood, combined with a rejection of class-based notions about the nature of art, is typical of many of his West German contemporaries Their attitude towards the pop world is ambivalent. Most would claim to be critical of it, but recognise its important position in contemporary society, and therefore often draw on it for their material. Pop literature is 'the reaction of art to total trivialisation, the reduction of the world to commodities, of things to consumer products'.[4] Younger writers particularly have been strangely attracted to it, even mesmerised by it. Examples

include Brinkmann's preoccupation with Marilyn Monroe and
Elizabeth Taylor, Wondratschek's with Mick Jagger (the subject of
a couple of his texts), and the interest in so-called 'beat' poetry.
The term suggests parallels with the earlier beat movement in
America, whereas the main stimulus for the German beat poets of
the later sixties came from the 'popular' sources of rock and music.
Beat is seen as

> a very rhythmic life-style suited to young people
> the ridiculing of a world exclusively controlled by rationality
> vitality, directness and bite
> a non-authoritarian, challenging self-consciousness
> spontaneous liking for people and things.[5]

If one looks at the poetry of, say, Paul Gerhard Hübsch, with
its many references to songs and singers and its adulation of the
stars of the pop world, there is no sign of any awareness of the extent
to which this itself is part of the kind of society which the West
German beat poets claim to be challenging. So the poems, instead
of opening up new kinds of experience, read like rather mannered
copies of pop lyrics (and have dated just as fast):

> Es hat sich viel verändert in den letzen jahren
> nur die guten alten JEANS, die alten JEANS, sind
> schon lange verrottet, das kannst du mir glauben
>   denn wir
>   denn wir
>   wir lieben den schlag-sahne-beat
>   wir lieben die poppige twen-hose
>   wir lieben siebzehn-jahr-blondes haar
>   wir lieben uns
>   wir lieben uns
>   wir
>   wir
>   wir sind die irrsten typen, die rumlaufen
>   wir sind die modischsten, modernsten MODS
>   dieser welt, schöne-neue welt
>   schöne-neue welt
>   HEY GIVE ME THE MONEY:

Such poetry is colourless in comparison with the vitality of many
pop songs. It is a peripheral phenomenon for all those young people
for whom literature, even when it seeks to express the values of the
pop sub-culture, has diminishing importance. This is true of West
Germany, and it applies elsewhere. As far as the cultural expressions

of their micro-world are concerned, what matter are films, clothes, comics, magazines—and, above all, gramophone records. These came to acquire a special importance for the sub-cultural movement, having 'to some extent even taken over the function of spreading information. The importance of the writer for the movement has correspondingly sunk.'[6] As regards the novel, sub-culture as a movement produced only one example of any particular interest, Fred Viebahn's *Die Schwarzen Tauben* (1969). This is the more striking because it opened up the milieu of the pop world—in this case an amateur rock group—beyond the limits of the in-group references characteristic of so many of the poems. It is a picture of young people determined not to accept a prescribed social existence and searching for a happy, carefree life: 'We're making a new start, taking life by the hand and dancing gaily with it. We want to be happy, to play—*play the game existence to the end.*' The quotation from the Beatles' 'Tomorrow never knows' shows them feeling very much part of the generation of flower-children, the hippie 'Kinder von Sergeant Pepper' (Uwe Nettelbeck), rejecting everything, to quote the Black Doves in the novel, 'that will spoil their ideals, their enjoyment, their peaceful happiness and their uncontrolled fun'. Just having a good time, with only 'drugs and fucking in mind', is not enough. The narrator and the Black Doves see themselves rather as a progressive sub-culture, looking 'forward in anger', with their life-style felt as a conscious rejection of a Nazi past represented by their parents' generation: 'we'd like to put bright flowers in our hair and leap about in pumps, instead of tramping about in jackboots and trampling on things, rifle over the shoulder, and close-cropped hair stuck in a tin hat'. Above all they distance themselves from whatever smacks to them of fascism. This, rather than any real political involvement, is why the narrator writes an article for his school magazine against the Emergency Laws. The protest songs of the Black Doves, reminiscent of the rather naive idealism of the early Bob Dylan, and in a way typical of the hippie generation, do not offer political alternatives to the existing society and its values. They oppose it merely through the Black Doves' own voice, pop, and the life-style they embody, substituting the guitar for the gun.

Brinkmann said in a discussion with Jörg Schröder of the März Verlag that it was important 'that people invent a new world for themselves, invent it so totally and unrestrainedly that a new environment is actually created'.[7] This is not a bad definition, on its own terms, of the tasks of a radical sub-culture, to which literature then matters less than life-style. The revolution is to be accomplished by living it, and the function of literature is to mediate the image of the new environment. But then it would not be enough, like Brinkmann and other West German beat poets, just to challenge existing bourgeois ideas of what is appropriate in literature and to demand that account should be taken of what was previously excluded as merely sub-culture in the sense of being intrinsically inferior. A type of literature would be called for radically new in both content and form. Viebahn's book, however, is strangely conventional in style. It even adopts the fashionable literary trick of dispensing with capital letters. It does not advance beyond the point of presenting the environment of sub-culture in opposition to the values of the existing society, and so implicitly calling for change. Tiny Stricker's autobiographical novel *Trip Generation* (1970) is, formally speaking, more adventurous. It describes a hitch-hiking tour to Persia and India, and contains lengthy descriptions of drug and homosexual experiences. It does what Viebahn's novel does, with the same limitations. Neither can be seen as a very effective challenge, for all their intended radicalisation of attitude, to established habits and attitudes.

Prominent among these, as seen in sub-culture circles, are those concerning sex, which are held to be morally contradictory and repressive. Legislation against the uncontrolled personal expression of sexuality, such as anti-pornography laws, is viewed as part of the mechanism of the 'system', restricting the freedom of the individual. In theoretical works, and in literature, the attempt is made to expose the hypocrisy held to be inherent in sexual mores and to challenge society and authority by opening up a world free of such restraints:

> sexual emancipation and the integration of sexuality into everyday life as an integral part of human existence (which includes reading matter with a sexual content) must, in the long term, lead to the breakdown of the prevailing moral standards.[8]

As to the way in which literature with a bold sexual content could achieve this effect, there is the remark of Peter Weiss already in 1962 in *Fluchtpunkt* about Arthur Miller's *Tropic of Cancer*: 'from the pages of this green and red book revolt against authority hit me in the face'.

This is more blatantly apparent in Friedemann Hahn's *Fick in*

Gotham-City (1970). In 'Stellungen—Paare aus Gotham City und Umgebung zeigen über 150 Liebespositionen' he mocks the language of handbooks on sexual techniques by introducing figures from American comics as participants, and by carefully switching from pseudo-scientific jargon into crudeness he seeks to expose the moral ambivalence of a society that claims to adhere to 'decent' values, hiding the fascination of sexual experimentation behind a facade of intellectual interest. So in 'Harley Davison', in a way very similar to Henryk M. Broder's visual analysis of sexual suggestion in advertising in *Wer hat Angst vor Pornographie?* (1970) and making play with the same now rather stale theme, he renders explicit the sexual implications in the advertised image of a particular commercial product.

The moral inconsistency thus attributed to capitalist society constantly involves reference to the 'obscenity' of the Vietnam war —in the sense of Marcuse's well known definition. To this Friedemann Hahn's 'MY LAI MACHT SPASS' is clearly indebted:

> a massacre is amusing
> and beautiful and fun
> a massacre is
> a cleaning-up operation
>
> clean things are liked
> what is liked is permitted
>
> you are permitted
> to take pictures of war
> to make films about war
> you are permitted
> to wage war
>
> sex and love aren't amusing
> not even beautiful
> and no fun
> fucking is
> sin and defilement
>
> dirty things aren't liked
> what isn't liked is forbidden
>
> it is forbidden
> to take pictures of fucking
> to make films about fucking
> it is forbidden
> to fuck

so join in the war
forget about love
forget about sex
think about crime
play at war that's permitted
and is fun
show pictures of war
and pictures

pictures will only be banned
when the general's hard-on
peeps out of his shirt

The idea here, closely in line with Christian Enzensberger's *Grösserer Versuch über den Schmutz*, of the way social values are determined by the categories 'clean' and 'dirty', recurs in numerous other German writers. It is well represented in the pornography number (1969) of the *Streit—Zeit—Schrift*, and it is always associated with the notion that the *status quo* requires these categories, and radical social change their destruction. Some, like Friedemann Hahn, here too evidently influenced by Marcuse's *An Essay on Liberation*, go even further:

The beginnings of a new life outside the law are to be found in the negation of all social values. A personally created world offers scope for your own sensations. The future belongs to the criminal, the drug addict and the asocial.
SEX, DRUGS AND VIOLENCE!
It's not so much a question of criticising society as living in an anti-society.

In this sense to 'go underground' is to build up the essence of a new life and, writing from within the society, to wage war against it.

Many West German writers, drawing often on the models of the American 'dirty speech' movement and 'Fuck you' magazines, have attempted, that is to say, to break through 'society's ordained linking of moral and political dogmas with matters of literary concern' by making, in a particularly radical and polemical way, sexual taboos a theme of literature. Hahn's 'Nasses Gedicht' and 'Super Garde' are masturbatory fantasies, the latter a series of conjectures about the genitalia of film stars: 'Keine Vorhaut' describes masturbation, intercourse and cunnilingus without restraint or inhibition:

meistens kommt es ihr wenn nicht dann
Fotze lecken
meine Nase in ihren Haaren
meine Zunge in ihrem Loch
das erregt mich
ich weiss nicht
dann will ich wieder und ich kann dann auch
manchmal kann ich nur einmal
wenn sie ihre Tage hat legen wir ein Handtuch unter
wenn sie nicht da ist wichse ich
ich muss einfach dafür kann ich nichts

The result is poems calculated to shock on first reading, but, as could be argued, with an integrity contrasting with the titillating of commercial pornography and the coy euphemisms of conventional descriptions of sex. The effect, however, can be to offer an easy target to those with a different moral position, like Jost Hermand, who labels Hahn's *Fick in Gotham-City* 'a sadistic and anti-sadistic porno shocker reaching towards the limits of the imagination in both illustrations and text'. The one view would be that the mere mention of certain commonly tabooed words is obscene. The other, represented by Viebahn's comments in the 'Plakat-Nachwort' to Broder's *Wer hat Angst vor Pornographie?*, would be that it can act as a release mechanism to free sexual practices from restrictive convention. The argument then is that what is commonly called pornography has 'the important function of working against the reality principle (which includes sex as prescribed by society) by developing sexual utopias (in whatever isolated form they may be) as analogues to social utopias'.[9]

This familiar challenge to the *status quo* from the underground goes in a direction similar to that advocated, from a position also clearly influenced by Marcuse, in Charles Reich's *The Greening of America*. The aim for him is a 'revolution by consciousness', the method is for the individual to feel himself an outsider. Cultivating if necessary a life-style at odds with legality, he will strive for a 'subversion through culture', particularly through the expression of radical ideas in the channels of mass culture. On this showing the role of literature, as conventionally understood, must be a minor one. However, those close to the world of sub-culture in West Germany who, like Brinkmann, felt that literature in some new form could play a significant part in bringing about social change received powerful support from Leslie Fiedler's informal lecture 'The case for post-modernism'. This was delivered in English in June 1968 at the

University of Freiburg and then first published in German (in the same year). In his lecture, quoted approvingly by Brinkmann, it is argued that the age we are now entering is of a new kind, 'apocalyptic, anti-rational, blatantly romantic and sentimental', dedicated to 'joyous misology and prophetic irresponsibility', with literature concerned with 'the dream, the vision, *ekstasis*', and writers as 'holy disturbers of the peace of the devout'. It is in this context that Fiedler cites Leonard Cohen's *Beautiful Losers*. Baumgart does so too in putting forward similar ideas—and it was the März Verlag that published the German translation of Cohen's book. On this view literature should challenge society's values, depict not romantic love but fellatio, buggery and flagellation, and, turning to the anti-gods and anti-heroes of the new pop culture, call the power structure of society into question:

> The notion of one art for the 'cultured' and a sub-art for the 'uncultured' represents the last survival in mass industrial societies of an invidious distinction proper only to a class-structured community. Precisely because it carries on, as it has carried on ever since the middle of the eighteenth century, a war against that anachronistic survival, pop art is, whatever its overt politics, subversive, a threat to all hierarchies in so far as it is hostile to order.

This is also Chotjewitz's position. The concern of bourgeois culture with humanity, justice and progress having had regard only for a privileged minority, it is to be replaced by the 'Unkultur' of the alternative world of pop:

> Our classics are called Julie Driscoll and Jimmy Hendricks [*sic*]. They're it. They reveal an un-culture no one would have ever thought possible. They were thrust on the world, but, now they're here, they do more than make money for it. The It reveals a human warmth no one would have ever thought possible. No more dying for culture, for the Shah of Persia, for Air Marshal Ky. No more fighting for culture, no starving, no more suffering for culture.[10]

The change to the 'It' thus proclaimed will be hurried on by a few record harvests of best quality marijuana, and the 'new man'— shades of Expressionism!—will reject a narrowly purposive rationality on the principle of the 'principle of pleasure in place of achievement' (*Lust statt Leistung*).

As to the revolution thus envisaged, we might turn to Helmut Salzinger's 'Das lange Gedicht'. A 'revolution with guitars and sex and pot and giving up and refusing and laughing', it will be a quest for personal freedom and happiness through defiance of existing values, escape into a new consciousness, discovery of a new experience of life:

now I'm simply talking about the revolution
I'm talking about giving up
    about rebellion
    about doubt
I'm talking about certainty
    about resistance
    about refusal about scorn about insults
    about revolts about breaking all commandments
I'm talking about changing the pattern of ownership
    about the abolition of property
        (not only that involving the means of production)
    about changing good manners and the law
       and good taste
I'm talking about love about sex about drugs about reality
    about hope and possibility about imagination
    about work
        about happiness
           about life . . .[11]

Certain popularised Marxist ideas figure here, but political ideas, as Brinkmann and Rygulla said in their postscript to *ACID*, are not of great relevance to the development of the 'new sensibility'. The spirit of the revolution is embodied rather in its folk heroes, especially pop stars. It is conceived of as a great sensory experience, reflected in the way the rhythm of the poem drives on, as in a rock number, resoundingly to its climactic 'now', the fulfilment of what Timothy Leary called the 'Politics of Ecstasy':

THE REVOLUTION IS AN ETERNAL GLORIOUS ORGASM
AND SPURTS AND SPURTS AND
THAT IS THE THIRD STONE FROM THE SUN.

The 'third stone from the sun' referred to is the title of a track of Jimi Hendrix's LP *Are you experienced?*, and the revolution here projected is best embodied in the figure of Hendrix (likewise quoted, along with Mick Jagger, by Salzinger with great approval), with his drug-taking, the blatant sexuality of his lyrics, the euphoric eroticism of his playing, his phallic guitar.

For all this, the supposedly revolutionary sensibility of the kind described is hardly a real threat to the structure of society. Certainly it is not if the way Brinkmann talks is anything to go by. From a position close to Fiedler's, in a way reminiscent sometimes of the Expressionist generation, and revealing the influence of writers like William Burroughs and J. G. Ballard, he states that the post-revolutionary world will be above all a state of inner experience:

> We are indebted to the poets and 'junkies' for pointing out to us that the 'new' world, to be inhabited by the 'new' man of the second half of the twentieth century, can only be discovered by the conquering of inner space: through an adventure of the mind, the expansion of the psychical possibilities of man.[12]

Above all for anyone expecting literature to bring about political change, this is very open to criticism. For Peter Hamm it is too like the stress on 'Geist' in the nineteen-twenties and thirties, as a way of avoiding conflict and political involvement. For Martin Walser the new 'inwardness', while a possible means of escaping from the 'miseries of bourgeois capitalism', does not promote a critical awareness set on radical social change. He approves of the trend represented by Fiedler in so far as it points to the lack of personal satisfaction offered by the existing society. But the literature it produces is, as in his phrase abut Brinkmann, merely 'narcissistic posturing'. It could lead only to a 'society in which everyone seeks his own liberation by following the path to inwardness, with the help of drugs, with the help of a literature that delights in myths and falsified trivialities, or even with the help of a literature which acts as an ancillary drug to chemical drugs'.[13] This may be a literature claiming to strive for the breaking down of class barriers, but for Walser it is inherently fascist. Propagated by white, middle-class writers, those who really need liberation have no place in it. The works of people like Brinkmann are 'privileged dances of liberation', tolerated because of the licence afforded but, in terms of social change, ineffectual. When Michael Buselmeier and Günther Schehl, writing in the left-wing *kürbiskern*, stress society's capacity to absorb dissent by integrating the avant-garde into the existing cultural pattern as a feature of capitalism, their argument links aspects discussed earlier in this book with the specific problem of sub-culture:

> The function of the avant-garde in late capitalism has not been changed by the 'experiments' of artists from sub-culture or underground. They are suppliers to the affirmative culture and consciousness industries, industries which serve to deceive the masses. The system tolerates and even sets up vacuums in which anti-bourgeois behaviour patterns are allowed.[14]

Manfred Grunert's novel *Die verkommenen Engel* (1970) adds the further, though not original, point that, with the fashions created by pop culture enlarging the market, capitalist society can even turn criticism directed against it to its own economic advantage: 'from you industry is already earning millions. Capitalism has made you into a new market area. You dance as soon as it calls the tune. And you're still surprised that your revolution is just running on the spot.' 'If you've revolutionised anything,' Baku goes on, 'then it's international fashion. You're so chic, so much the tops, so high, that you're *in* again.' It was thus that Hubert Fichte's novel *Die Palette*, exploiting curiosity about the 'underground', could be a commercial success in a ready market. Jimi Hendrix, the embodiment of Salzinger's concept of revolution, was turned into a large-scale business enterprise, with his seemingly revolutionary, asocial behaviour as a major sales attraction. For Tom Schroeder 'underground' was becoming too respectable, a 'bogey now long since absorbed into the bourgeois set-up',[15] and by the end of the decade there were many who doubted whether it was not by this time too fashionable and trendy any longer effectively to serve a seriously subversive purpose. The need, it was being said, was for a new term to indicate a genuinely radical position. Hence the title of Rolf-Ulrich Kaiser's survey of the international protest scene *Underground? Pop? Nein! Gegenkultur* (1970). But ironically, like his *Das Songbuch* (1967) and *Protestfibel* (1968), it has all the outward appearance of just another modish product to suit the market and, without apparently realising it, merely cashes in on the commercialisation of the underground.

This highlights the important role of the circle associated with the magazine *Song*, edited by Rolf Gekeler, Tom Schroeder and Reinhard Hippen, and the significance of its change of sub-title in 1969 from 'Underground-Zeitschrift' to 'Zeitschrift für progressive Subkultur'. It is useful to consider it in conjunction with the views of Rolf Schwendtner, one of the most outspoken critics of the impasse in which sub-culture now found itself. In his *Theorie der Subkultur* (1971) he was to call for the development of radical sub-cultures which, in Peter Schütt's term, would be emancipatory rather than otherwise. He distinguished what he regarded as retrogressive sub-cultures—notably pop and earlier the Bohème, both a 'waste-product of the bourgeoisie'—from progressive ones, characterised by their vision of a better society. The latter, said the editors of *Song*, have to be seen as dynamic forces for social change: 'a sub-culture is only a counter-culture, firstly, when it strives for a fundamental change of society aimed at its humanisation and emancipation, and, secondly, when it cannot easily be integrated or made to conform'. This is in line with Schwendtner's insistence that, to have any hope of bringing about the desired transformation and to avoid the danger of integration into the culture of the 'system', sub-cultures must involve political action. The shift of attitude is vividly demonstrated in the development of the German literary chanson in the sixties.

Its emergence—or re-emergence—in this period is closely linked with Burg Waldeck (in the Hunsrück) where annual song festivals were held from 1964 to 1969, sponsored by the Arbeitsgemeinschaft Burg Waldeck which had developed out of the post-war youth movement. The theorists of the group, notably Jürgen Kahle and Diethart Kerbs, saw post-war Germany as a country now without a folk tradition. As Franz-Josef Degenhardt put it:

> Tot sind unsere Lieder,
> unsere alten Lieder.
> Lehrer haben sie zerbissen,
> Kurzbehoste sie verklampft,
> braune Horden totgeschrien,
> Stiefel in den Dreck gestampft.[16]

The idea was to discover, with the help of singers from abroad, whether it was possible to regenerate a German folk tradition—unsuccessfully, as it proved. English and American folk and protest songs were introduced at Burg Waldeck, only to be taken over by the mass media and copied in mannered imitations. But there emerged from within the Waldeck movement, to some extent under French influence (particularly that of Jacques Brel and Georges Brassens), a type of literary chanson with socio-critical overtones and close affinities with the German cabaret tradition, particularly with the songs of Brecht, Tucholsky, Klabund and, among modern cabaret artists, Wolfgang Neuss. Of these new German chansonniers the more important include Dieter Süverkrüp, Hanns Dieter Hüsch, Walter Hademann, Kristin Bauer-Horn, Walter Mossmann and Hannes Wader. The most representative figure is Degenhardt.

The characteristic songs of his early period, from 1963 to 1967, put irony in the service of a critique of West German petty-bourgeois society. The setting of most of them is the small town. In 'Zug durch die Gemeinde' and 'Deutscher Sonntag' the aim is to present it as parochial and claustrophobic, revealing the negative features—

intolerance of minorities, for instance—of petty-bourgeois society. 'Spiel nicht mit den Schmuddelkindern' is about a boy who, having none of the set ideas of the older generation, to the horror of his parents and the pastor likes to play with the 'dirty children' of the town, but is gradually drawn away from them to keep him respectable:

> So trieben sie ihn in eine Schule in der Oberstadt,
> kämmten ihm die Haare und die krause Sprache glatt.
> Lernte Rumpf und Wörter beugen.
> Und statt Rattenfängerweisen
> musste er das Largo geigen . . .

He is made into someone outwardly quite different from the 'Schmuddelkinder', and is rejected by them, but in later life, becoming a complete conformist, he tries to get his revenge by leading a life that is the antithesis of theirs, and even to eliminate the area they live in. When his son in his turn is discovered to have been playing with the 'Schmuddelkinder' he is duly thrashed. The father then has a car accident which affects his mind in such a way as to wipe out the social veneer he has acquired, whereupon he is revealed as basically like those he had earlier spurned and attacked:

> Als er später durch die Strassen
> hinkte, sah man ihn an Tagen
> auf 'nem Haarkamm Lieder blasen,
> Rattenfell am Kragen tragen.
> Hinkte hüpfend hinter Kindern,
> wollte sie am Schulgang hindern
> und schlich um Kaninchenställe . . .

Unprincipled opportunism of this kind is a recurrent theme in Degenhardt's earlier songs. 'Wenn der Senator erzählt' depicts a self-made man who from humble beginnings builds a steelworks and then exploits the depression between the wars to build up a large industrial empire. After the war he uses his contacts with the Minister of Transport, an 'old friend from darker days', to turn the land he still owns into a holiday resort, and with the profits rebuilds his steel business. The conformist taking advantage of his opportunities is also the theme of 'Horsti Schmandhoff'. Horsti appears in turn as a model child in traditional costume, a standardbearer in the Hitler Youth, an arrogant soldier in a tank regiment, a gum-chewing friend of the Americans, a successful post-war businessman and, finally, personal adviser to the president of some developing country.

The point is to make him a typical figure and to issue a warning ('Kumpanen, da, gesteht euch ein, / da wolltet ihr genau wie Horsti Schmandhoff sein'), and, as in many songs of this phase, to criticise features of the German middle-class life which once had facilitated the rise of National Socialism. At this stage the danger of its resurgence was Degenhardt's constant theme, as in a song about the influence and prestige of people who once actively promoted it:

> Wie oft hat man sie schon totgesagt, doch
> hier im Innern des Landes leben sie noch
> nach den alten Sitten und alten Gebräuchen,
> kaum dezimiert durch Kriege und Seuchen,
> stämmig und stark ein beharrliches Leben,
> den alten Führern in Treue ergeben . . .

All the same, Degenhardt could say of himself at this time: 'I'm not a political person, I know that I have too little political passion.'[17] One senses in his work a concern about West German society, but no great feeling of urgency or alarm. There are limits to his involvement, and sometimes, as in 'Adieu, Kumpanen' there is a tone of withdrawal. In numerous other songs he retreats into the circle of his drinking companions. His texts embody indirect, subtle criticism, but more in the guise rather of satire and the grotesque. His style of singing and playing was subdued and melodic rather than strident or declamatory, with simple patterns of rhythm and rhyme. In the mid-sixties, influenced by events at home and abroad, his chansons undergo a rapid transformation in the context of the general politicisation, and for the same reasons. The escalation of the war in Vietnam, the growing awareness of the problems of the Third World, the coming of the Grand Coalition in 1966, the Emergency Laws, the economic difficulties—all figure as themes of songs written between 1967 and 1970. For Degenhardt himself, as we know from his 'Fast autobiographischer Lebenslauf eines westdeutschen Linken', the decisive influence was the police handling of the student demonstrations, and his first really political song, '2. Juni '67' was written in direct response to the shooting of Benno Ohnesorg. It displays a shift towards a more direct kind of statement, but is still very much in the more lyrical style of his earlier work. The songs written from 1968 are less rhythmical, less 'musical' than his previous ones, the statements bolder, the delivery (usually in 'Sprechgesang') is harsher, with strident chords on the guitar. The imagery characteristic of his preceding songs disappears and his work acquires features influenced by a change towards a more sharply focused political position:

> The move towards change, daring to make counter-proposals clearly marks off agitatory literature from the prevalent protest wave of American origin, be it called beat, pop, hippies or happenings. Correspondingly, the 'politniks' use parody and the grotesque less and less, because these admittedly denounce the *status quo* but don't offer any alternatives to it.[18]

In the case of Degenhardt the change in style was so rapid that those of his admirers who had not followed him in his political development began to express their disapproval. He was himself aware of this, but, as he states in a song indicating the change his work had undergone, his priorities were now different:

> Manchmal sagen die Kumpanen
> jetzt, was soll dieser Scheiss?
> Wo sind deine Zwischentöne?
> Du malst bloss noch schwarz und weiss.
> Na schön, sag ich, das ist ja richtig,
> aber das ist jetzt nicht wichtig.
> Zwischentöne sind bloss Krampf
> im Klassenkampf.

A similar change can be observed in the songs of Dieter Süverkrüp, Hanns Dieter Hüsch and Walter Mossmann, in those of more recent poet–singers like Dittrich Kittner and Rolf Schwendter, and in the Floh de Cologne group (as well as, for that matter, certain songs which Wolf Biermann released in the West at this time, such as 'Drei Kugeln auf Rudi Dutschke'). The point was to avoid songs that were too easily enjoyed and therefore too attractive as commercial propositions:

> Und der Dichter, der poetisch
> protestiert in seinem Lied,
> bringt den Herrschenden ein Ständchen
> und erhöht ihren (und seinen) Profit.
> Und genau das ist nicht richtig,
> und genau das ist nicht wichtig.
> Protestieren ist bloss Krampf
> im Klassenkampf.

The problem of commercialisation brought about a radical rethinking of the nature and function of the Waldeck festivals. By 1968 they had become big business, heavily dependent for financial support on the media. These emasculated the more political songs in edited recordings and concentrated primarily on the non-controversial foreign songs. As a counter-measure the scale of the 1969 festival was reduced, and there was a good deal of theoretical discussion on the theme of 'Gegenkultur'. The political song was now seen as just one component in a more widely based subversive subculture within which the aim of the singers was to induce more radical attitudes in the service of political change. In this matter the political chansonniers were better placed than other writers. Their medium of distribution—concert and record—were more in line with the tastes of the majority of the young, and there is ample evidence of political activity having been induced at this time by involvement in political songs.

The new situation was commented on in these terms:

> It has been said that the aim of the Waldeck movement, and of the political song movement in general, is political effectiveness, and if you take that as your yardstick, then you have to start with the question of quality, but not in an aesthetic sense. You have to ask whether the political statements being made in the songs are really worthy of being taken seriously, whether the singers who perform political songs here are really up with the latest political developments, and whether they really have some sort of feeling for the real political problems that crop up.[19]

The song, that is to say, was now being called into question by the need to be more specific, even if more ephemeral. Its most effective form 'will in future be the sung fly-sheet'. Concert performance, as was usual up to now, began to seem less appropriate. Reflecting the impact on the Waldeck movement of worker–singers such as the Four Conrads, as well as Marxist critics like Peter Schütt, the songs came more and more to be seen as belonging within the setting of political action, in the street, outside the factory gate, or at a political rally. As with some of the agitprop songs of the nineteen-twenties, they were now often being used to draw the attention of passers-by, to introduce themes for discussion, or as a means of fostering or expressing political solidarity. Practice varied. The worker–singers apart, of the leading figures only Mossmann presented his songs like this. Others, even Hüsch and Degenhardt, continued to sing in concerts.

The effort to find an appropriate form of literature for agitatory or informative purposes on behalf of the extra-parliamentary opposition in the late sixties produced also the so-called 'street theatre', initially stimulated by American companies such as the Bread and Puppet Theatre and by the Teatro Campesino, though its fore-runners go back to the Weimar Republic. It was a medium, as some would say, forced on the radical left by the difficulty of gaining adequate access to the mass media: 'as long as the left has no access to technical media, it will have to use primitive media: fly-sheet, wall-newspaper, street theatre'.[20] Or, one might say, the street was the opposition's only daily newspaper free of some form of censor-ship. The street theatre was felt to lend itself particularly to the imparting of political information, largely because of the directness of its language:

> Whilst the language of the ruling class uses more and more new forms of circumlocution and concealment, the agitprop authors are concerned with reality; they name the things that oppress them by name, so as to make the situation more graspable, and they portray social con-ditions in just the way they are.[21]

Once a crowd is attracted by songs or the handing out of leaflets, a dramatic sketch can be used as a way exposing the 'lies' of the mass media and giving the 'truth'. Short speeches and discussion can follow. So street theatre is really a form of documentary theatre, with its 'tangible proof', 'density of documentation' and 'truth to facts'.[22] What is depicted claims to be typical, except that street theatre as used by very radical left-wing groups (who virtually came to monopolise it), deliberately over-simplifies in order to make its case about the exploitation of the working class.

The way street theatre works may be illustrated by reference to *Tendenz: Immer besser* by the Interpol group from Cologne. Its starting point is an optimistic article in a Cologne newspaper on rising wages:

> *Speaker 1.* It 'was calculated that male industrial workers at the present time have an average weekly wage of almost 240 marks and thus this year have reached for the first time a gross wage scale of more than 1,000 marks a month . . .' (*Kölner Stadt-Anzeiger*, 17–18 June 1969).
> *Speaker 2.* What wonderful times we live in!
> *Speaker 3.* Indeed, we've never had it so good!
> *Speaker 4.* A thousand marks a month!
> *Speaker 5.* That's something granddad never dreamt of!

It is then shown how, in the case of the average worker of forty with

two children, this income is eroded, leaving nothing for other necessi-
ties, not to mention little luxuries:

> *Speaker 1.* Thus Herr Müller has no money left.
> *Speaker 5.* No money for:
>
>> clothes and shoes and cleaning bills,
>> for cigars, cigarettes, wine and beer,
>> the children's birthdays, the parents' birthdays,
>> the Easter hare and Father Christmas . . .

Having proved how difficult it is for a man to survive on such a
wage, the folly of the article is further exposed by another quotation
showing how misleading the *Kölner Stadt-Anzeiger* had been in
looking only at industrial workers:

> *Speaker 1.* 'But by no means all workers earn 1,000 marks. A third of
> all wage-earners receive no more than 500 marks a month' (*Spiegel*,
> 28 June 1969).

The impact of such plays was exceedingly small, and the uncon-
vinced worker, at whom they were aimed, was little influenced by
them. Enzensberger said that the worker rejected such attempts to
enlighten him as merely patronising, though he might have mentioned that workers were often actively involved in the writing and
performance. An audience used to the more sophisticated techniques
of the mass media easily saw through the over-simplification. There
was a danger, too, in being so offhand about aesthetic considerations
just because they were thought to be bourgeois. Handke has some
comments about this. In the nineteen-twenties, he said, agitprop 'did
not use old play forms, which were bound to distract the audience's
attention in the direction of old, harmless *significances*, but it showed
through play new possibilities of play for the audience and not just
(and that's what it's all about) for the *players*'. By contrast, street-
theatre groups 'spielen nach, statt vor, und äffen nach, statt den
Leuten etwas vorzuäffen'.[23]

The implied call for a new art form to replace the street theatre,
but carrying out its avowed aims, was to some extent answered by
the Floh de Cologne group, which began as a student cabaret act.
Their early programme, such as 'Trari, trara, die Pest ist da' (1966),
shows the close relationship between the 'politisch-engagiertes Lied'
and these new developments in cabaret at this time. The targets of
their attack were the emergency laws, the 'formierte Gesellschaft',
the NPD, the Vietnam war and the situation in Berlin. Their next

programme, 'SimSAladimbambaSAladUSAladim' (1967) concentrated on similar topics but showed a definite move away from a straight
cabaret performance. Spoken interludes were introduced, readings
supported the songs, the flow of the music was broken, and the
audience kept more alert. With growing political involvement their
material became increasingly militant, their act much more un-
comfortable. Under the influence of the American group The Fugs
(headed by figures as important for West German sub-culture as
Ed Sanders and Tuli Kupferberg), it developed into a collage of
songs, a barrage of sound and aggressive sexuality, the purpose being
so to shock the audience as to prevent them merely enjoying the
performance and taking it too easily in their stride. More and more,
however, they become frustrated because as a socialist

> you can't achieve anything in the bourgeois cabaret with a bourgeois
> audience. You can rake in the cash, help the people who scribble the
> newspaper supplements to make a bit more money, you can stand on
> your head and shout 'socialism' and the audience will applaud, because
> no one has said it like that before. People want to enjoy sharp criticism,
> to be shouted at and find the whole thing a shade too one-sided. You
> can even piss on these people, if it's well resolved in formal terms.[24]

In their 'Siebtes Programm' (1969), therefore, the Floh de Cologne
decided to 'kill off' the cabaret, and in a savage attack, monstrously
amplified, on the mentality of the consumer society and on middle-
class values they succeeded in driving a good part of their audience
in Recklinghausen out of the hall. Since then, using pop music as
more appropriate to the reactions of their new audience, they have
tried to bring a sort of socialist post-cabaret to young workers and
apprentices, and have also campaigned for the German Communist
Party. Their most recent programmes, 'Fliessbandbabys Beat-Show'
(1969) and 'Profitgeier (1971), have continued to attack the 'throw-
away paradise' conjured up by 'the top 10,000' who are said to
control the capitalist system, backing up their songs with reportage,
pamphlets and discussions.

Another attempt to develop a new political art form is suggested
in Manfred Grunert's novel *Die verkommenen Engel*. By a series of
apparent monologues illuminating the story from various perspectives, it depicts the destruction of the existence of Karl Böhm, a
successful businessman. Böhm, his narrative accompanied by a series
of authorial, theoretical 'introductions to capitalism' in footnotes,
tells how some years earlier he had married his 'angel', a beautiful

younger woman. The relationship, for him just another desirable possession, affords him great personal satisfaction, with marital sex a duty punctiliously fulfilled every Saturday. After three years of marriage his wife, unsatisfied by the monotony of her sex life, rebels against her husband with a display of unbridled sexuality that horrifies Böhm—who stands for 'decency' and 'das gesunde Volksempfinden'—and ruins the relationship for him. His wife, in her frustration, turns to the central character of the novel, Uwe Kutschenreuter. Böhm finds them in bed together, is so horrified that he has a stroke, thenceforth being confined to a wheel-chair. Kutschenreuter, however, is no casual lover taking advantage of the easy favours of Böhm's wife. He is merely following the policies advocated by his friend and political mentor Baku, designed to help to bring about the downfall of capitalism by striking at individual capitalists:

> Dispossess capitalists in the same way as they got rich. Tap the money-bags of your idols. Marry rich tools and fannies. Screw with the pluto-crats' wives and frustrated capitalist studs. Break up their rotten families in full view of the public, and make money out of it. With the money you make set up production co-operatives, the foundations of our future society.

Following this idea through, they set up a touring multi-media show which lays bare Böhm's story, exposes the true nature of his apparently respectable bourgeois marriage, illustrates it with photographs of the 'repressive' sex life that his wife rebelled against, and shows its final destruction by Uwe's intervention. Böhm, in his wheel-chair, is part of the show, during which he tells his side of the story. The idea is that he, the capitalist, should expose himself to the audience: 'Baku is using me to kill myself.'

In *Die verkommenen Engel* the monologues are a composite part of the multi-media show. The suggestion, therefore, is of a new art form genuinely able to help to bring about a radical change in society. Like most of the ideas for revolutionary art emanating from the sub-culture within the extra-parliamentary opposition, this represents a fundamental questioning of important aspects of literature, as regards both its function and its form. The former is seen as above all political, the latter as challenging the authority of the separate genres. Also, many of the works produced by this movement in the last two years of the decade deal a blow at the established concept of the book as such. Two of the most significant products of the German left at this time, *Klau mich* by Fritz Teufel and Rainer Langhans, and *Subkultur Berlin* (1969), evocative of the style of the underground press, can better be described as 'happenings' than as books. They are both essentially collages of ready-mades, and, as a matter of fact, very similar to the pop products which the radical left claims to reject. *Subkultur Berlin* comprises a leaflet of the women's branch of the Frankfurt SDS on sexual emancipation, various other political pamphlets, data about communes, transcripts of discussions, a report on marijuana, an extract from a handbook of sexual techniques, documentation of a famous department store trial, selections from radical newspapers, pictures of cunnilingus, a Donald Duck cartoon, and a record of prominent left-wing people discussing a demonstration. What is thus created is thought of as an oppositional world to that of bourgeois society, and, reflecting the belief in the death of bourgeois literature, resorts to devices calculated to declare its fatuity. From the point of view of the protagonists of sub-culture literature is necessarily reactionary and irrelevant.

Not everyone concerned, however, was prepared to leave it quite like that. Rolf Schwendter rejected Enzensberger's claim that the only literature now acceptable is agitatory 'Reportagen', and Hans Christoph Buch went on record with the view that 'Reportagen', however useful they may be, 'can never be a substitute for literary techniques of a more complex kind and on which, as ever, the writer has to rely'.[25] Thus by the end of the decade a division of opinion became apparent within radical left-wing circles as to the role of literature within a progressive sub-culture. Grunert's *Die verkommenen Engel* puts forward the idea of non-literary political art, but cannot disguise the fact that, whatever we may think of it, it regards itself as a work of literature. This underlines the situation within the wider debate about the 'end of literature' as we have analysed it in a previous chapter—the confident rejection of literature as irrelevant, followed by counter-moves, within the sub-culture and beyond it, expressing themselves with equal force and confidence. The view is maintained of literature as serving first and foremost the cause of radical political change, but the importance of literature as fantasy is reasserted. Even critics like Peter Schütt, Hannes Stütz and Wolfgang Heise, who take this line and at the same time champion agitprop, are seen to occupy a position remarkably similar to those of the Fiedler school of thought, like Brinkmann. That is to say, in the sub-culture too the category of bourgeois literature is rejected, but the value of literature comes to be affirmed as appealing to and enriching the imagination, and thereby holding out the hope of 'emancipation'.

Notes

1 Helmut Kreuzer, *Die Boheme*, Stuttgart, 1968, p. v.
2 'Die Lyrik Frank O'Haras', in *Lunch Poems und andere Gedichte*, Cologne, 1969, p. 73.
3 In his lecture 'The case for post-modernism', printed under the title 'cross the border, close the gap', *Playboy*, December 1969, p. 230.
4 Hermann Peter Piwitt, 'Pop, Protest, Sex, Vitalismus', *Der Monat*, 242, November 1968, p. 71.
5 *pro* 6, Krefeld, June 1967, p. 2.
6 Werner Diepholz, 'Modern Pop', *SOUND TRACK. zeitschrift für gegen medien*, 3, quoted in Helmut Salzinger, *Rock Power*, Frankfurt a M., 1972, p. 223.
7 'Interview mit einem Verleger', *März Texte 1*, Darmstadt, 1969, p. 294.
8 Henryk M. Broder, 'Der literarische Jugendschutz', *Song*, 5, 1969, p. 38.
9 Gisela Dischner, 'Säuberungsmissionare', *Pornographie (Streit—Zeit—Schrift*, VII, 1), Frankfurt a. M., 1969, p. 104.
10 *Vom Leben und Lernen*, Darmstadt, 1969, p. 22.
11 In V. Tsakaridis (ed.), *Super Garde*, Düsseldorf, 1969, pp. 167–91.
12 'Angriff aufs Monopol', *Christ und Welt*, 15 November 1968, p. 15.
13 'Über die Neueste Stimmung im Westen', *Kursbuch*, 20, 1970, p. 36.
14 'Die Kinder von Coca Cola', *kürbiskern*, 1, 1970, p. 78.
15 *Song*, 8, 1969, p. 8.
16 This and the other songs of Franz-Josef Degenhardt quoted are contained in *Spiel nicht mit den Schmuddelkindern*, Reinbek, 1969.
17 'Tüte voll Angst', *Der Spiegel*, 21 February 1966, p. 126.
18 Peter Schütt, *Asphalt-Literatur, ed. cit.*, p. 11.
19 Ingo Weihe, in the press conference of Chanson Folklore International V, Burg Waldeck, 13 June 1968.
20 Michael Buselmeier, 'Bedingungen des Strassentheaters', in Agnes Hüfner (ed.), *Strassentheater*, Frankfurt a. M., 1970, p. 332.
21 Peter Schütt, *Asphalt-Literatur, ed. cit.*, p. 6.
22 Agnes Hüfner, foreword to *Strassentheater, ed. cit.* This volume contains Interpol's *Tendenz: Immer besser*, quoted below.
23 'Für das Strassentheater—gegen das Strassentheater', *Theater heute*, July 1968.
24 *Profitgeier und andere Vögel*, Berlin, 1971, p. 61. This volume contains extracts from the programmes referred to.
25 'Von der möglichen Funktion der Literatur', *Kursbuch*, 20, 1970, p. 44.

Conclusion

Retrospect and assessment

The inclusion of a chapter on sub-culture in a book on West German literature may seem surprising. It is not yet academically respectable, and our comments about it have not been enthusiastic. However, as an academic subject German has too long been too narrowly concerned with the more refined and elegant aspects of literary history. Whatever may have been the reasons for this in the past, it is least justified the nearer one gets to the modern and contemporary field. In any case the close connections existing between sub-culture and other aspects of the sixties are such that to ignore it is unrealistic. There is a clear relationship between the question of identity discussed in our first chapter and, in the area of sub-culture, the urge to recover the sense of self. Sub-culture is in large measure about a life-style—commune, spontaneity, pleasure principle—in and through which the discomfiture of alienation is, or is imagined to be, overcome and the self released. There are connections also with our second chapter, in the interplay of a concern with institutional change and a subjectivism that can be so at odds with political organisation as to make them uneasy partners. The debate examined in our third chapter has its bearing too, since at the extreme the logic of the argument directed against literature extends as far as the affirmation of what in part sub-culture represents—and in the area of sub-culture, too, the case against literature ends by being a defence of it.

The material we have been dealing with, however, militates against too neatly co-ordinated results. It comprises emergent issues, new starts and unsolved problems. Trends and developments show themselves without it being possible to reach final decisions on the moral and aesthetic aspects involved. In the sixties, as always in the past but at this time more obviously than usual, literature arose from the deep processes of personal and social life and conflict. For the writer the problems express themselves in aesthetic forms, but they derive from the total experience of a society. We have been

investigating the area of social experience in which needs, desires,
longings, hatreds and frustrations form and change, coalesce, diversify, discover objectives, alter direction. What writers strive to do is
to give them significant shape and to examine their profounder
character and justification.

Many factors in the sixties, however, were militating against a
writer's occupying as easily as before a representative position. They
include the pressures of a market hungry for new talent, however
ephemeral in the long term, and geared as much to a quick turnover
and to a diversification of the product as to investment in what is
already successful; of a younger generation absorbing from the consumer society, however much they may think they dislike it, famili-
arity with phenomena of obsolescence and suspicion of yesterday's
model; of intolerance of continuity and stability. The writer might
still be a star in the public image, but so likewise are TV personalities
and footballers. In the ideological tensions of the sixties, for a writer
to establish himself could prompt a desire to disestablish him. This
would have applied to Walser if he had not adapted himself to
changing pressures in the way he did, and to Böll but for the way
his sympathies seemed to go in his latest novel, where attitudes of
the kind cultivated most obviously in the world of sub-culture have
positive associations. There was also, at a critical point and on a
telling issue, his concern for a more humane understanding of the
Baader-Meinhoff group, which had been setting fire to buildings as
a protest against capitalism. Radical opinion never became much
troubled about Uwe Johnson one way or the other. He was away in
America for some time and absent from the West German scene at
a crucial and aggressive phase. Grass was in the thick of the ideological battles and in radical quarters his standing was held against
him. Consistently representing a moderate socialist position, committed to the SPD and its role within the institutions of parliamentary democratic government, unambiguous in his attitude to
left-wing violence and excess, he was an obvious target for the enthusiasts of revolution.

For various reasons, then, the sixties were hardly a time for the
consolidations of 'major' figures. Of those falling into this category,
Böll had reached this position some time before, and Grass, Johnson
and Walser had already established eminence around the beginning of the decade. The sixties were a time marked rather by the
emergence of writers coming quickly into prominence and then, as

attention was directed elsewhere, fading from foreground attention. West German literature was restless, impatient, hurried and hectic. The cliché of the 'Literaturbetrieb' conveys this very well. The effect may be to seem to blur distinctions of imaginative and artistic quality, but the situation would be poorly described by reference to only a few writers selected for their intrinsic excellence. In respect to the clash of ideologies, to the diversity of interests and attitudes represented overall, to the number of writers needing to be taken account of, and to the variety of their work, it was far too differentiated for this to be adequate. There would be missing, too, a body of evidence about social pressures and literary responses necessary in any study of individual writers whom one might then wish to single out as deserving special treatment. There is also to be borne in mind the factor of the reading public, consisting now to a significant extent of a younger generation drawn to radically critical attitudes and intolerant of established culture. This was a new factor as compared even with the fifties, and its effect was felt on writers, publishers and criticism, and in many other ways.

From there emanated the main force of the idea that the 'great book' had lost its aura and authority, and of the calling into question of the individual imagination as a privileged guide to truth and values. The argument was ideologically intentioned and it was pushed to extremes. It would have made less impact had there not been a rather more general sense that nowadays more than ever there were effective alternatives—film, press, television, psychology, sociology—for informing oneself about the problems of man and society. There was more than merely a sectarian foundation for the belief that literature could no longer be so exclusively equated with belles lettres. The line dividing literature from what is not literature was becoming so tenuous that even the identity of literature itself seemed sometimes to be in doubt. Symptomatic was the increasingly frequent transgression of a frontier—of values, form and style— which once had been more clearly delineated and more jealously protected.

West Germany was not unique in any or all of these matters. Characteristic of the sixties there was the force of ideological pressure, the energy and extent of theory, and the radical consequences in terms of dogma and practice. In the English literary situation of the sixties there was greater stability and consistency, in general and as far as the work and standing of individual writers was concerned.

It needed no term equivalent to 'Literaturbetrieb' to describe it, and
the word is hard to translate anyway. Belles lettres, for long a less
exclusive, less self-conscious and more broadly accommodating
category, never became an issue as it did in the Federal Republic.
A major debate dominating the literary scene for a while about the
demise of literature would have been inconceivable. A book about
English literature would have naturally found itself talking as much
about poetry as would a book on German writers in the fifties. The
similarities are closer in the case of America. There too, for example,
the problem of identity and its ramifications was a central concern.
No book on English literature in the sixties would have that as a
paramount topic.

As in America, but not in England, alienation was in the foreground as an ideological concern. In West Germany it was an intellectual obsession that sprang not from the experience of alienation
in real life but from a predisposition to utopian patterns of thought.
There was, above all, the dream of man at one with himself and
with the world—the dream that particularly in sub-cultural circles
made out of the revival of Hermann Hesse a cult of religious force
and character. It was a dream that in times past others too had
dreamt. Prominent among them in Germany were those whose thinking dated from the latter part of the nineteenth century, commonly
and with good reason regarded as anticipating the manifestations of
irrationalism which so embarrassed Weimar democracy, and the
effects of which did not stop there. It was a kind of thinking energised
by a romantic anti-capitalism expressive of a general contempt for
modern industrial society. The idea was the release of the authentic
and submerged essence of existence, of the individual's and society's,
as a counter to circumstances felt to be hampering natural creativity
and self-expression.

Julius Langbehn in his once best-selling *Rembrandt als Erzieher*
(1890) made much of this. It led him to want a type of community
on a more popular basis and with a more natural and more spontaneous kind of inner cohesion. 'Volkstümlichkeit' was his word for
it. The haziness of such romanticism in the midst of advancing industrialisation is obvious enough. A good deal of West German literature and ideology in the sixties indicates a romantic yearning for
a community ideal which one is tempted to describe in Langbehn's
phrase.

What was demanded in the sixties is frequently set forth in the terminology of politics and sociology. This may seem deceptive if in the light of a characteristic figure like Langbehn we consider the obsession with whatever is thought to weaken or disrupt the cohesion of individual and social existence—class divisions, division of labour, authority—and, complementary to this, the romantic cult of 'the workers', the fascination with simple people, and the idealisation of folk heroes from Che Guevara to Rudi Dutschke, from Benno Ohnesorg to figures from beat and pop. The yearning was to 'get the whole of life in one's grasp' and as such in the circumstances it was—as it came to be called by one young left-wing intellectual—a 'mystical social romanticism'.[1] It had disquieting implications. Langbehn's doctrine of 'Volkstümlichkeit' came to be associated for him with the need to exclude elements—notably Jews—alien to its cohesion. In the romantic radicalism of the sixties, and not only in Germany, capitalists sometimes figure in a similar role, but there the way people were called upon, for example, physically to attack one particular publishing house was eerily reminiscent of the language of the Nazis against the Jews.[2] Inherent also in Langbehn's philosophy was an impatient reaction against the civilising restraints of 'Kultur'. As a way out he advocated 'barbarism'. This was synonymous for him with 'Unkultur', and this a term that crops up in the sixties with associations of return to more primitive and sensuous experience.

We have been comparing radical trends in the sixties with writers of an earlier period whose thinking was fundamentally conservative in its motivation. This, paradoxical as it may seem, was why their ideals so conspicuously contained features with the outward appearance of being 'progressive'—the rejection of specialisation, of the division of labour and the 'totes Wissen' attributed to the established system of education. What they were doing was to oppose life and essence, cohesion and totality—concepts by that time well established in the philosophy of German conservatism—to the hated and disruptive force of industrial society, of modern life. Already in *Kunst und Revolution* (1849) Richard Wagner makes much of the 'man-destroying march' of 'Kultur' and of the 'crushing pressures' of 'Zivilisation', glorifies 'instinct', demands to savour to the full the 'joys of life', attacks education as an instrument of repression, and sets up the ideal of man restored to his essence as 'true living man'. The art directed to this end, he said, was art as 'revolution'. It was at the same time, he insisted, 'conservative'.

The comparison is striking enough to reinforce the impression that, had the revolution of the sixties succeeded, it would have been marked as much by regression from a complex and demanding society as by genuinely progressive solutions as a way of advance into the future. What is certain is that, while the literature of this decade reveals many features in the category of innovation and emancipation, it turned out in the end to be marked often by return from radical positions to conformity to the less hazardous and the more familiar. The 'politicisation of literature' got mixed up with attitudes attaching a vaguer and more inward significance to the idea of the political. Literature, called into question, was reaffirmed. Documentary methods, with their promise of 'authenticity', began to look less convincing when some belief in fantasy returned. Attempts to involve writers in themes from the industrial world proved little more than an episode, helpful though they were to the cause of literature, hard pressed at an awkward juncture. Sub-culture, starting from a critical concern with established culture, came to operate as a ritual release of certain areas of feeling through which writers were the better able to reassert what began to look like a simple version of a well known notion of literature. Its narcissistic inwardness made its political effectiveness doubtful. It became involved, as entertainment and even economic advantage, in the capitalism it despised, and as one of the luxuries which this, with all its waste and plenty, so naturally facilitated and could so easily afford.

All the same, in the intellectual turmoil of the sixties genuine problems of modern society and modern culture had been pushed into the foreground and subjected to intense and even brutal scrutiny. Traditional assumptions, unaccustomed to the need to justify themselves, had been called to account. The experience will have weakened some and invigorated others. New possibilities had been opened up, some plainly ridiculous, others deserving of attention. The sixties, that is to say, leave future writers with a challenge not lightly to be disregarded, and its effect, negatively and positively, will be with them for some time yet.

Notes

1 Hans Christopher Buch, *Kritische Wälder. Essays, Kritiken, Glossen*, Reinbeck, 1972, p. 86.
2 Compare, for example, 'Macht den bürgerlichen Linksgeschäftemachern

ihr Geschäft kaputt' and 'Lasst euch nicht von den Rowohlts ver-schachern, Genossen' with equivalent phrases in Nazi times urging the destruction of Jewish businesses, the idea being at the same time that the 'community' of Germans was being 'cheated' by the alien Jews.

Selected bibliography

Primary works

Achternbusch, Herbert, *Die Macht des Löwengebrülls*, Frankfurt a. M., 1970.
— *Die Alexanderschlacht*, Frankfurt a. M., 1971.
Bachmann, Ingeborg, *Malina*, Frankfurt a. M., 1971.
Becker, Jürgen, *Felder*, Frankfurt a. M., 1964.
Bernhard, Thomas, *Frost*, Frankfurt a. M., 1963.
— *Verstörung*, Frankfurt a. M., 1967.
— *Das Kalkwerk*, Frankfurt a. M., 1970.
Böll, Heinrich, *Billard um halbzehn*, Cologne, 1959.
— *Gruppenbild mit Dame*, Cologne, 1961.
Chotjewitz, Peter O., *Vom Leben und Lernen*, Darmstadt, 1969.
Degenhardt, Franz-Josef, *Spiel nicht mit den Schmuddelkindern*, Reinbek, 1969.
Delius, F. C., *Wir Unternehmer*, Berlin, 1966.
Enzensberger, Hans Magnus, *Einzelheiten*, Frankfurt a. M., 1962.
— *Politik und Verbrechen*, Frankfurt a. M., 1964.
— *Das Verhör von Habana*, Frankfurt a. M., 1970.
— *Der kurze Sommer der Anarchie*, Frankfurt a. M., 1972.
Cologne, Floh de, *Profitgeier und andere Vögel*, Berlin, 1971.
Grass, Günter, *Über das Selbstverständliche*, Neuwied, 1968.
— *Örtlich betäubt*, Neuwied, 1969.
— *Aus dem Tagebuch einer Schnecke*, Neuwied, 1972.
Grunert, Manfred, *Die verkommenen Engel*, Munich, 1970.
Gruppe 61, *Aus der Welt der Arbeit*, Neuwied, 1966.
Hahn, Friedemann, *Fick in Gotham-City*, Berlin, 1970.
Handke, Peter, *Selbstbezichtigung*, Frankfurt a. M., 1966.
— *Kaspar*, Frankfurt a. M., 1966.
Härtling, Peter, *Das Familienfest*, Frankfurt a. M., 1969.
Heissenbüttel, Helmut, *Das Textbuch*, Neuwied, 1970.
— *Projekt Nr. 1: D'Alemberts Ende*, Neuwied, 1970.
Hochhuth, Rolf, *Der Stellvertreter*, Reinbek, 1963.
— *Soldaten*, Reinbek, 1967.
Hüfner, Agnes (ed.), *Strassentheater*, Frankfurt a. M., 1970.
Kipphardt, Heinar, *In der Sache J. Robert Oppenheimer*, Frankfurt a. M., 1964.
— *Joel Brand*, Frankfurt a. M., 1965.
Kluge, Alexander, *Schlachtbeschreibung*, Olten, 1964.

Kühn, Dieter, *N*, Frankfurt a. M., 1970.
— *Ausflüge im Luftballon*, Frankfurt a. M., 1971.
Lenz, Siegfried, *Deutschstunde*, Hamburg, 1968.
Rother, Rosalie, *Rosalka oder Wie es eben so ist*, Frankfurt a. M., 1969.
Runge, Erika, *Bottroper Protokolle*, Frankfurt a. M., 1968.
Tsakaridis, V., (ed.), *Super Garde*, Düsseldorf, 1969.
von der Grün, Max, *Männer in zweifacher Nacht*, Recklinghausen, 1962.
— *Irrlicht und Feuer*, Recklinghausen, 1963.
— *Zwei Briefe an Pospischiel*, Neuwied, 1968.
Viebahn, Fred, *Die Schwarzen Tauben*, Hamburg, 1969.
Wallraff, Günter, *Wir brauchen Dich*, Gütersloh, 1966.
— *Nachspiele*, Frankfurt a. M., 1968.
— *13 unerwünschte Reportagen*, Cologne, 1969.
Walser, Martin, *Erfahrungen und Lese erfahrungen*, Frankfurt a. M., 1965.
— *Das Einhorn*, Frankfurt a. M., 1966.
— *Fiction*, Frankfurt a. M., 1970.
— *Die Gallistl'sche Krankheit*, Frankfurt a. M., 1972.
Weiss, Peter, *Die Ermittlung*, Frankfurt a. M., 1965.
— *Notizen zum kulturellen Leben der Demokratischen Republik Viet Nam*, Frankfurt a. M., 1968.
Wellershoff, Dieter, *Ein schöner Tag*, Cologne, 1966.
— *Die Schattengrenze*, Cologne, 1969.
Werner, Wolfgang, *Vom Waisenhaus ins Zuchthaus*, Frankfurt a. M., 1969.
Wolf, Ror, *Fortsetzung des Berichts*, Frankfurt a. M., 1964.
— *Pilzer und Pelzer*, Frankfurt a. M., 1967.
— *Danke schön. Nichts zu danken*, Frankfurt a. M., 1969.
Wondratschek, Wolf, *Ein Bauer zeugt mit einer Bäuerin einen Bauernjungen, der unbedingt Knecht werden will*, Munich, 1970.
— *Omnibus*, Munich, 1972.

Secondary literature

Arnold, H. L. (ed.), *Gruppe 61: Arbeiterliteratur—Literatur der Arbeitswelt?*, Munich, 1971.
Baumgart, Reinhard, 'Unmenschlichkeit beschreiben', in *Literatur für Zeitgenossen*, Frankfurt a. M., 1966.
Benjamin, Walter, *Das Kunstwerk im Zeitalter seiner technischen Reproduzierbarkeit*, Frankfurt a. M., 1963.
— 'Der Autor als Produzent', in *Versuche über Brecht*, Frankfurt a. M., 1966.
Bohrer, Karl Heinz, *Die gefährdete Phantasie*, Munich, 1970.
Brinkmann, Rolf-Dieter, 'Angriff aufs Monopol', *Christ und Welt*, 15 November 1968.
— 'Anmerkungen zu meinem Gedicht "Vanille"'. in *März Texte 1*, Darmstadt, 1969.
— 'Die Lyrik Frank O'Haras', in *Lunch Poems und andere Gedichte*, Cologne, 1969.
Buch, Hans Christoph, 'Von der möglichen Funktion der Literatur', *Kursbuch*, 20, 1970.

Enzensberger, Hans Magnus, 'Gemeinplätze, die Neueste Literatur betreffend' *Kursbuch*, 15, 1968.
Fiedler, Leslie, 'Close the border, cross the gap', *Playboy*, December 1969.
Heissenbüttel, Helmut, and Vormweg, Heinrich, *Briefwechsel über Literatur*, Neuwied, 1969.
Marcuse, Herbert, *One-dimensional Man: Studies in the Ideology of Advanced Industrial Society*, London, 1964.
— *An Essay on Liberation*, London, 1969.
Michel, Karl Markus, 'Ein Kranz für die Literatur', *Kursbuch*, 15, 1968.
Piwitt, Hermann Peter, *Das Bein des Bergmanns Wu*, Frankfurt a. M., 1971.
Reich, Charles, *The Greening of America*, London, 1971.
Scharang, Michael, *Zur Emanzipation der Kunst*, Neuwied, 1971.
Schneider, Peter, 'Die Phantasie im Spätkapitalismus und die Kulturrevolution', *Kursbuch*, 20, 1970.
Walser, Martin, 'Über die Neueste Stimmung im Westen', *Kursbuch*, 20, 1970.
Weiss, Peter, and Enzensberger, Hans Magnus, 'Eine Kontroverse', *Kursbuch*, 6, 1966.
Widmer, Urs, *Das Normale und die Sehnsucht*, Zürich, 1972.

Suggested further reading

Durzak, Manfred (ed), *Die deutsche Literatur der Gegenwart. Aspekte und Tendenzen*, Stuttgart, 1971.
Heissenbüttel, Helmut, *Über Literatur*, Olten, 1966.
Hermand, Jost, *Pop International. Eine kritische Analyse*, Frankfurt a. M., 1971.
Koebner, Thomas (ed.), *Tendenzen der deutschen Literatur seit 1945*, Stuttgart, 1971.
Matthaei, Renate (ed.), *Grenzverschiebung. Neue Tendenzen in der deutschen Literatur der 6oer Jahre*, Cologne and Berlin, 1970.
Paulsen, Wolfgang (ed.), *Revolte und Experiment. Die Literatur der sechziger Jahre in Ost und West*, Heidelberg, 1972.
Reich-Ranicki, Marcel, *Deutsche Literatur in West und Ost*, Munich, 1963.
— *Literatur der kleinen Schritte. Deutsche Schriftsteller heute*, Munich, 1967.
Thomas, R. Hinton, and Bullivant, Keith, *German Literature since 1945*, Sussex Tapes, London, 1974.
Thomas, R. Hinton, and van der Will, Wilfried, *German Literature and the Affluent Society*, Manchester, 1968.
Vormweg, Heinrich, *Eine andere Lesart, Über neue Literatur*, Neuwied, 1972.
Weber, Dietrich (ed.), *Deutsche Literatur seit 1945 in Einzeldarstellungen*, Stuttgart, 1968.

Index